Dynamic WILDLIFE PHOTOGRAPHY

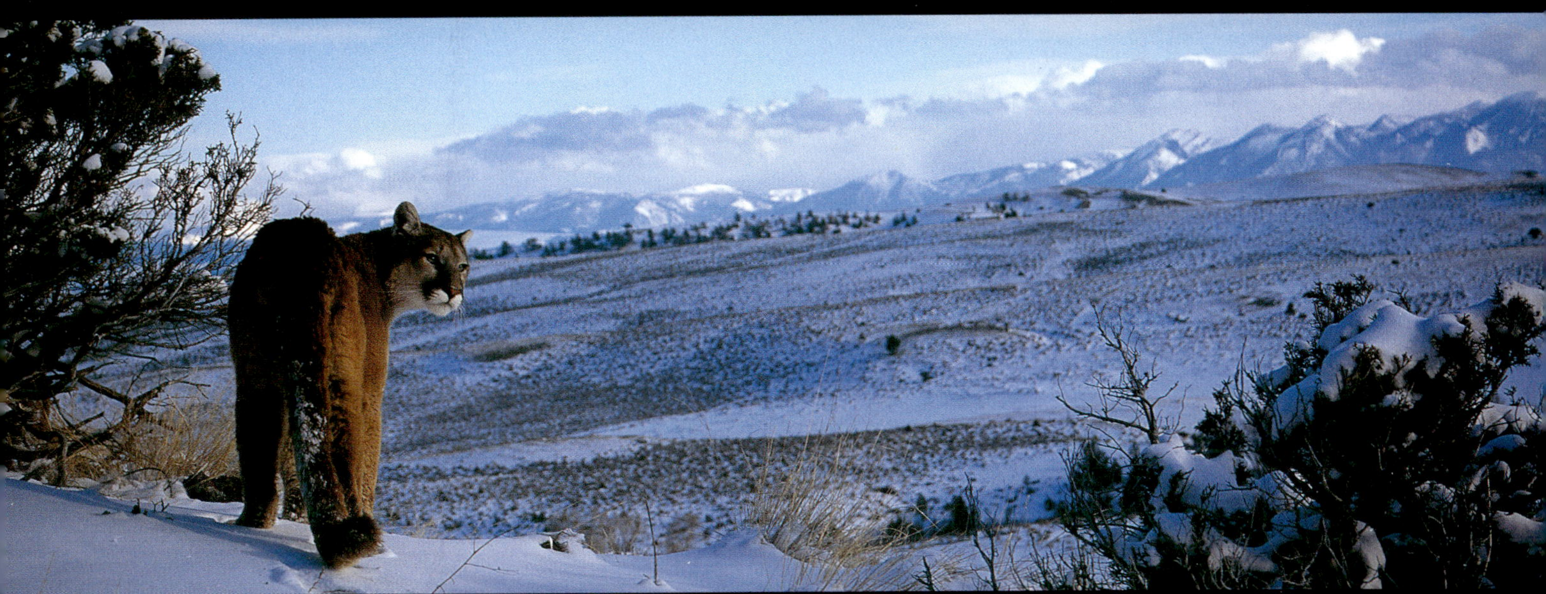

TECHNIQUES FOR CREATING CAPTIVATING IMAGES

Amherst Media, Inc. ■ Buffalo, NY

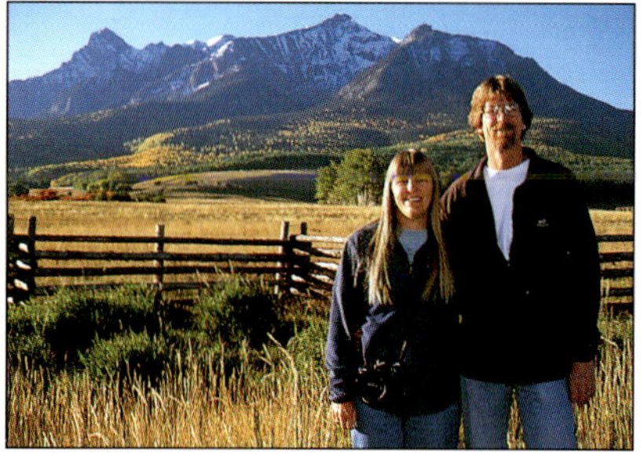

About the Authors

Cathy and Gordon Illg are a professional photographic team specializing in wildlife, nature, and outdoor recreation. For more than twenty years, they've been exploring North America, searching for great places to photograph, even going so far as to maroon themselves on a deserted, tropical island. However, in spite of spending time at these nature photography hotspots, they have found that many of their strongest images were taken right in their own Colorado backyard.

Gordon's degree in wildlife biology has been a big help in providing insight into the lives of the animals they photograph. Cathy's background in business administration kept them afloat while they worked toward becoming full-time photographers.

They have been published in nearly all of the major nature publications as well as numerous calendars, books, and other publications. They have received many awards in the Nature's Best International Photography Competition, and in 2003, they had a second-place winner in the BG Wildlife Photographer of the Year contest. Their writing has appeared in a number of magazines, and they are the authors of *Rocky Mountain Safari* (Rinehart Publishing, 1994).

Because they enjoy meeting new people and sharing the beauty of nature with them, Cathy and Gordon became Certified International Tour Managers. They now lead instructional photography tours under the name Adventure Photography. This is currently keeping them out of trouble, as well as killing any social life they may have had.

Copyright © 2004 by Cathy and Gordon Illg
All rights reserved.

Published by:
Amherst Media, Inc.
P.O. Box 586
Buffalo, N.Y. 14226
Fax: 716-874-4508
www.AmherstMedia.com

Publisher: Craig Alesse
Senior Editor/Production Manager: Michelle Perkins
Assistant Editor: Barbara A. Lynch-Johnt

ISBN: 1-58428-128-6
Library of Congress Card Catalog Number: 2003112486

Printed in Korea.
10 9 8 7 6 5 4 3 2 1

No part of this publication may be reproduced, stored, or transmitted in any form or by any means, electronic, mechanical, photocopied, recorded or otherwise, without prior written consent from the publisher.

Notice of Disclaimer: The information contained in this book is based on the author's experience and opinions. The author and publisher will not be held liable for the use or misuse of the information in this book.

Table of Contents

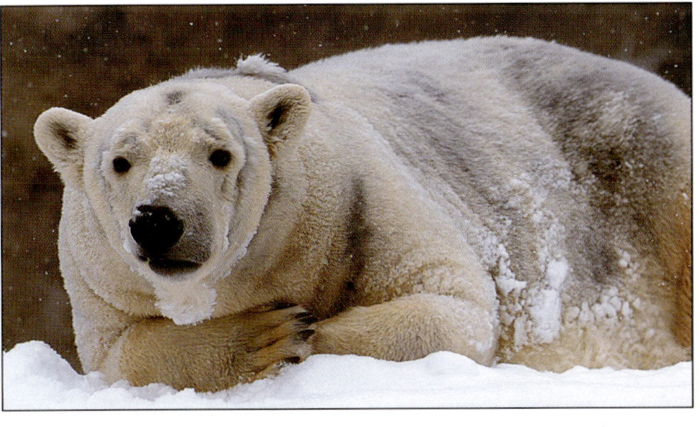

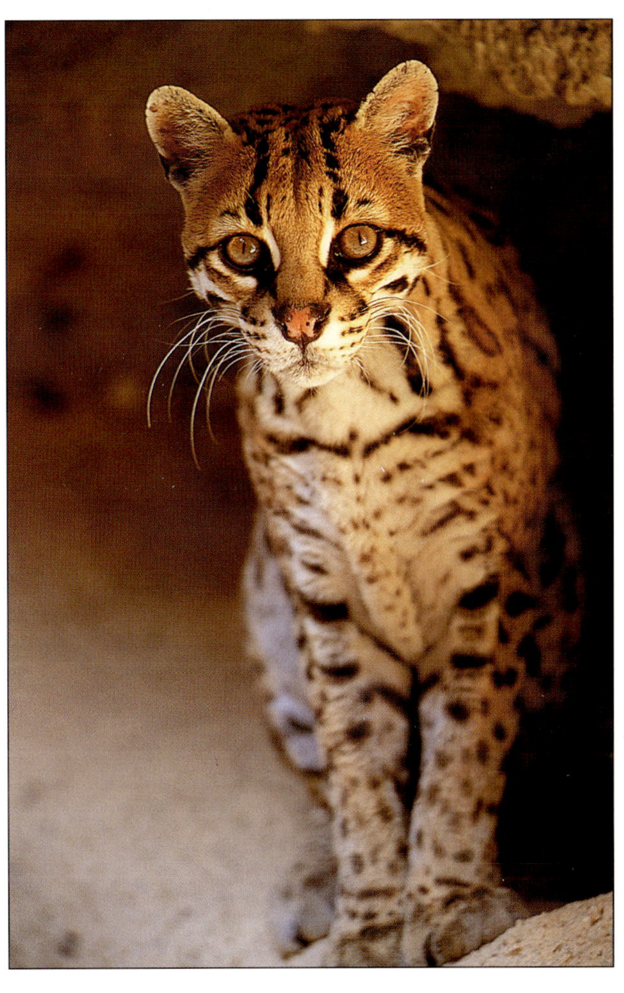

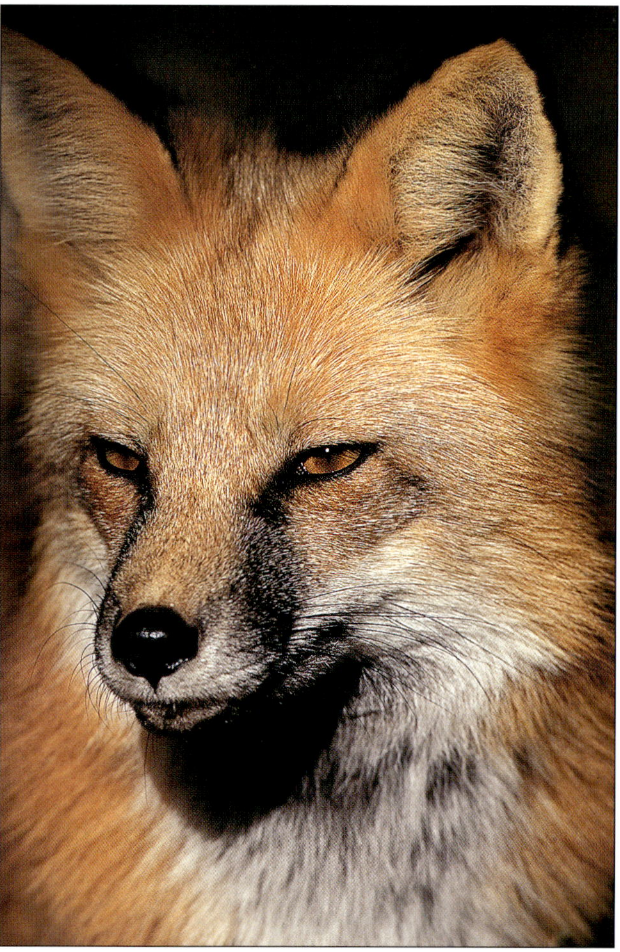

Preface

I never planned to get into wildlife photography. In fact, I thought I was happy and content without lugging a long lens and heavy tripod around the countryside. However, no one could have been more wrong.

It was during a backpacking trip in Colorado's San Juan Mountains that I discovered what was missing in my life. Gravity didn't affect me nearly so much back then, and I was climbing to the top of a ridge just for something to do, carrying a borrowed camera that actually had interchangeable lenses. I felt just like a real photographer.

Climbing up the steep grade, I didn't notice much except the ground before my feet. And oddly enough, that's where the elk was. Halfway up the avalanche chute I was using as a trail, I encountered a newborn elk calf lying right where I wanted to plant my foot. If not for its large, unblinking eyes and the subtle rising and falling of the animal's chest, I would have thought it was dead. I had never before seen anything so magical. Animals of all kinds had always been special to me, but never before had I seen a large, wild creature this close.

I didn't realize what a rare opportunity this was for a photographer. Of course, I also didn't realize that I should have switched the 28mm

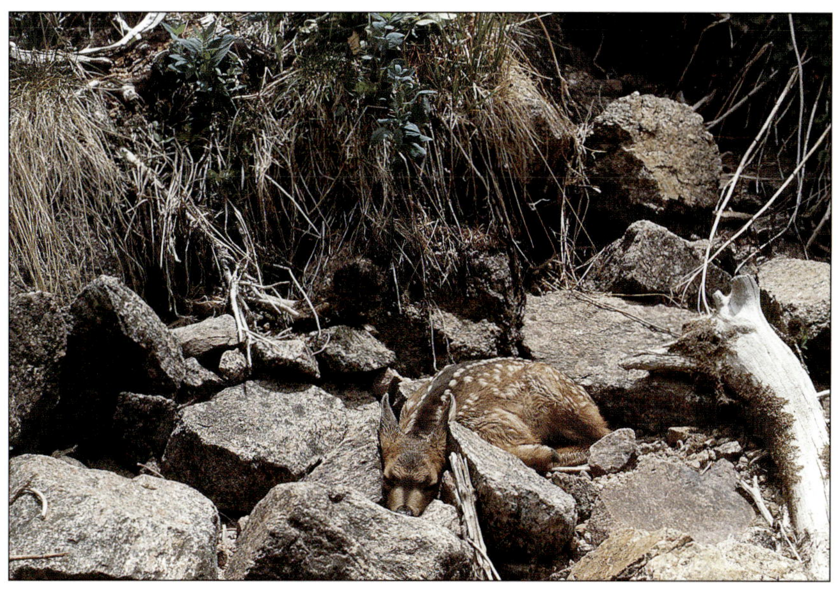

This was my first attempt at a wildlife photo. Notice the clever use of clutter and negative space. I only wish I could have a similar opportunity again, so I could compose an image worthy of the situation. I've been waiting more than a quarter of a century for the situation to repeat itself, though, and I'm still waiting. San Juan Mountains, Colorado. 28mm lens.

lens on the camera for the small telephoto I was also carrying. However, as I centered the tiny elk in my viewfinder, apparently taking great pains to include plenty of negative space and clutter all around it, I knew what I wanted to do with the rest of my life. I wanted to photograph animals.

There is something about wildlife photography that is immensely soul-satisfying. Just watch the visitors at a national park when some creature shows its face. Even if the subject will only appear as a small dot in the resulting image, nearly everyone with a camera takes a photo. We want to show others that our vacation was special because we saw wild animals. Perhaps it reaffirms the ties we humans have had with the natural world for most of our existence.

There is something about wildlife photography that is immensely soul-satisfying.

1. Beyond Documentation

The finest images—the images that stir our souls—combine documentation of natural things with a sense of what they mean to us.
—Freeman Patterson

Only three or four decades ago now, wildlife photography was terribly difficult. Obtaining even the poorest wildlife images was an incredible challenge. Quality film was slow and so were the lenses. The animals photographers wanted to photograph, on the other hand, were usually fast and preferred low-light situations—not the best combination for great photos. Not surprisingly, a well-exposed photograph with a subject that was close to being in focus was generally considered a good image.

Today's viewers are a spoiled bunch. They've seen a lot of great wildlife photos, and it's not always easy to make them sit up and take notice. What's one more picture of a tiger or a whale to them? That's where the first wildlife photographers had an advantage. Their audience had seen very few animal images, which made it easy to impress them. Now we have equipment that makes getting the photos relatively easy, but we have to work just as hard as our predecessors did because we need much stronger images to impress our audience. If our photos are only documentary, we're not going to get much of a reaction.

As Simon King, noted wildlife filmmaker and judge for the BG Wildlife Photographer of the Year competition, remarked in *Wildlife Photographer of the Year: Portfolio 10* (December, 2000),

> Taking photographs isn't rocket science. . . . With the advent of hi-tech camera and lighting equipment, many of the practical problems of this work have been reduced or eliminated. But far from making the photographer's life easier, it makes it a whole lot tougher. Gone are the days when simply recording a well-focused image of a fox was worthy of praise. Now the fox has to be doing something interesting. Not only that, but it has to be doing it in gorgeous light. And there is always that little something extra, the composition, the light in the eye, the intangible ingredient that lifts an image out of the mass of good photographs into the elite of the great ones.

Yes, technologically, wildlife photographers have it much easier today. In the last two decades, the improvements in equipment have been nothing short of fantastic. We now have film choices out the wazoo, and the film is not only two to three stops faster than what it used to be, it now has better grain and color. Most of the cameras sold today don't even use film anymore. They record images as a series of zeros and ones, and the photographers can even delete photos they don't like. No one need ever know how many poor photos they took.

Today's cameras not only focus wherever you point them; they can also track incredibly fast-moving objects. The lenses we put on our cameras are both faster and sharper than ever before and give more magnification. I don't know how many old-timers I've heard complaining about how easy today's wildlife photographers have it. And it's true. Of course, I've noticed that most of the old-timers have also switched to the new equipment, which means they have it easier too.

All technology aside, another benefit to photographers is that the world has become a much smaller place. Anyone with a few weeks' time and the money to travel the world can visit locations where exotic animals will share their lives with you. If you have the time and the money, incredibly endangered species like mountain gorillas and Indian rhinos can be seen through your viewfinder. But you don't need to travel the world to find wonderful wildlife subjects. Even photographers who have to settle for photographing in their own backyards can usually find great subjects. A little bit of habitat around a bird feeder can provide outstanding photo opportunities.

Even photographers who have to settle for photographing in their own backyards can usually find great subjects.

Additionally, many of our subjects are much more approachable than they were in the past, and there are several explanations for this.

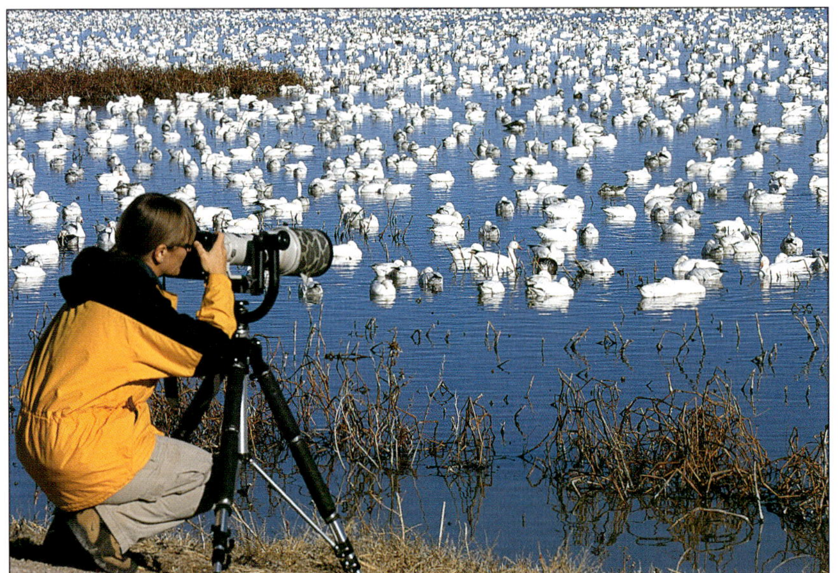

Cathy uses a 500mm lens to photograph snow geese at Bosque del Apache National Wildlife Refuge in New Mexico. Today, it's relatively easy to find photographable animals.

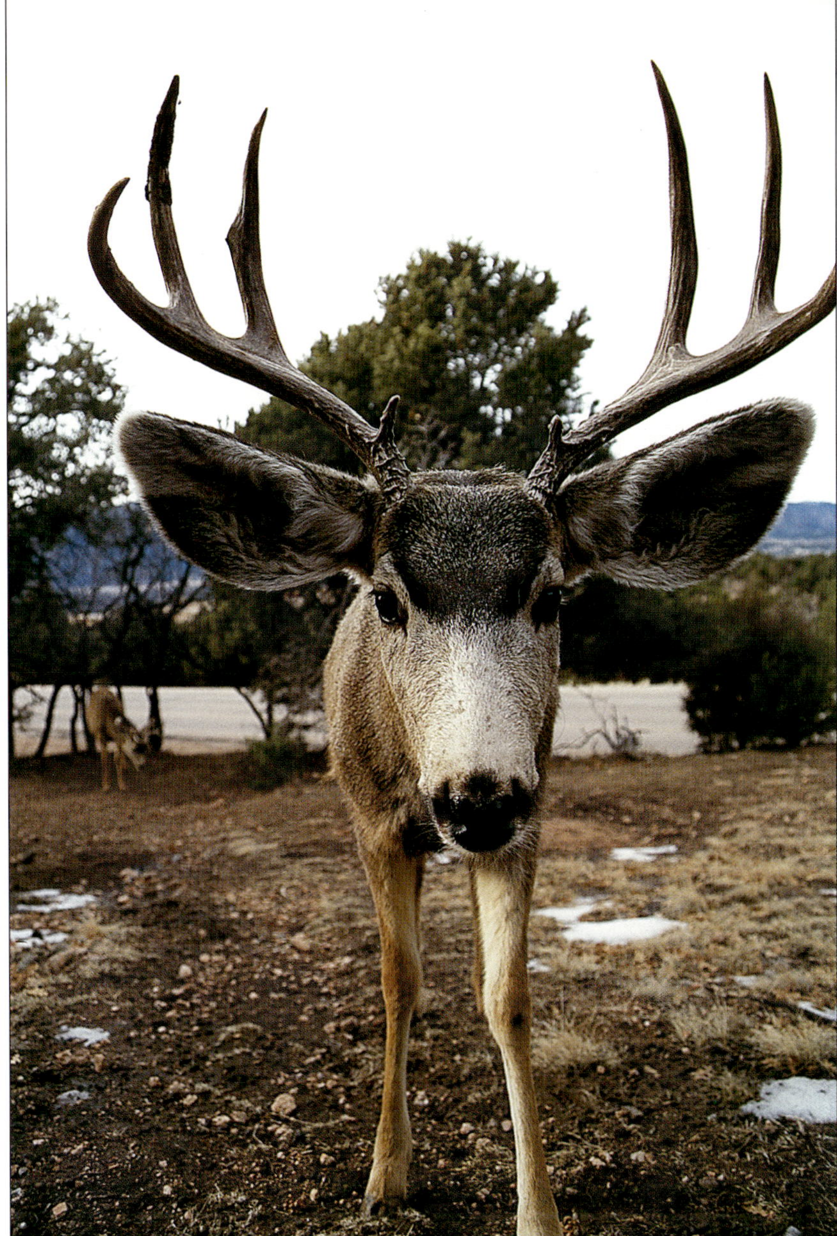

This photo of a wild mule deer buck was taken with a 28mm lens as the animal stuck his nose in my face. Historically, a mule deer this tame would have been dinner for some lucky family long before he became this habituated to humans. Royal Gorge, Colorado.

Traditionally, many animals were hunted throughout their range. Today, hunting is losing its popularity, and there are many locations where the animals are protected. There are now places where mule deer and white-tailed bucks will allow point-blank photography. Such a thing would have been almost unheard of several decades ago. Many of the animals today have also been forced to adapt to the presence of lots of people, making it much easier to approach them. In some parts of Florida and California, the egrets will not even look up from their fishing to check out the parade of wildlife watchers filing past.

Between advances in technology and subjects becoming more accessible, today's photographers are finding it much easier to capture wildlife on film than their predecessors did. With the proper equipment, it is now no big deal to obtain wildlife photos that are properly exposed and in focus. And today so many of us have the necessary gear that our viewers are being bombarded with technically correct images. As Mr. King said, though, just being technically correct is no longer enough to make a photo worthy of praise.

THE NEW IMAGE REQUIREMENTS

Although it has become relatively easy to take photos that are sharp and well exposed, most of today's wildlife images document little more than the fact that the photographer saw an animal. They give viewers the bare minimum of information: There isn't enough happening in the image to hold the viewers' attention for very long; the subject isn't engaged in any observable behavior; the image isn't tight enough to show any real detail in the subject's expression; and it's not wide enough to show the subject's relationship with its environment. Have you ever heard someone say, "That's a nice enough picture of a deer, but it doesn't do anything for me?" Well, they were probably describing a documentary photo.

On the other hand, some images grab and hold our attention with their beauty, cuteness, strangeness, the emotions they evoke, the behavior they show, the environmental relationships they portray, and the details about the subject they allow us to see. These elements take images beyond the realm of mere documentation; the photos that successfully incorporate them draw the viewer into the creature's world and bring out the "oohs" and "aahs" at slide shows. These are the kind of photos that come to mind when we think of cover or calendar photos (although there are also plenty of published cover and calendar shots that are only documentary).

These elements take images beyond the realm of mere documentation . . .

GOING THE EXTRA MILE

Photographers want to create images that captivate their viewers, that present something interesting about the subject. But if these are the type of photos that wildlife photographers want to take, why do they account for such a small percentage of the images we produce?

Beginning wildlife photographers, especially those working in locations with lots of animal activity, are inclined to take a few quick photos of an animal, then move on to another subject. If the center of interest is in focus and the image is relatively clutter-free, the photographer's job is done. Their goal is diversity instead of quality, and they may capture a great many decent, technically correct images in this way. Shooting like this, however, they will not take many photos that go beyond documentation.

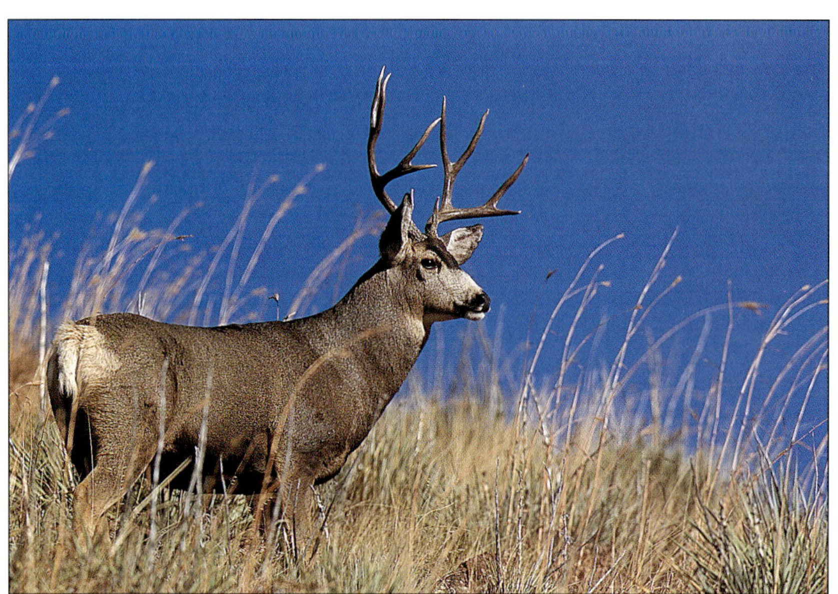

This is a fine shot of a mule deer buck. It's sharp. It's properly exposed. And the composition is fine. With all of the deer photos we've seen, though, it's nothing special. This image doesn't give the viewer a lot of information to play with. It pretty much just documents that the photographer saw a mule deer buck. Boulder County, Colorado. 500mm lens.

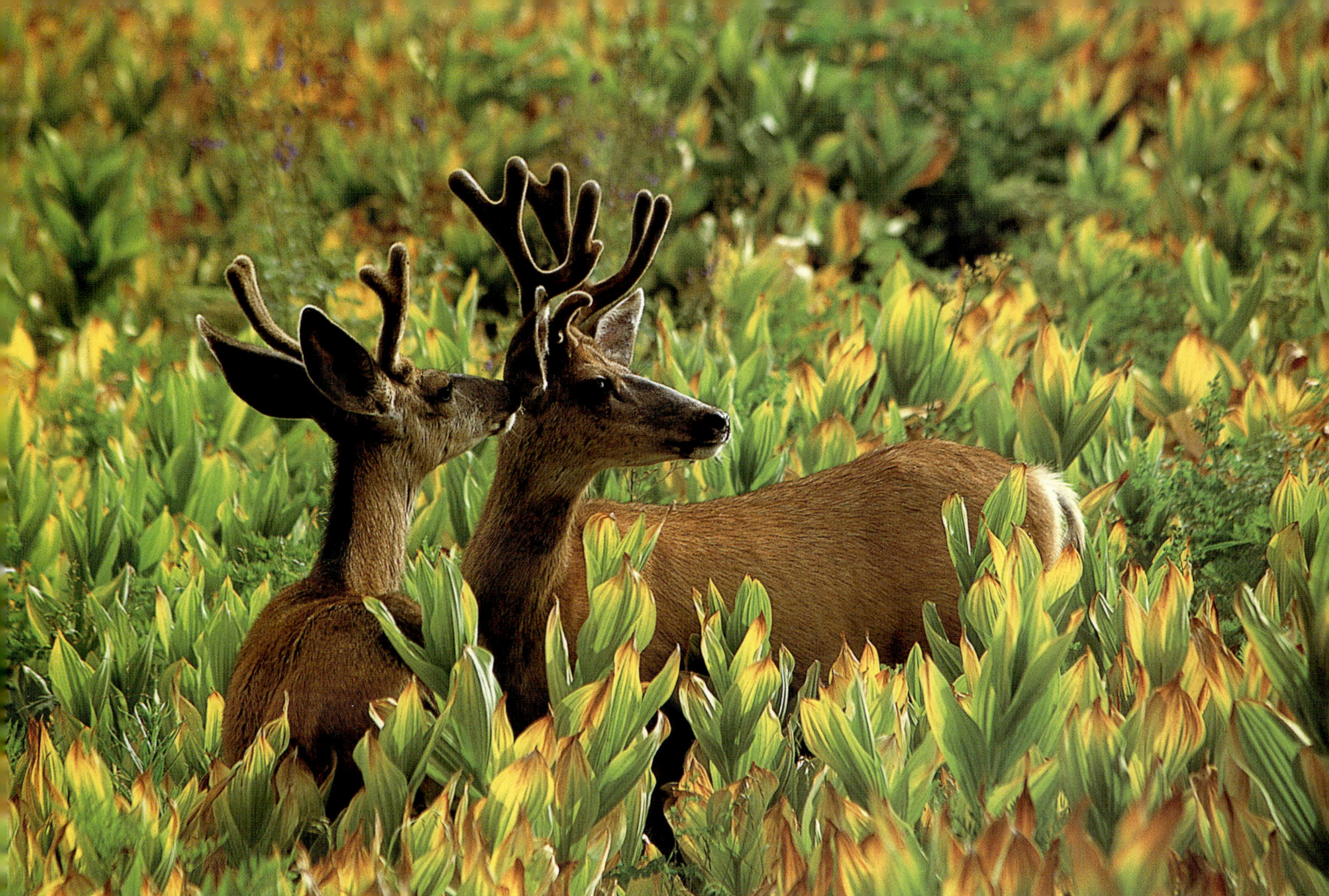

Mule deer bucks greeting each other. Not only does this photo have behavior working for it, but a touch of back light shows off the velvet on the deer antlers and makes the old skunk cabbage leaves glow. Gunnison National Forest, Colorado. 75–300mm lens.

The difference between a snapshot and a serious photograph is how much work is put into it, and the most satisfying images rarely result from snapshots. Getting images that go beyond documentary requires more patience, more perseverance, more skill, more knowledge about your subject, and many times, a lot more luck. For this reason, great photographers will often stay with a subject as long as the subject will allow. They may not get as much variety, but they come back with a much higher percentage of attention-grabbing images.

While all wildlife photos, even the poorest ones, tell us something about the subject, photos that go beyond documentary show viewers why the image was taken. We can show the beauty/majesty/spirit of the animal. We can show how it feels about the cold as well as whether it's happy to see friends, angry about seeing rivals, or just bummed because it's all alone.

Many scientists get upset by the attribution of human emotions to the "lower orders." They say these creatures don't have the brain power to experience these feelings. Hogwash! Recent studies have shown that quite a few of the "lower orders" experience many of the same emotions as you and I. And besides, the subject doesn't need to be happy

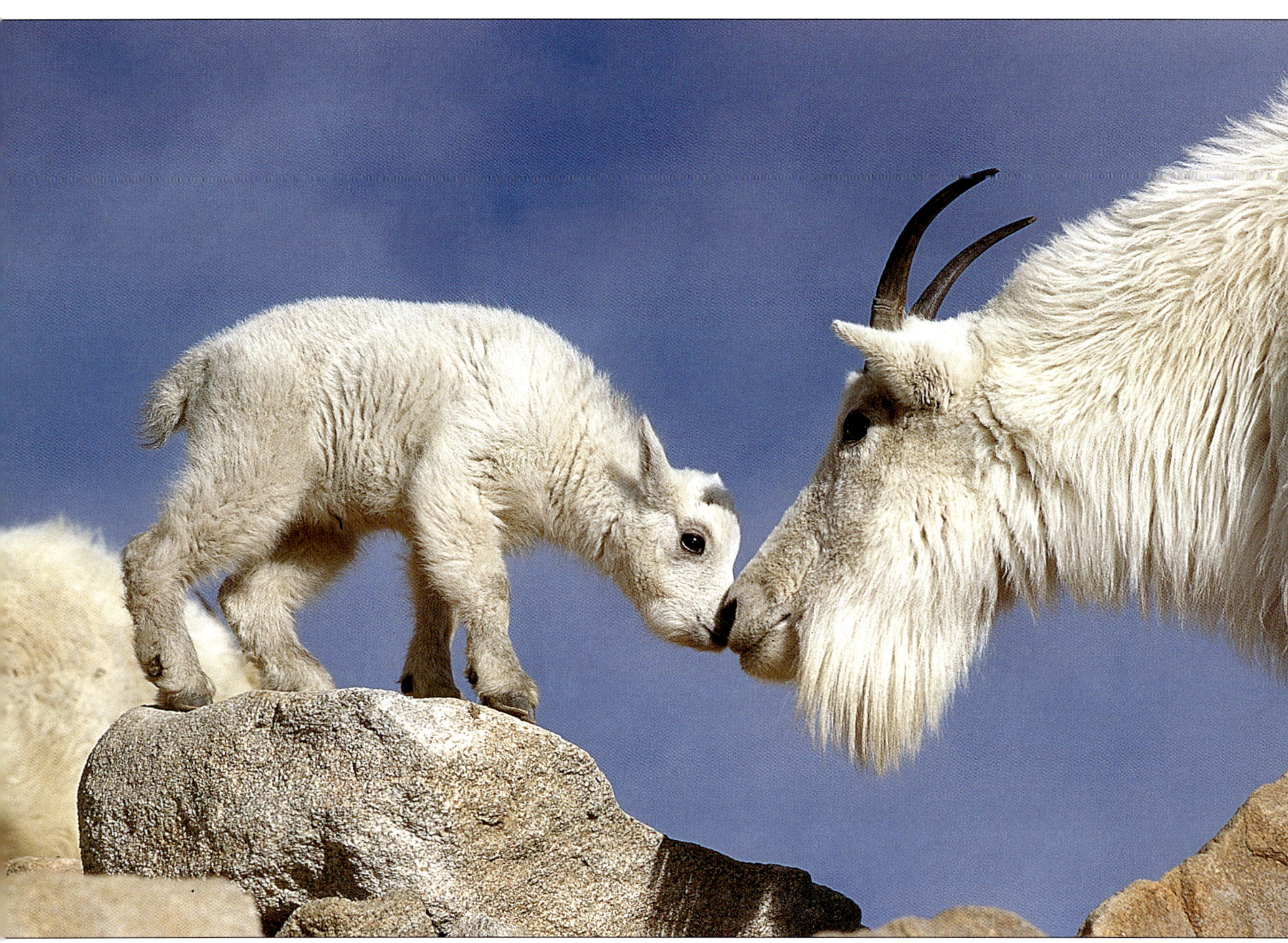

Mountain goat mother and kid greeting each other. Evoking emotions, like motherly love, is a good way to draw the viewer into your image. Mt. Evans, Colorado. 75–300mm lens.

or sad. It just needs to look that way. If the viewer has a common bond, like an emotion, with the subject, it helps draw the viewer into the picture. And we want the viewer to spend lots of time looking at our pictures.

DOCUMENTARY VS. BEYOND DOCUMENTARY

Since Cathy and I know the secret of taking these great photos, surely every image we capture these days sings to the viewer's soul, and after you read this book, you'll be in the same enviable position, right? Hardly. The reason we're willing to share these secrets is because it still takes a lot of work to go beyond documentary with any regularity, and many photographers are not willing or are unable to put in the time. Most of the photos we take, as well as those of every other wildlife photographer, are still just documentary. It isn't easy to go beyond that. So don't feel bad if most of your photos seem to only be documenting the fact that you've seen an animal. You're not alone in that boat.

If you only took wildlife images that went beyond documentation, you wouldn't take many photos, and we love to take photos. In fact, you'd probably take so few pictures that you would be out of practice and mess up the shot when a truly great moment occurred. So when you find that great egret or desert tortoise, take a few documentary shots just to make sure you get something. After you have some good documentary images under your belt, then you're ready to attempt something more. Try for behavior, or environmental shots, or closeups, or move to put a better background behind your subject. Use your imagination. In *National Geographic Photography Field Guide: Secrets to Making Great Pictures* (Peter Burian and Robert Caputo, The National Geographic Society, 1999), photographer Chris Johns said, "If every picture on your roll is perfect, then you've failed."

By the way, there is nothing wrong with never taking anything but documentary photos. The activity gets you outside and in the presence of some wonderful company (the animals, not other photographers). Photos that go beyond documentation do not always do better in competitions. If you're looking to sell your work, photos that go beyond documentation do not necessarily get published any more often than documentary ones. Just check the magazines. Editors use the photos they need, not the ones they like.

For example, a magazine used some of our images in an article on where to see birds around Tucson, Arizona. We sent them some great stuff on the local avifauna, and they did use some bird photos that went beyond documentation, but only as tiny inserts. Our largest photo in the article ran almost a full page, and it was a straightforward shot showing the entrance to the Arizona–Sonora Desert Museum. A kid with a point and shoot could have taken the same shot.

Taking your wildlife photography beyond documentation will definitely give your viewers a lot more to ponder.

Be sure of your reasons for stretching your horizons. This is something to undertake only if some artistic urge within you will not let you settle for images that look much like everyone else's. The techniques offered here will not ensure that you win any more ribbons in photography contests or that you are published any more often than you are now. However, taking your wildlife photography beyond documentation will definitely give your viewers a lot more to ponder in your pictures.

2. What Should I Photograph?

Photograph what interests you, something you're passionate about.
—Jodi Cobb, National Geographic Society Photographer

It wasn't a photo opportunity that many people would expect while tent camping, but as we crawled out of our sleeping bags, wondering how best to capture the sunrise, a dolphin surfaced not thirty feet away. We were camped on Isla Magdalena, a barrier island on the Pacific Coast of Baja California, and the shore dropped off quite quickly on the east side of the island, so the dolphin could swim almost right next to the beach. That dolphin exhaling a big cloud of spray silhouetted against the sunrise was what I wanted to photograph.

The animal wasn't particularly afraid of me, restricted as I was to the beach, but it wasn't exactly posing for photos either. It was swimming parallel to the shore, sometimes so close it seemed like I could have jumped on its back and ridden away. But it would only take one or two breaths in quick succession then disappear underwater only to surface sixty to one hundred feet farther along the shore. I was running along the water's edge and then setting up for my shot while trying to catch my breath. All of this while trying to estimate where the animal would reappear so I could silhouette it against the sunrise.

After fifteen minutes worth of hundred-yard dashes down the beach, I didn't get a single photo of the dolphin with the sunrise. Every time

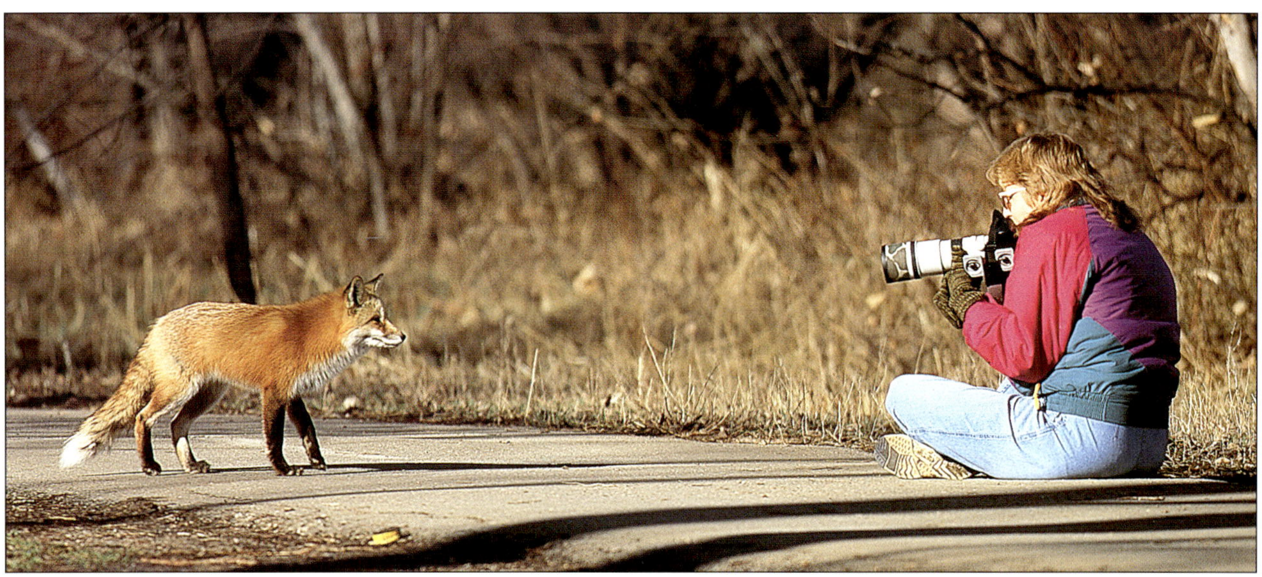

Cathy being checked out by a wild red fox. Finding a tolerant subject and being willing and able to spend lots of time with it are important if you want to capture images that go beyond documentation. Jefferson County, Colorado. 500mm lens.

I was getting ready to put away my gear when this desert cottontail came up and sat down beside me. I don't even know why. On another day it might have been afraid to come close. As I sat there watching it, the rabbit began washing its face. Take advantage of tolerant subjects. Arapaho National Wildlife Refuge, Colorado. 500mm lens with 1.4x teleconverter.

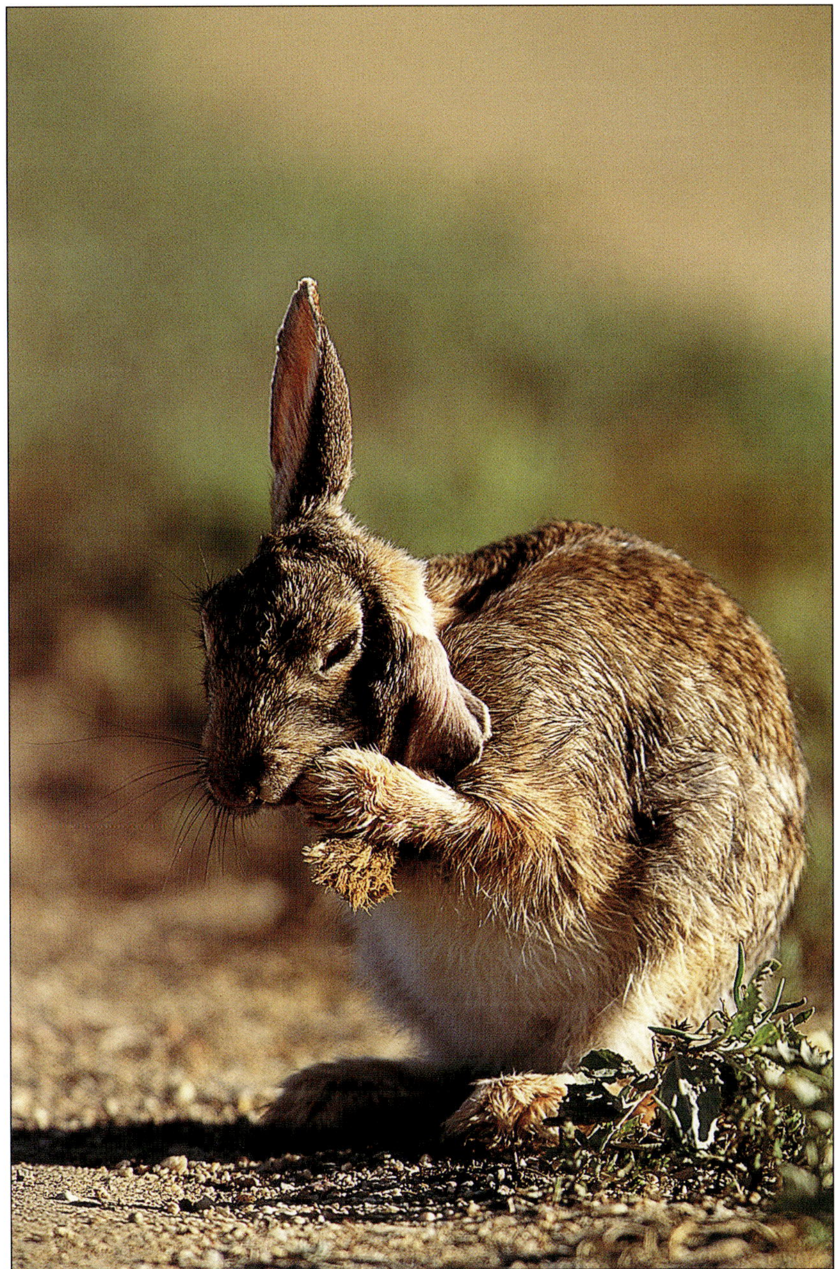

it came up, it had either already passed me or hadn't reached me yet. All I had to show for my effort that morning were some wobbly legs and burning lungs.

Every wildlife photographer has encountered subjects that just won't cooperate. In fact, it happens most of the time. The hard truth is that most animals just don't trust us enough to allow photographers to get close enough for meaningful photography. And overcoming this handicap is a big part of the secret to exceptional wildlife photography.

Patience, determination, and perseverance are all good traits to have if you want to be a good wildlife photographer, and all the great photographers have these characteristics in spades. However, the one thing that is almost a necessity in shooting photos that go beyond documentation is a tolerant subject. If you have a subject that will not tolerate your presence, your only shots are going to be of the animal's rear end as it disappears over a hill.

You may luck out and sneak up on your subject or have it look back for a second as it's leaving, giving you the chance for one or two decent photos. You will not, however, be able to work the subject at all, and that's what is required to go beyond documentation with any dependability. Oh sure, most photographers will luck out every now and then, but going beyond documentation usually requires spending a considerable amount of time with your subject.

WILL THE ANIMAL LET YOU PHOTOGRAPH IT?

Now when we talk about tolerant subjects, we're not just talking about animals who have been forced to accept us because their habitat has been inundated with a flood of humanity. There are other reasons animals might tolerate photographers. The animals may not know the photographer is there because he's using a blind; the animals might not be familiar with humans and may have no fear of us; the animals may be so much bigger than us that they ignore us or look upon us as a prey item; the animals' senses may not be keen enough to detect our presence; the subject may be in a controlled situation; or the subject may be captive. The important thing, though, is to have an animal that will allow you to spend time with it, capturing moments that most people never see, mostly because they either can't or won't spend lots of time with these creatures.

Going beyond documentation usually requires spending a considerable amount of time with your subject.

Why do you think there are so many endearing photos of penguins in the media (despite the fact that the cost of visiting them limits the number of potential photographers considerably)? There are a lot more photographers out there photographing elk, for example, but, even including hunting magazines, there are many times the number of penguin photos in print than there are elk photos. Of course, penguins are popular subjects because they walk on their hind feet and wear those nifty tuxedos (let's just say the appeal may be rooted in anthropomorphism). Another reason, though, is these birds are so incredibly tolerant of camera-toting humans. They'll walk right up to you. You just have to pick a lens, any lens.

EVERY ANIMAL HAS A STORY TO TELL

So if you want to take photos that are more than just documentary, photograph tolerant subjects. It doesn't matter what species it is. Don't

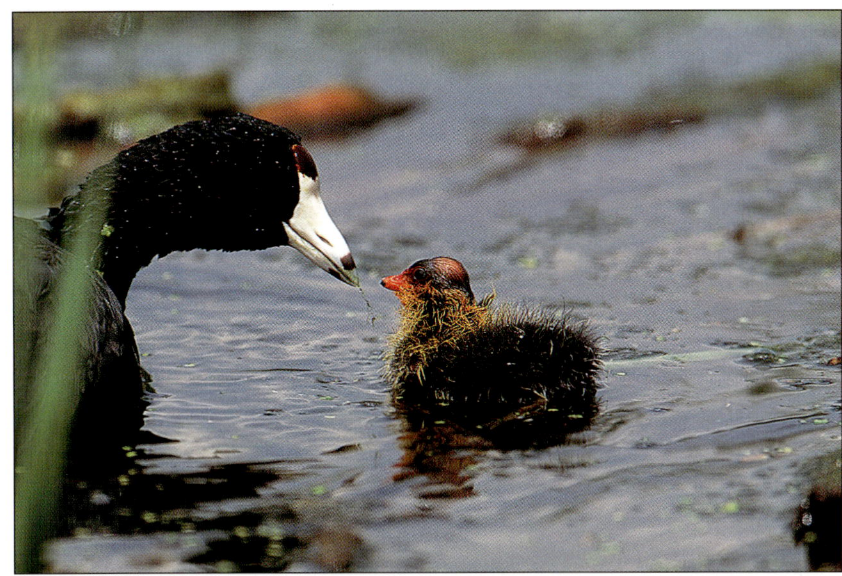

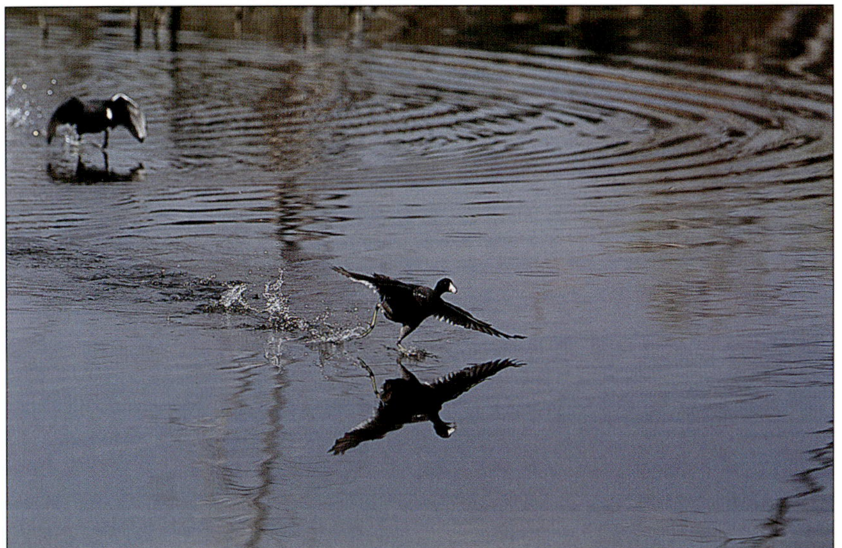

TOP—Adult coot feeding a chick. Every species, no matter how apparently dull and drab, has a story worth photographing. Jefferson County, Colorado. 500mm lens with 1.4x teleconverter. **BOTTOM**—Capturing coots running across the water would have been almost impossible without spending lots of time with these birds. Jefferson County, Colorado. 300mm lens.

make the mistake that Cathy and I did when we first began photographing wildlife. If an animal wasn't colorful or exciting enough, we just didn't bother with it. We spent lots of time looking for charismatic megafauna and colorful birds because those were the first species to attract our attention.

Coots were very high on our list of uninteresting animals, and even when they were quite tame, we looked down on photographing them. If we had not lucked out and stumbled upon a nest of newly-hatched coot chicks, who knows how long we would have continued along this path of ignorance? The chicks, with their bald, red heads, purple eyeshadow, and clown feet, more than made up for their parents' drab colors. And as we photographed the chicks, we noticed behaviors in the adults that were worth many rolls of film. If not for the chicks, we would never have captured the adults running across the water, or seen two pairs "mooning" each other in a territorial dispute. Coots, of all things, are now one of our favorite wildlife subjects.

Every wildlife subject is interesting and has its own story to tell. Granted, some animals require a lot more research and observation before they reveal exactly what makes them so interesting, but that element of discovery is part of what makes wildlife photography so exciting. And many of the species that are commonly perceived as boring are rarely photographed. Capturing new or at least rarely photographed activities featuring these "uninteresting" species is a good deal easier than competing with the crowds photographing elk or egrets.

Something to keep in mind is that your viewer's perception has a great deal to do with whether or not your images of wildlife are merely documentary or something more. As we mentioned earlier, wildlife photographers of several decades ago had a much easier task trying to impress their audience. If you could find a similar group of unsophisticated viewers, who knows, maybe most of your images would bring out the "oohs" and "aahs" from the crowd. Most viewers, however, have seen many, many wildlife photos, and the more images they see of a particular species, the harder it is to impress them with pictures of that animal. Show them a species that they may not have ever seen a photo of, and it's much easier to impress them.

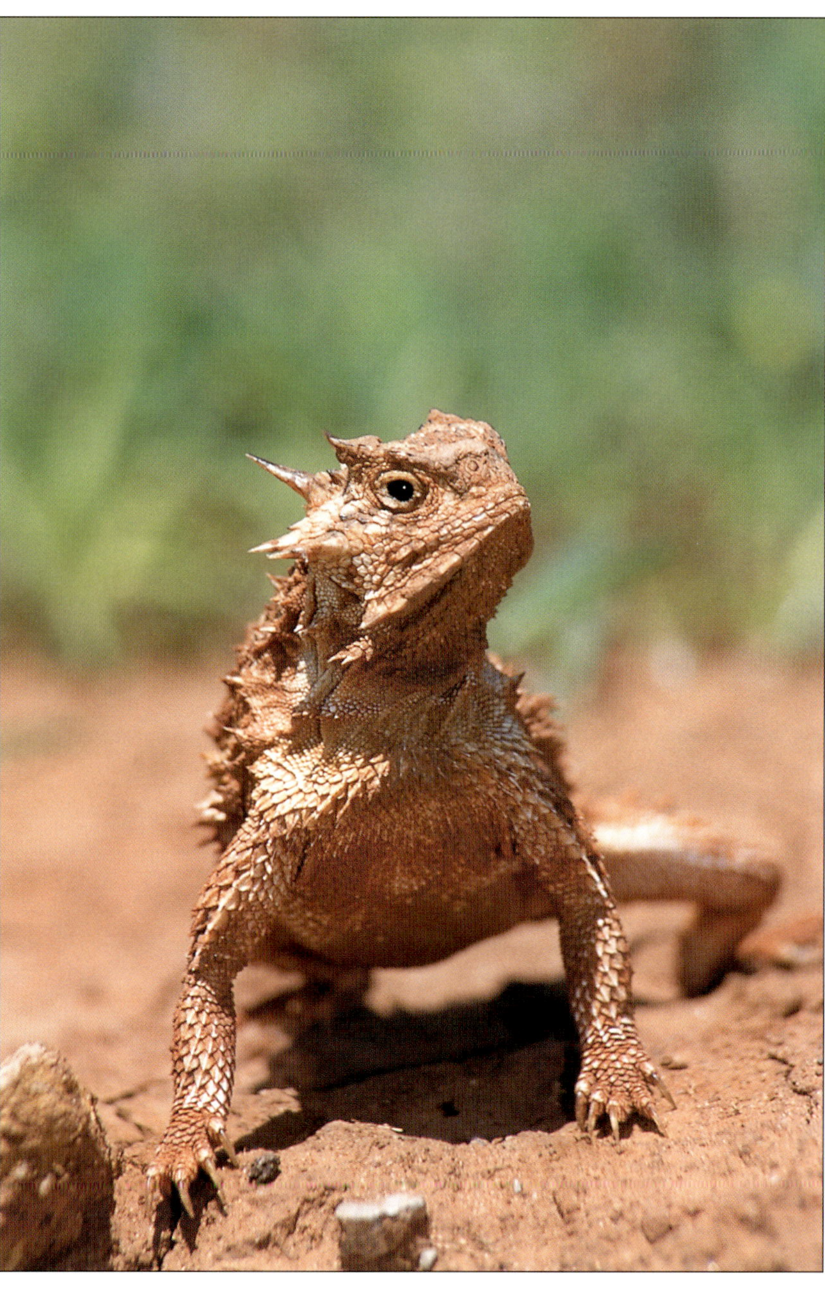

It's easier to get your viewers' attention with images of species they haven't seen many photos of. Horned lizards are relatively common in the Southwest deserts, but they are not often photographed. Working from a low position helped make this a strong image. Black Kettle National Grassland, Oklahoma. 75–300mm lens with extension tubes and fill flash.

For example, if you're showing photos of egrets, especially if you're showing them to a group of other wildlife photographers, you need something pretty special in order to impress them. Nearly everyone has already seen lots of pictures of egrets, even if they haven't photographed them personally. Most viewers have seen every aspect of these birds' lives, from flying with nest twigs in their beaks, to fishing, to feeding their chicks. How many people, though, have seen photos of coots feeding their chicks? The only ones we've seen are the ones we have taken ourselves. And these photos always get a good reaction from the viewers.

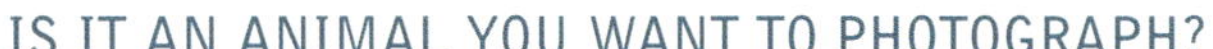

IS IT AN ANIMAL YOU WANT TO PHOTOGRAPH?

When you are picking a subject to photograph, the most important criteria is how you feel about the creature. Choose an animal you want to photograph, even if it is an egret. We still photograph these beautiful birds every chance we get. Photographing a subject just because you think the images might sell or do well in a contest is a sure way to end up with documentary photos. This doesn't mean that the photos won't sell or won't do well in a competition. It just means that the photos probably won't be anything special. On the other hand, if you're photographing a species you really want to photograph, you'll be much more inclined to put in the time and effort necessary to capture images that go beyond documentation.

Don't lose any sleep worrying that your subject has already been over-photographed, its essence already captured. There is always something new to show, a different way to portray your subject. Every species out there still has secrets it's just waiting to share with some lucky photographer. It might as well be you.

In that same vein, it is not necessary to travel halfway around the world to take photos that go beyond documentation. Almost all of us have suitable subjects nearby. It's hard to find an urban area that doesn't have a greenbelt, open space, or park where wildlife can be found. We've seen incredible wildlife images that have come from ordinary backyards. And concentrating on animals that you find close to home gives you more time to work them, more time to capture those special moments and compose those special scenes.

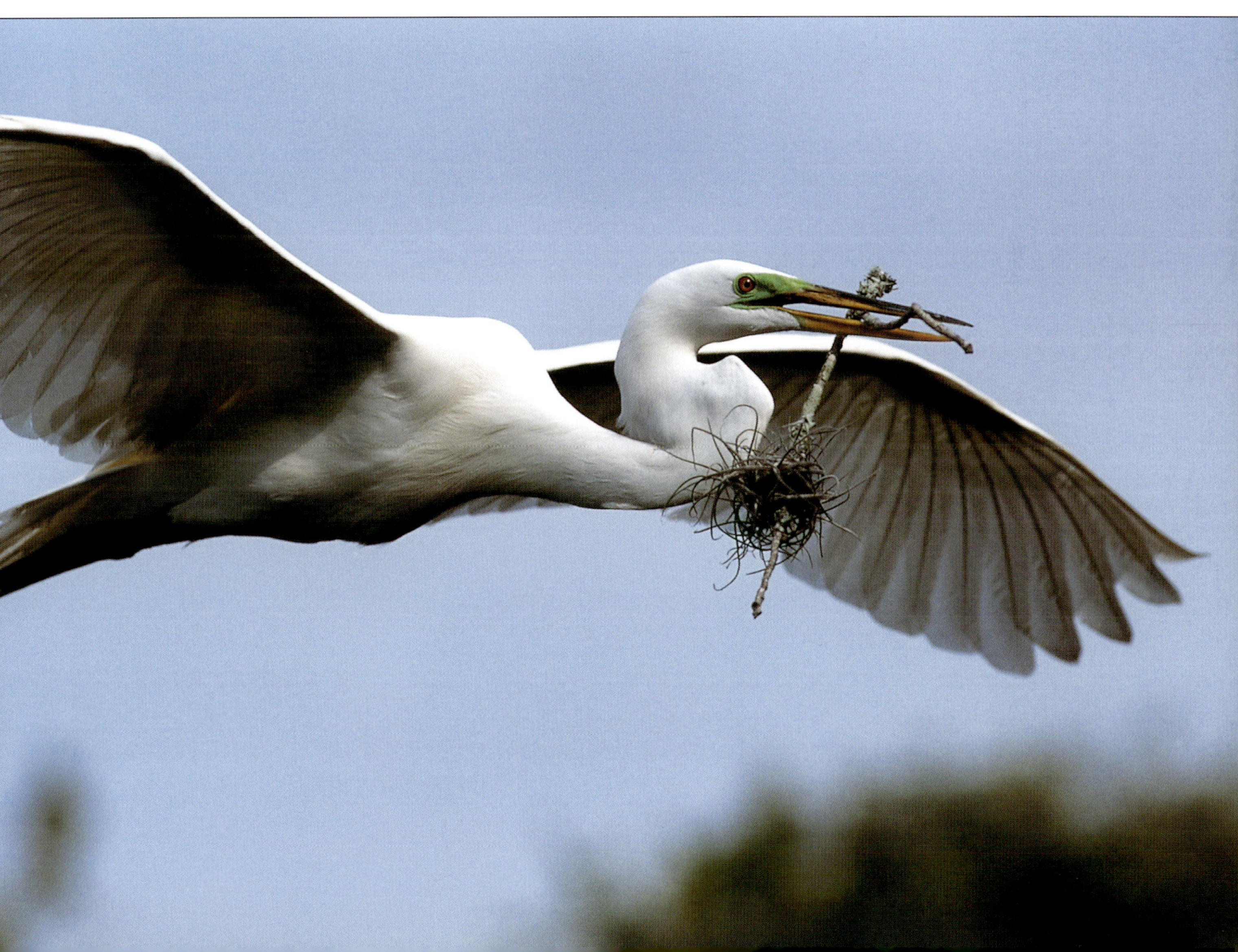

Most viewers have seen lots of photos of egrets, and it can be hard to impress them even with dramatic shots, like this great egret bringing sticks back to its nest. Anastasia Island, Florida. 100–400mm lens.

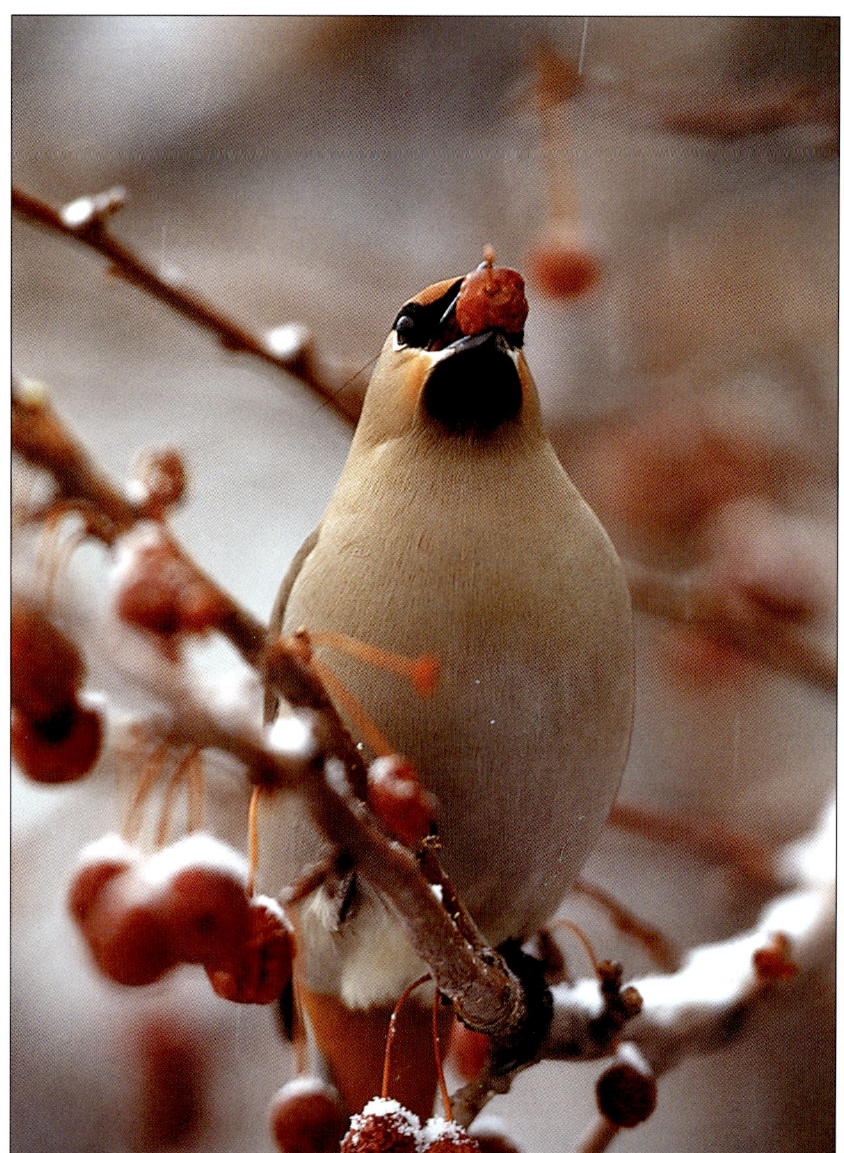

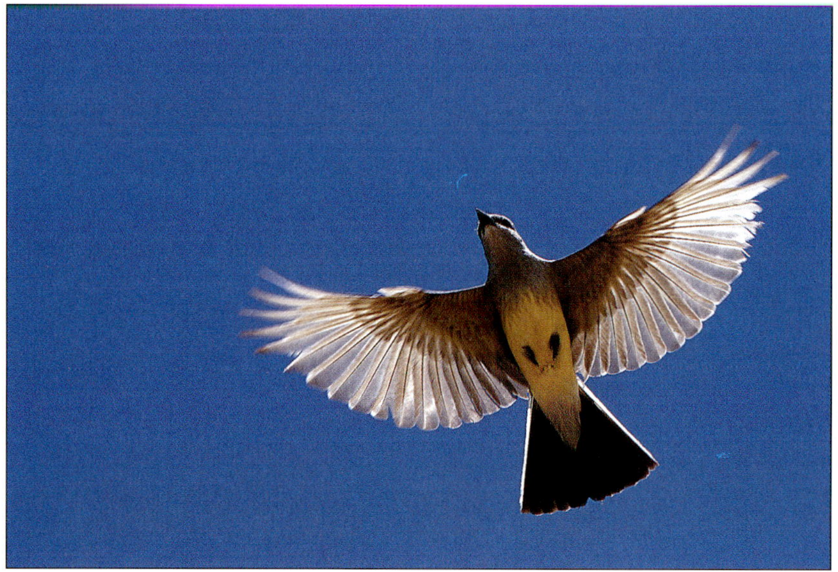

TOP—Every species has something new to share with photographers who are willing to spend some time with them. Here a Bohemian waxwing is eating crab apples in a snowstorm. Jefferson County, Colorado. 500mm lens with extension tubes. BOTTOM—This western kingbird nested at a bend in a rain gutter on a house on the Colorado prairie. The bird became very used to people because of where it nested, and it hovered almost every time it approached the nest, making it relatively easy to get this shot. Barr Lake State Park, Colorado. 300mm lens.

So when you're choosing the ideal subject to help you take photos that are more than just documentary, pick a subject you'll enjoy photographing. Then try to find a location or a situation in which that subject will tolerate your presence. If that means setting up a blind, do it. If it means finding a location where that species is friendly to photographers, search for it. It might require some combination of tactics, but whatever it takes, as long as it doesn't harm your subject or break any laws, go for it.

3. Throw Some Light on the Subject

There's an incredible number of people running around with incredible equipment who don't think of the image as much. They think if they get the right film and a long enough lens, and they go to the right national park . . . I used to think like that.
—Jim Brandenburg

The sun is about to rise, and you've just stumbled across a small herd of mule deer bucks in velvet. The deer are moving, and you have to decide: do you try to position yourself for front light, side light, or back light shooting? Cathy and I found ourselves in just this situation a number of years ago. It looked like we would only have time for one series of photos before the deer disappeared, and we just guessed about where we should position ourselves.

If we knew then what we do now about how light from different directions will affect an image, we would not have had to guess. Most wildlife photographers learn early in the game that all light is not the same. It varies in intensity, color, and direction, and if a person is serious about this craft, they are going to be seeing lots of sunrises and sunsets. Not only is the quality of the light better early and late in the day, but our subjects are often more active then.

We're also taught to keep the sun at our backs to get the best results. And front lighting not only gives good results, it is probably the easiest light direction to deal with in terms of getting an accurate meter reading. In most situations it is probably the best way to go. It is not the only way, though, and wildlife photographers should know what changing the direction of their light source will do to their image.

WHICH WOULD YOU CHOOSE?

So which type of light did we choose with the mule deer bucks at sunrise? We ignored everything we had been taught and took a chance on some back-lit photos. It turned out to be a lucky guess. The velvet antlers came back looking like they were charged with electricity, and the late summer grass took on a golden glow. Would the deer have looked better front lit? You can judge for yourself. After we took a handful of shots, the deer stopped their march into the forest and started eating again. So we were able to photograph the deer from every side. Granted, it's very subjective, but we like the back-lit images best.

When photographing commonly photographed animals, like mule deer, you need to make your subject look different if you want it to be

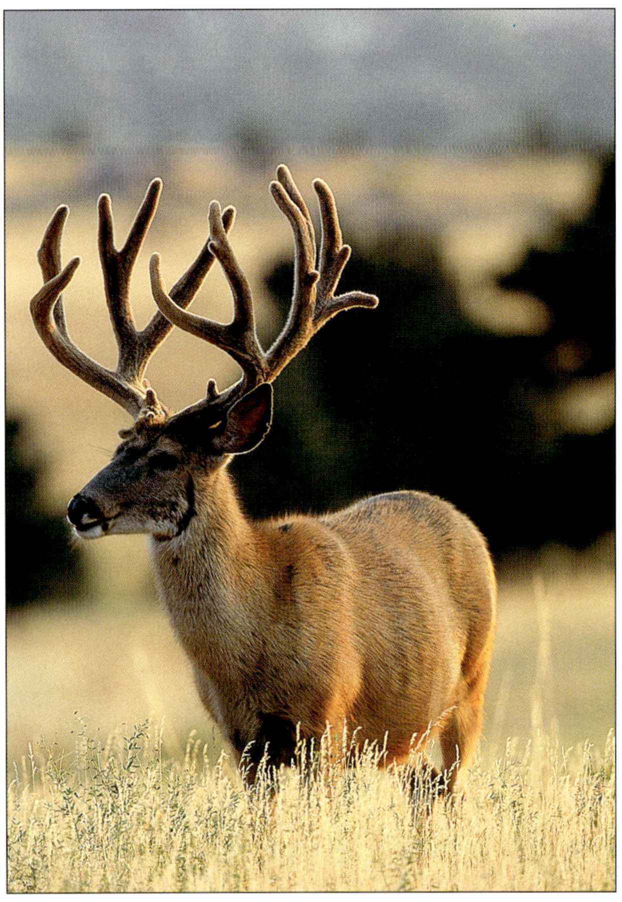

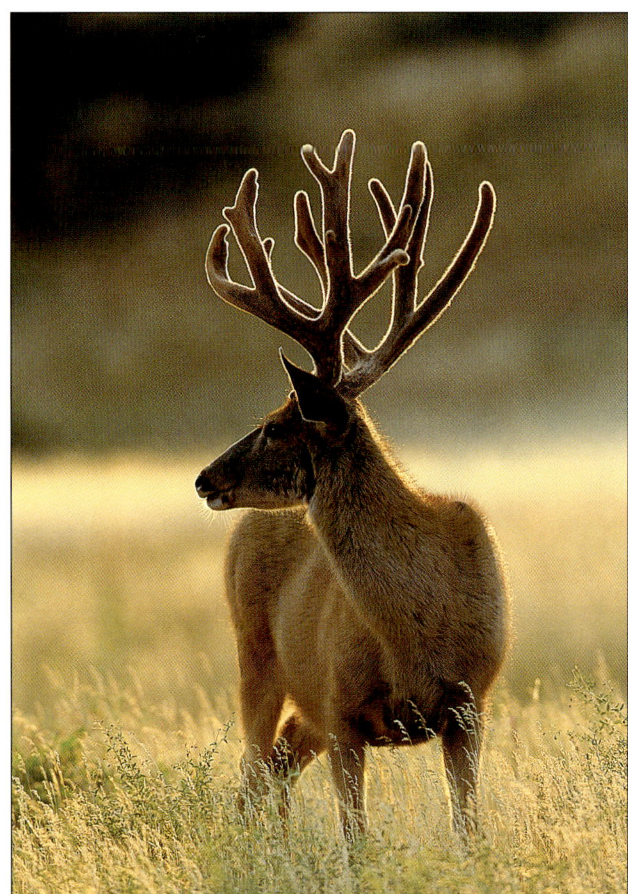

LEFT—This is a nice enough picture of a mule deer buck in velvet, but we've seen lots of mule deer images, and this one is nothing special. Boulder County, Colorado. 300mm lens with 1.4x. RIGHT—Changing the direction of the light source made all the difference in the world for this image. By adding the rim light on the buck's antlers and the golden glow on the grass, the back light takes this shot beyond documentation. Boulder County, Colorado. 300mm lens with 1.4x teleconverter.

noticed. Sometimes just changing the direction of the light is all it takes. The front-lit photos we took of the deer were fine: they're sharp, well composed, in warm light, and they've even been published in some prominent places. They also don't give a whole lot of information to the viewer, and we've seen a lot of nice photos of deer in velvet. To Cathy and me, these are basically documentary photos.

The back-lit photos actually don't show a lot more than the front-lit ones do. So why do we feel the back-lit images go beyond documentation? The rim light on the antlers and the golden glow of the grass not only add an air of beauty, they add an element of strangeness, making the subject look almost supernatural. Viewers often take a moment to study the details in these images, and changing the direction of the light is all it took.

FRONT LIGHT

Front lighting is the traditional choice of photographers, and the lion's share of wildlife photos are handled in this way. Front lighting provides good color saturation, and short of shooting directly into the sun, it gives the photographer the most light to work with. This makes front lighting ideal for situations in which you want to stop the action of a quickly moving animal, say ducks in flight or a running deer. Not to take anything away from front-lit photos (Cathy and I shoot most of our wildlife photos this way), but it is also the most common way to present your subject, and hence, most of the images your viewers see are front lit.

There is no trick to shooting front-lit subjects, but it usually takes something special to go beyond documentation with these kinds of photos. To do so, either the creature you're photographing has to be so unusual in its own right the viewer wants to spend some time studying the photo; there is some interesting behavior going on; you've created an image of stunning beauty with your composition; or some combination of all three. If you anticipate some active behavior, front light would be a good choice since it provides the most light. If you have colorful picture elements you wish to include, front light would work well because it gives good color saturation.

Front light is also the right choice if you hope to capture the subject's reflection. Reflections are still possible with light coming from other directions, however, because of the high probability of glare on

Front light is a good choice for capturing behavior because it provides even light, and short of shooting directly into the sun, it provides the most light. Front light made it possible to stop this wood duck drake as it was landing. Pima County, Arizona. 500mm lens.

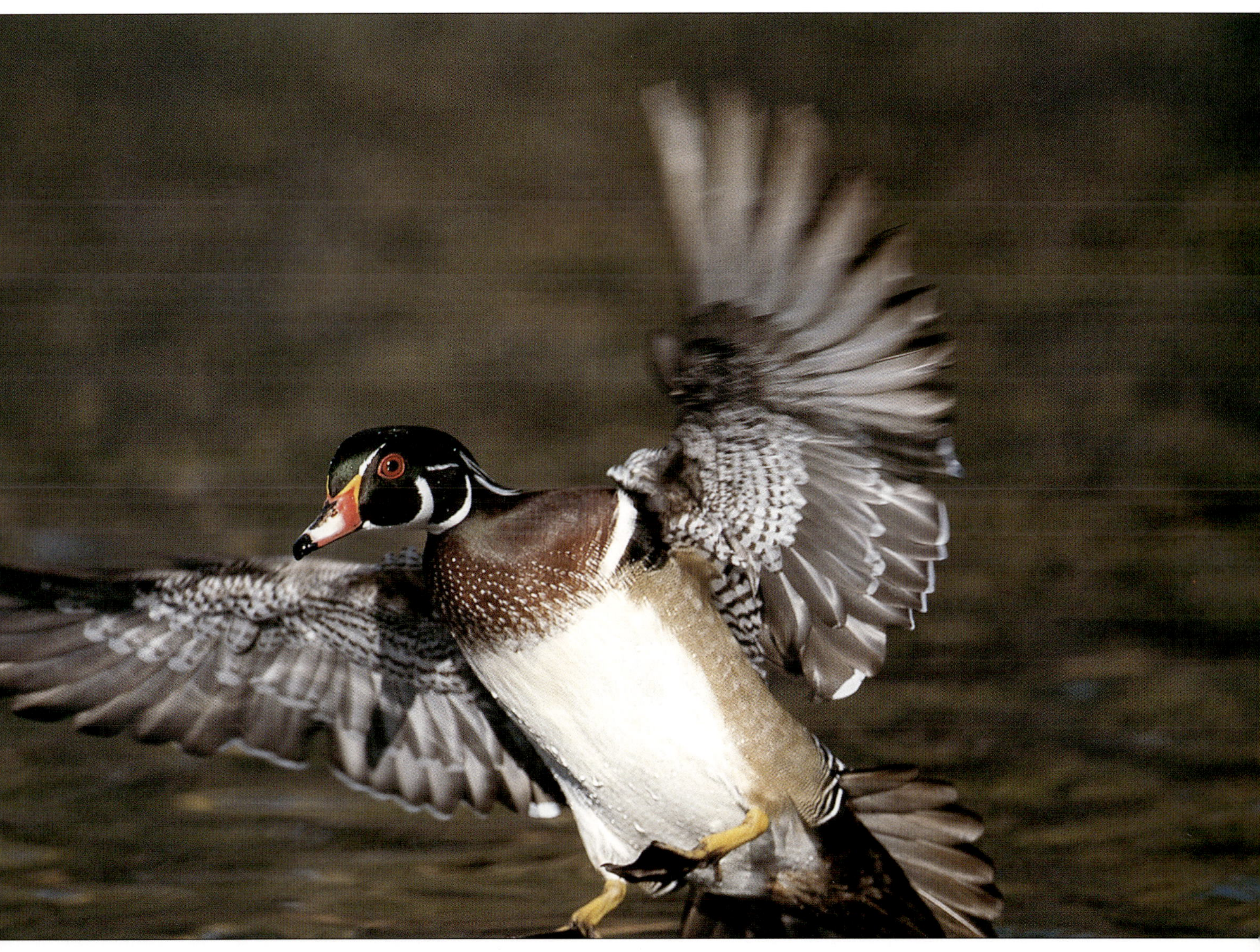

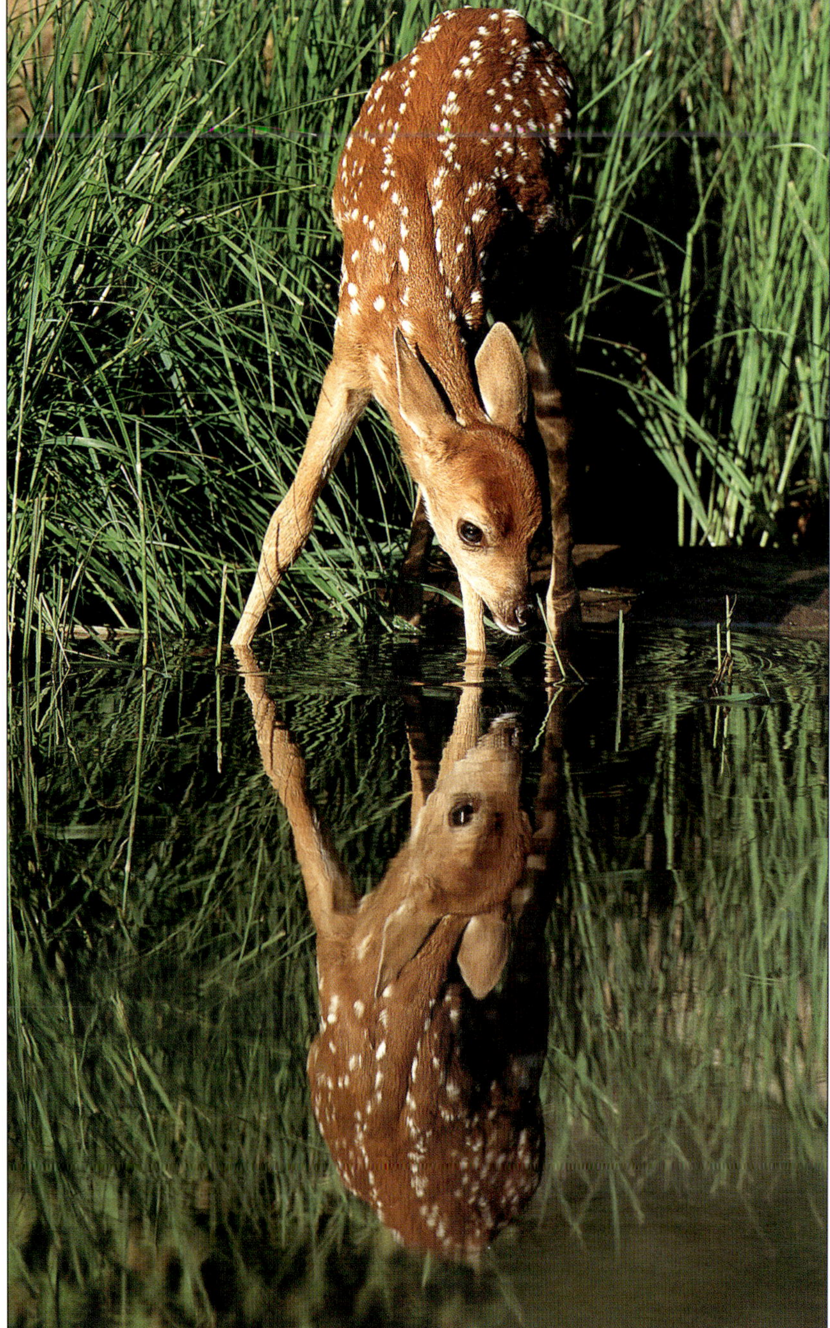

Front light is the best choice for shooting reflections. White-tailed deer fawns make cute subjects regardless of where they are photographed, but front light and the reflection helped take this image beyond documentation. Captive. Pine County, Minnesota. 500mm lens.

the water, and because much of the subject is often shaded in side light and back light situations, front lighting usually gives much better results. If you are not able to incorporate behavior or other attractive picture elements, give some thought to the light direction you want, especially if you want your images to stand out from the crowd.

SIDE LIGHT

Strong side light will leave part of your subject well exposed and part of it either under- or overexposed. Scenic photographers have long known

When you can highlight the sunlit part of your subject against a dark background, it can give your image a dramatic feel. Notice how this makes the feathers on the great blue heron's neck and breast stand out. Bosque del Apache National Wildlife Refuge, New Mexico. 500mm lens with 1.4x teleconverter.

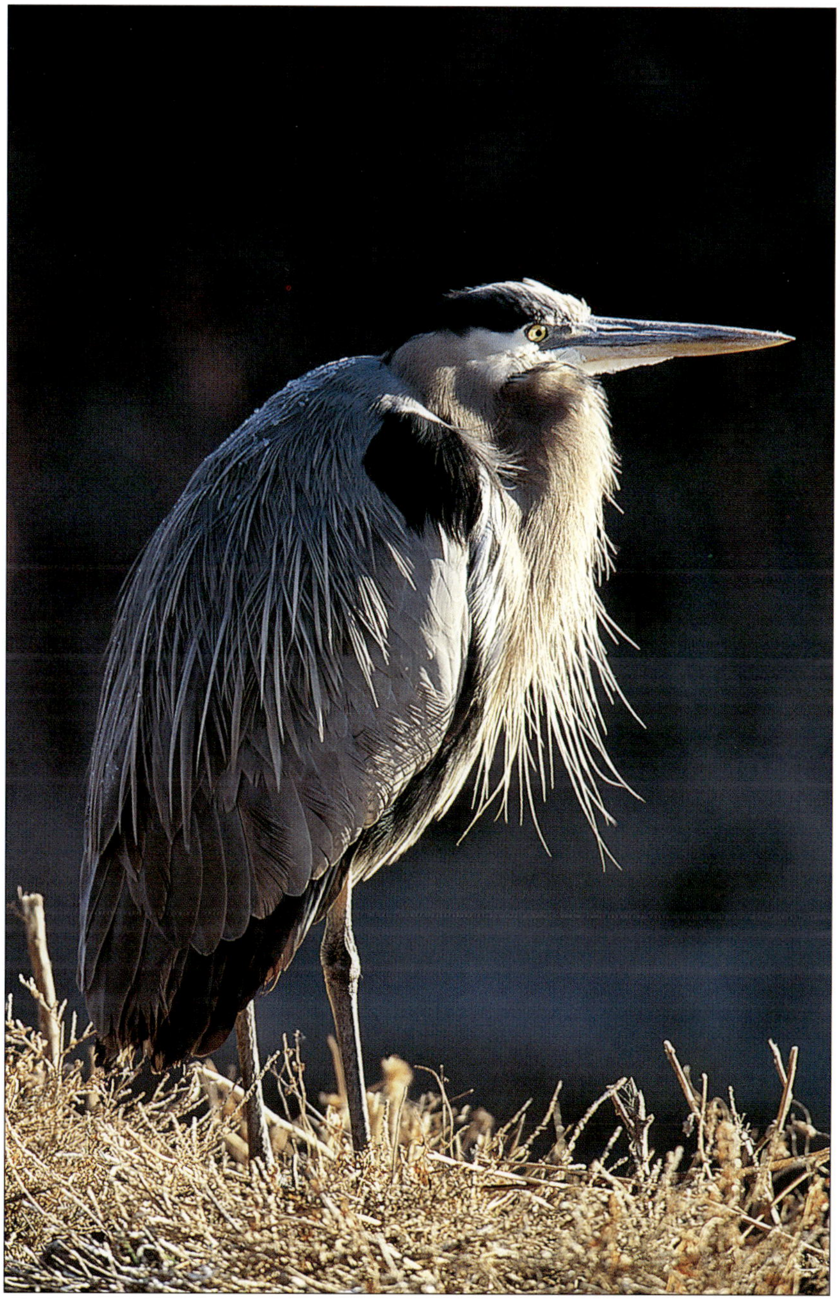

that side light is great for bringing out the texture of subjects because it creates strong shadows and adds depth to the image. This treatment can give a wildlife photo a very dramatic feel because it does the same for living things. It highlights the texture of the animal you're photographing. On a subject with large scales, fuzzy hair, or prominent feathers, side lighting can let your viewers know what it would be like to touch that animal.

When you're shooting with side light, unless you have a subject with a particularly photogenic butt, you will want to have at least part of the animal's face in sunlight. The face is usually what viewers find most interesting. Give them a good look at it, and let the shadows go dark. Unless the subject is very dark, highlight the sunlit portions of the subject against a dark background. Spotlighting the subject's face will call attention to any subtle textures there, and give the image a very dramatic feel.

BACK LIGHT

With the exception of silhouettes, back light is probably the most underused light direction. Shooting into the sun can cause some problems, like lens flare, but in the right situations it can also transform an ordinary image into something wonderful. When you want to give your subject an ethereal, spiritual quality, a feeling of freedom and lightness, consider shooting into the sun. When the sun is low in the sky, back light will often outline your subject with a brilliant rim light, especially if the animal is fuzzy or downy.

We've already talked about how well back light works on animals that are covered with short hair or downy feathers. When you're trying to create an image where rim light is a major element, highlight the most important pieces of rim light, like the antlers in our mule deer photos, against a darker background. If there's time and the subject allows it, Cathy and I will often bracket our exposure when we're trying to capture rim light on a subject. Different exposures will give the image a different feel, and the "correct" exposure is not always the one we like the best.

Obviously, you have to be aware of the sun if you're going to point your lens toward it. The closer to sea level you are, the lower the sun is; and the more humidity, dust, and pollution in the air, the less of a problem shooting toward the sun presents. In the high, thin air of Colorado, where we do much of our shooting, you have to be careful of the sun from the moment it rises to the time it sets. It's very easy to end up with an image in which the most visible element is a series of monstrous flares.

Ideally, you should be able to point just enough to the side of the sun that the lens hood will block the sun's rays from shining directly on the lens. If this isn't doing the trick, try using your diffuser/reflector or maybe an umbrella to block the sun. If these are not handy, find a tree, boulder, building, car, another photographer—anything that produces a nice shadow—and use that to shield your lens from the sun. Once you've learned how to effectively hide from the sun, there are a number of things you can do with back light.

Back light can work wonders when you have a subject with translucent body parts (don't laugh, you'd be surprised at how

Before we found this bird in a position that forced us to photograph it with back lighting, we had no idea that a great blue heron's bill was translucent. The result is an unusual image of a very commonly photographed subject. Port Aransas, Texas. 500mm lens.

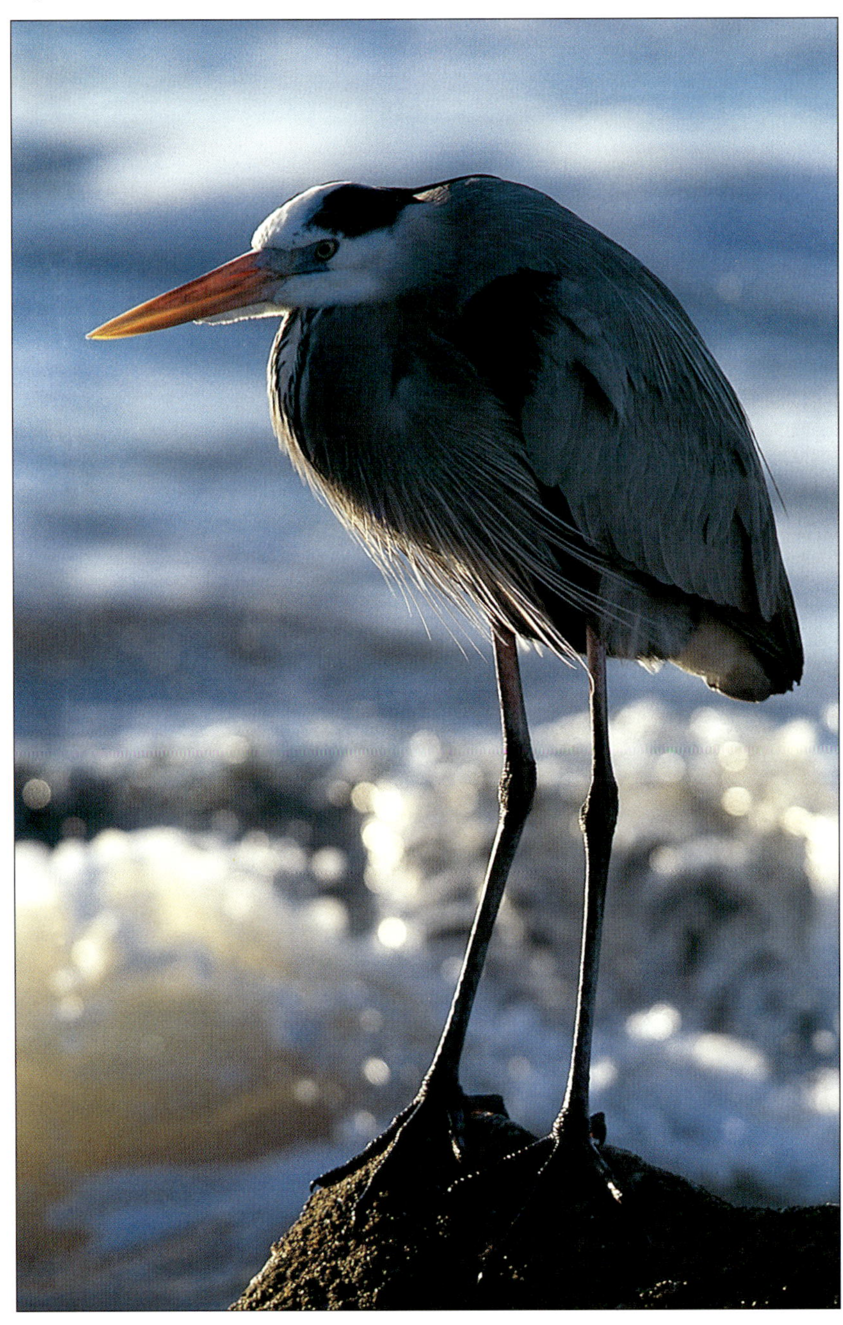

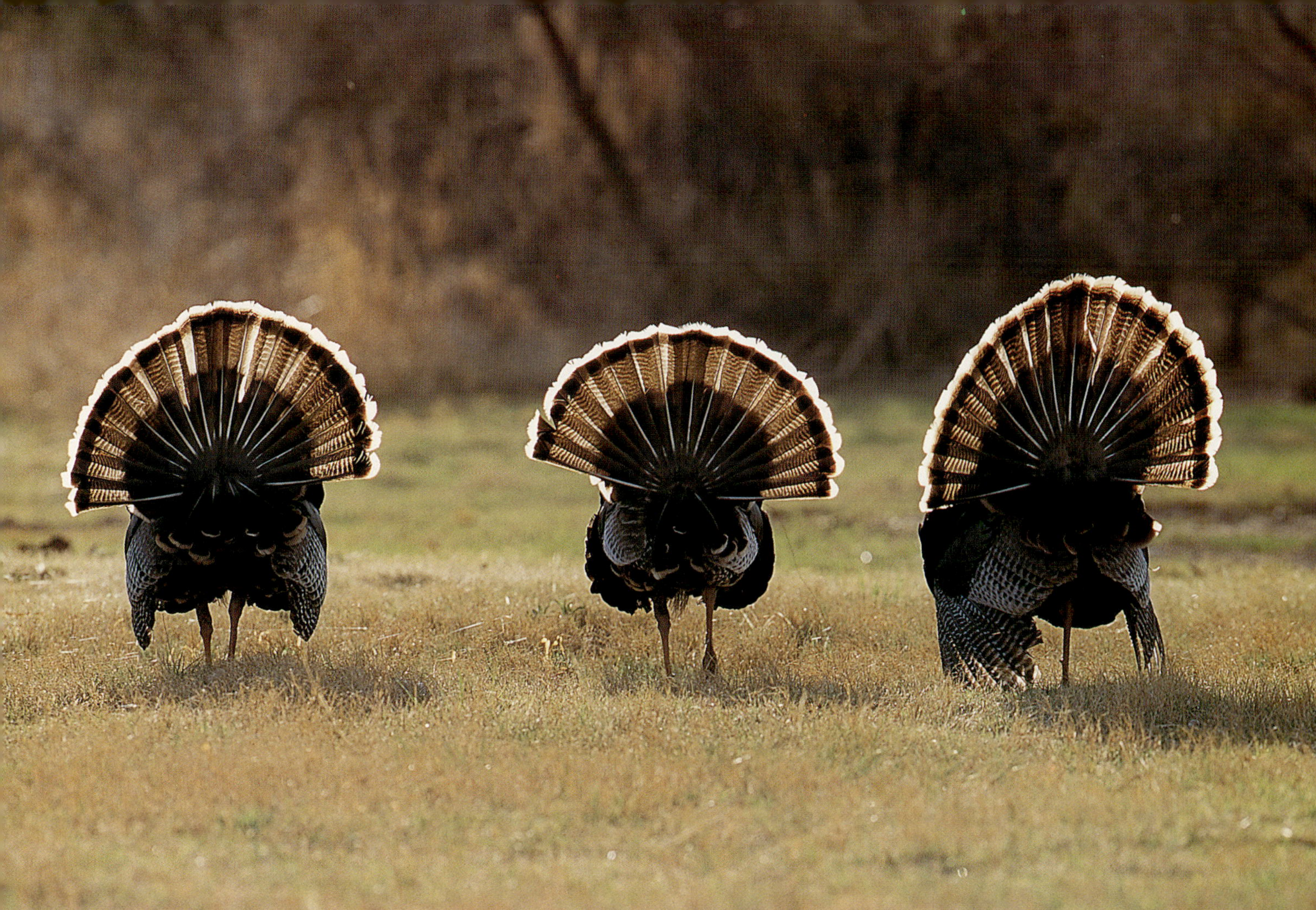

This is not the image we were looking for when we went photographing wild turkeys, but it's the one we liked the best, if only because we had never seen back-lit turkeys before. Palo Duro Canyon State Park, Texas. 500mm lens.

many there are). Most of the animals with translucent body parts are birds. The wings and tails are the obvious choices, but many of their beaks will also glow with the sun behind them. And some of them have throat sacs or pouches that sunlight will shine through.

Capturing this translucence is often just a case of being aware of its existence. Several years ago, we were photographing turkeys displaying. The shot we wanted, and the shot that most photographers try to get, is the tom with its tail spread and wings partially spread, gobbling to show what a fantastic specimen he is. The shot we ended up liking the most did indeed show a tom with its tail spread. In fact, there were three toms with spread tails, but they were walking away from us into the sun, and their tails were just glowing.

When the weather turns cold we start thinking about photographing animals blowing out steam. Most people don't think of breathing as an activity you can capture with still photography, but when the conditions are right, breathing becomes an easily observable behavior. On cold mornings, warm-blooded creatures blow out steam with every breath, so it should be a piece of cake to photograph. The problem is, steam doesn't show up against a bright background. If you want the subject's breath to show up, it needs to be highlighted against a dark background, and most subjects are just not that cooperative. Keep it in mind, though, when the conditions are right. Chapter 9 will cover this subject in more detail.

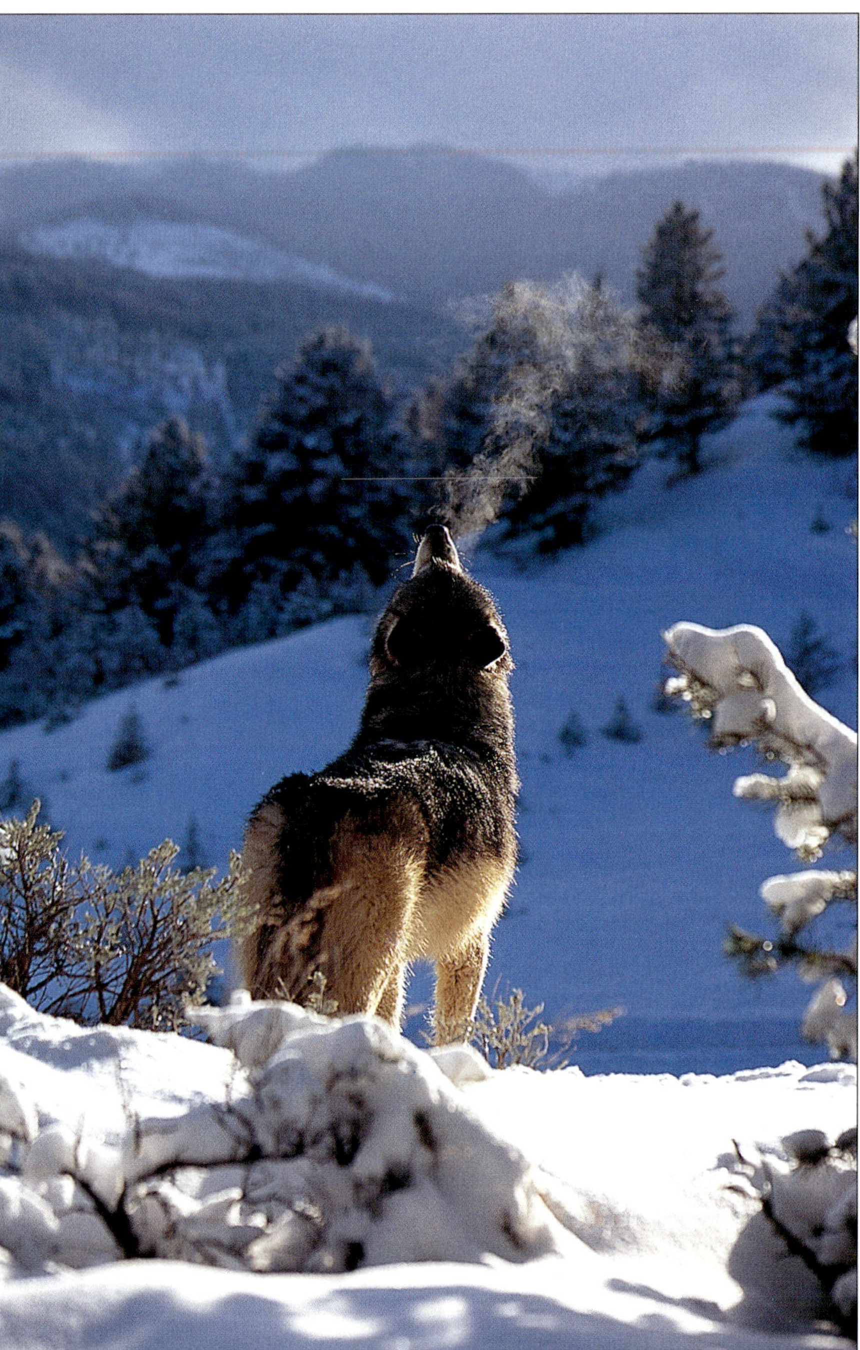

A warm-blooded subject, cold weather, and back or side light make an ideal combination for capturing your subject's breath. Notice how a dark background makes this howling wolf's breath stand out. Captive. Bridger Mountains, Montana. 75–300mm lens.

MAKING CONTRAST WORK

Regardless of which direction your light is coming from, you must be aware of your film's ability to handle contrast. The human eye can see detail throughout a scene where the bright areas are seventeen to nineteen (depending on your age) stops brighter than the dark areas. With slide film you have only three or four stops of latitude, and both print film and digital are only a little more forgiving.

This means that if the correct exposure for the bright spots in your image is 1/250 second at f8 and the correct exposure for the dark spots is 1/30 second or less at f8, you have several choices. You can expose for the sunny spots and let the shady ones go dark, expose for the shady spots and let the sunny ones get blown out, or pick an exposure in between with nothing properly exposed. After throwing away many, many photos where we unintentionally took our exposure reading from the shaded part of the animal, we can tell you that unless your entire subject is shaded, this kind of photo works best when the sunlit portion is well exposed and the shady portions are allowed to go dark.

It may seem like the camera's inability to handle contrast is just another in a long list of handicaps imposed upon the photographer, but there are times when you can use the film's shortcomings to your advantage. This limited ability of film to handle contrast can produce a very dramatic spotlight effect. Cathy photographed two flamingos roosting in dappled light at a zoo in Florida. The background included a bunch of clutter in addition to the usual manmade objects present in many zoo enclosures. For about ten minutes, though, the sunlight filtering through the trees only illuminated the flamingos. The rest of the scene was in deep shade. Cathy exposed for the sunlit portions of the scene, and in the resulting image it seemed as if two brilliant flamingos were floating there in the blackness.

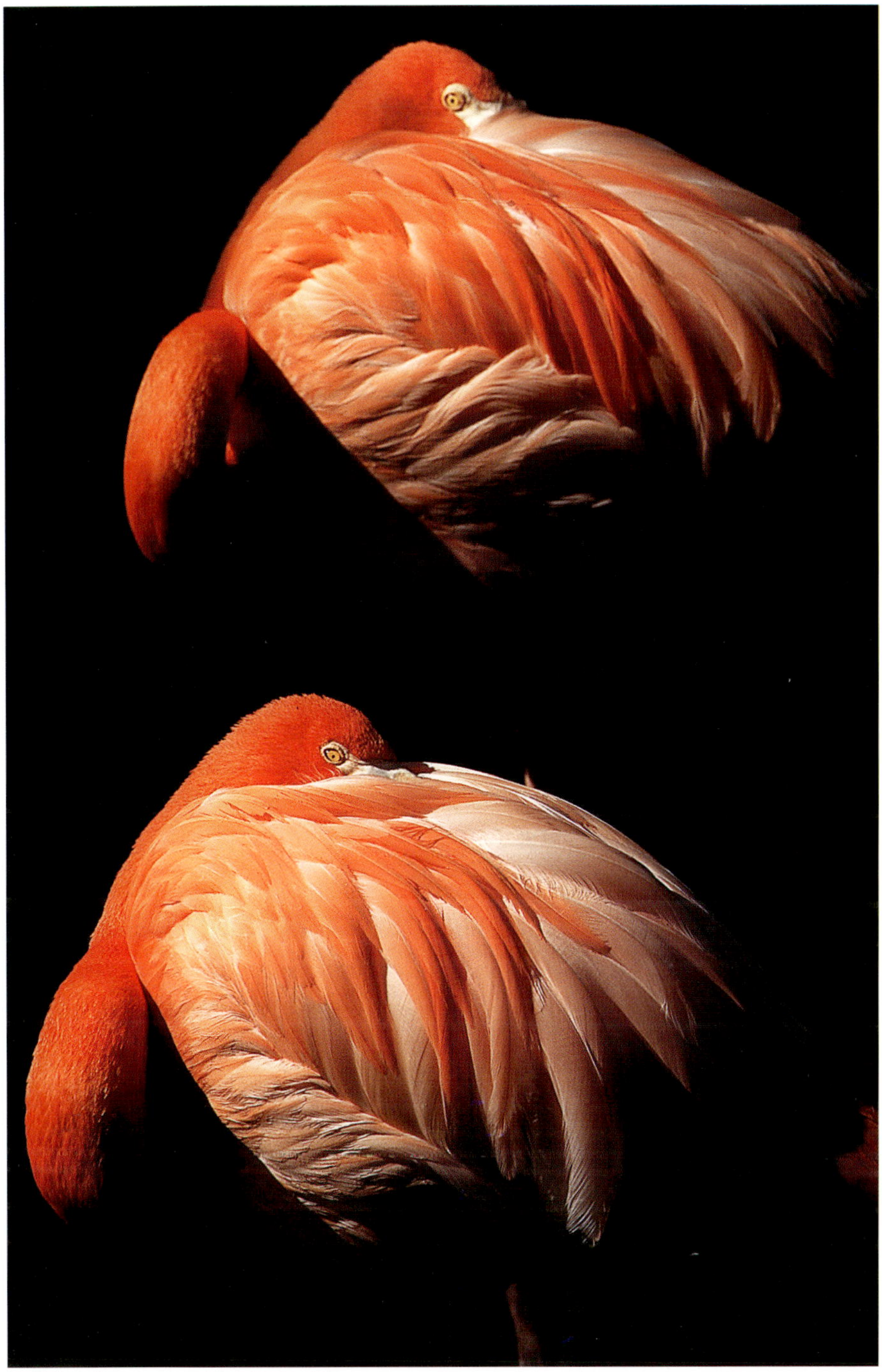

This is not what the scene looked like to the photographer. We could see the birds' legs, as well as the rest of the enclosure just fine. To the human eye, the birds appeared brighter than their surroundings, but it was easy to see detail in both. The film we were using, though, was totally blind to the shady surroundings when Cathy exposed for the sunlit birds.

This spotlight effect is not something that only occurs with front-lit subjects. It can also work with both side light and back light. Handle side light situations just like you would front light. Expose for the sunlit areas, and let the shadows go dark.

You can use your film or sensor's shortcomings to your advantage. By exposing for the sunlit portions of these flamingos and letting the film's inability to handle contrast do the rest, we ended up with this unusual image. Captive. Homosassa Springs State Wildlife Park, Florida. 300mm lens with 1.4x teleconverter.

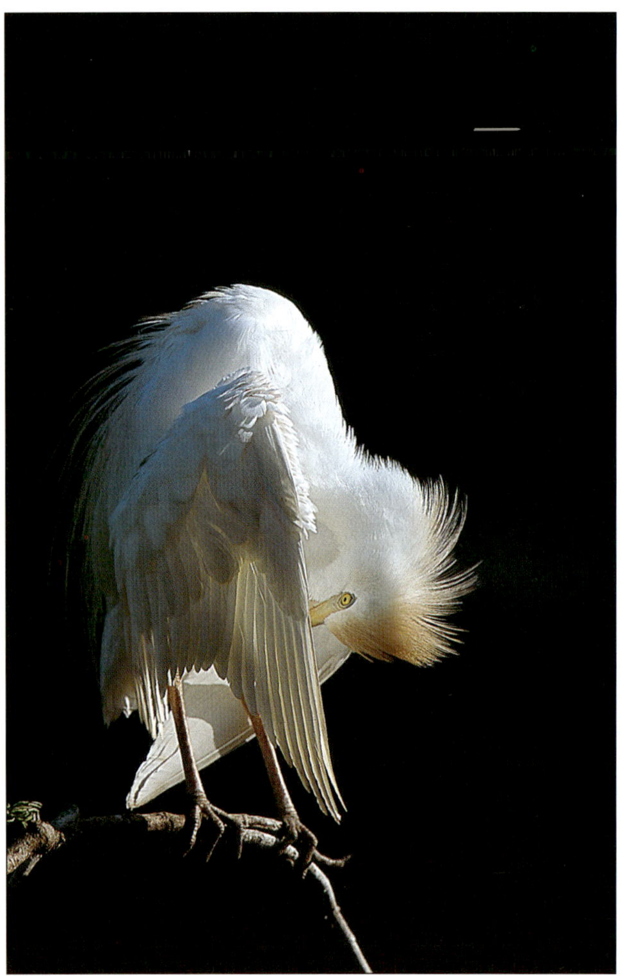

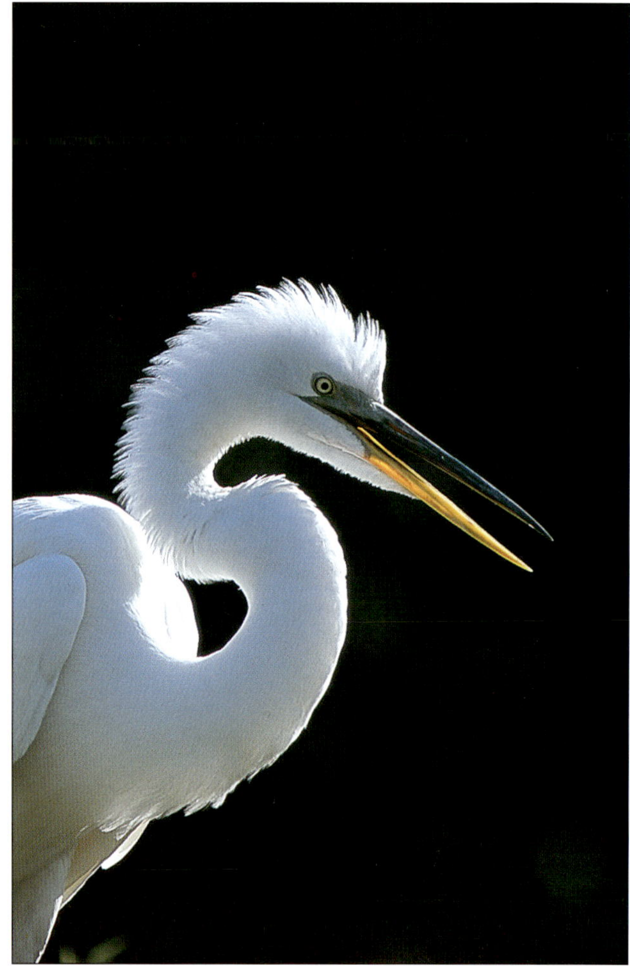

LEFT—This image of a cattle egret has several things going for it. Side light gives the bird's outstretched wing a translucent glow. The wing also makes a great reflector, shining light on the bird's face. And highlighting the subject against a dark background makes it stand out very nicely. Anastasia Island, Florida. 500mm lens with 2x teleconverter. RIGHT—Even the shady side of a white animal, like this great egret, is bright enough to make the subject stand out against a shaded background. The rim light and translucent bill are just icing on the cake. Anastasia Island, Florida. 500mm lens.

To create this spotlight effect with back light, a light-colored subject is often necessary because you are taking your meter reading from the shady side of the subject with a shaded background behind it. Unless it has a very strong rim light, a neutral-colored creature just will not stand out well because the side of the animal you can see and the shaded background will give almost the same meter reading. Your viewers will still be able to see your subject, but it won't exactly stand out. A white animal, though, like a great egret, affects the exposure enough so that it will be highlighted against the dark background, even though you're photographing the shady side of the bird.

SILHOUETTES

Silhouettes are something that we haven't touched on yet, and they can be a relatively easy way to capture graphic images of your subject. In this kind of image, you're photographing an animal against a much brighter background, and again, we're using the film's shortcomings to our advantage. Exposing for silhouettes, though, is the opposite of exposing for spot-lit images. To create a spotlight effect, you expose for

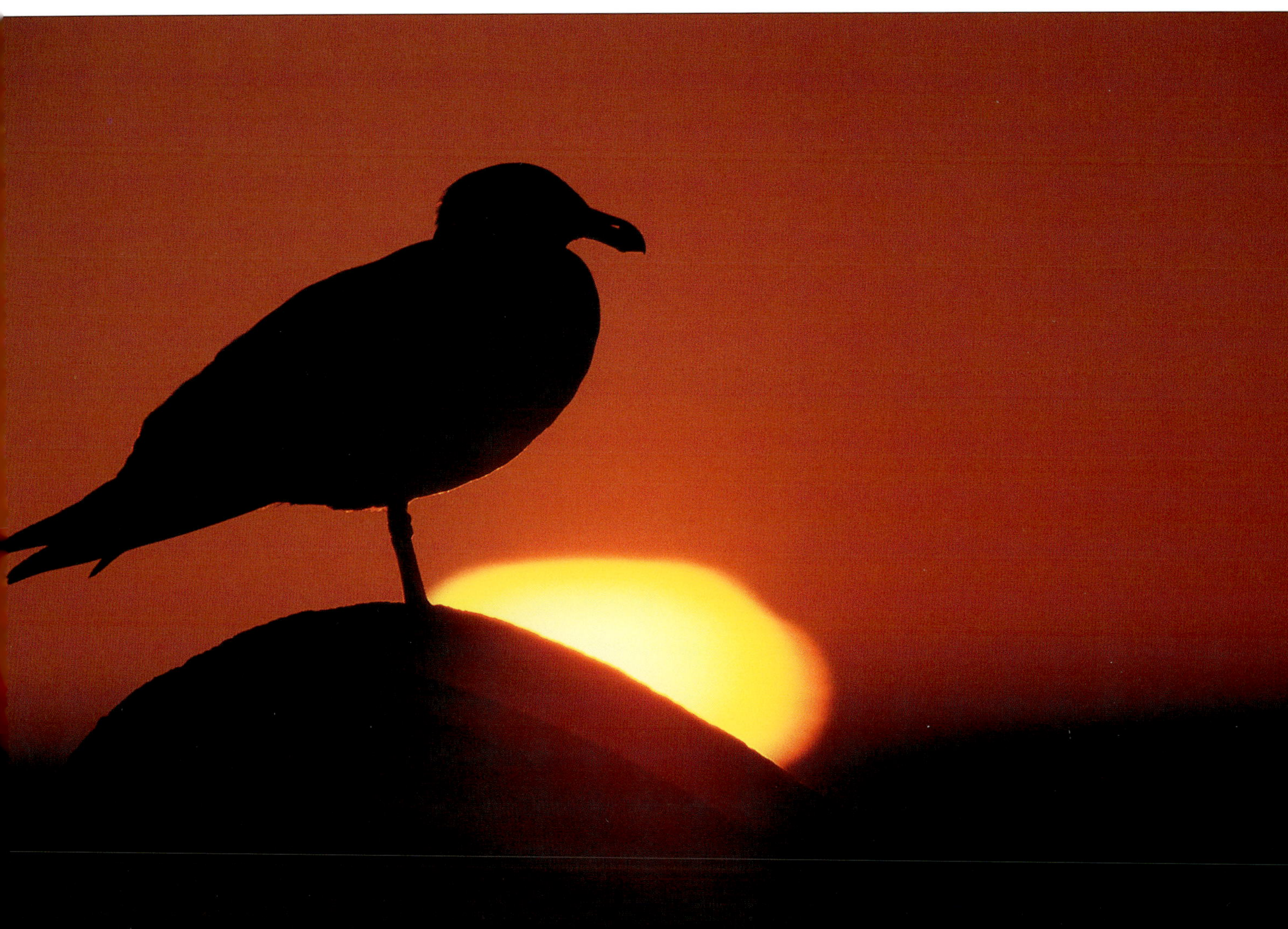

Silhouettes must be simple and easily recognized for them to work. This gull silhouette is graphic enough to hold the viewers' attention, even against the brightness of the setting sun. San Luis Obispo County, California. 500mm lens with 2x teleconverter.

the subject and let the background go dark. To create a silhouette, expose for the background and let your subject go black. It helps if there is not much contrast to your background, and it's ideal if the background is a warm color, like yellow, orange, or red. The trick to silhouettes is to keep the image very simple, and to photograph a subject that's very recognizable by its shape.

We photographed a bear silhouette once, and even though I rather liked it, many people could not tell what kind of creature it was. One editor didn't want to use it because he thought it looked like a cat. So make the subject easily recognizable. Your image isn't going to work if the subject is just a black blob, no matter how nice your background is.

OVERCAST LIGHT

Some photographers hang up their gear when the weather turns gloomy, which can be a big mistake. Overcast light is some of the best

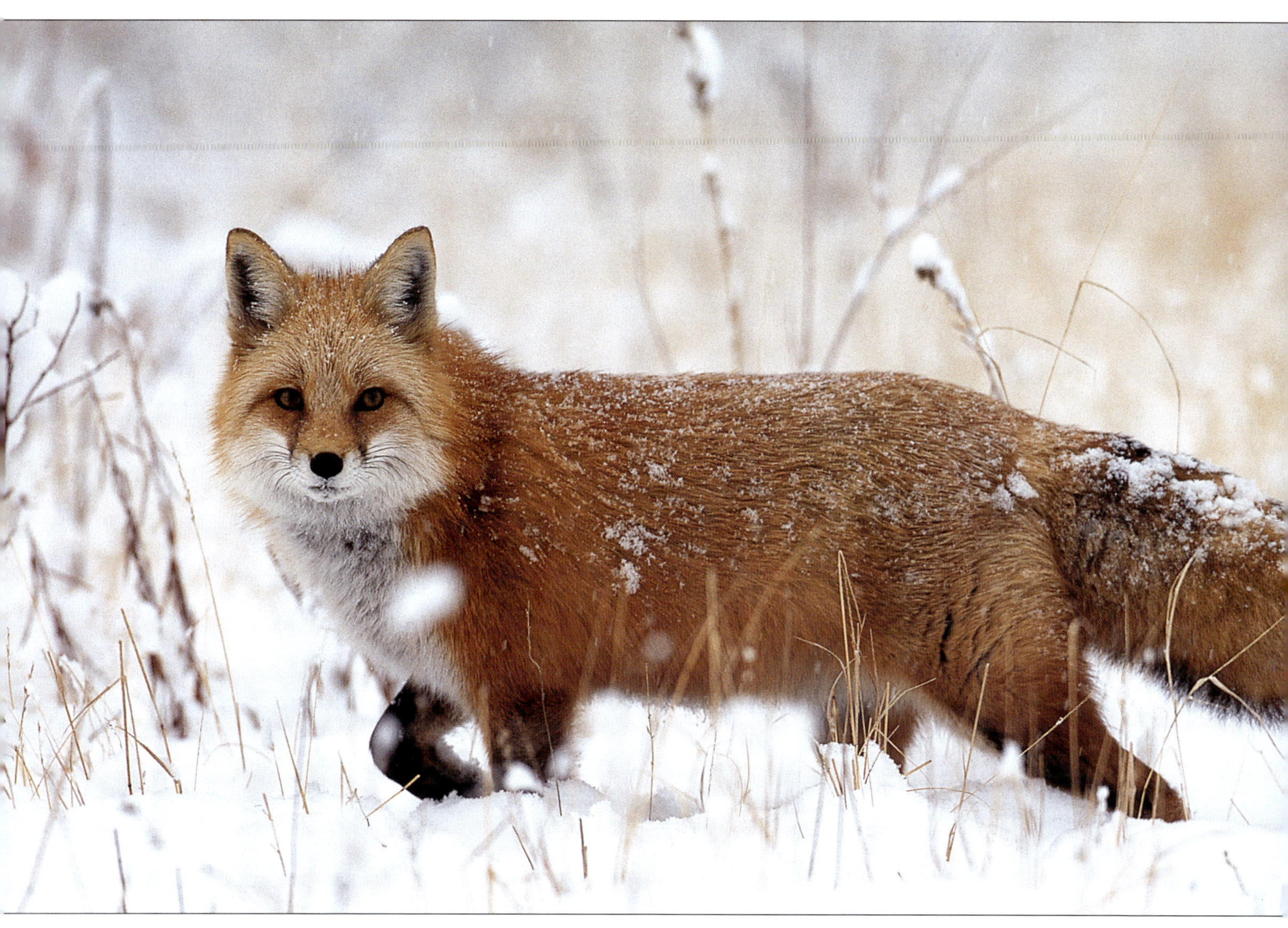

Overcast light is ideal for showing detail in fur and feathers because there is so little contrast under these conditions. In this image, light reflected off the snow helps eliminate any small shadows there might have been on this red fox. Jefferson County, Colorado. 500mm lens.

possible light in which to photograph wildlife. Because of the way light rays are bounced around inside clouds, overcast light is essentially light from every direction. And since the light is coming from every direction, there are no shadows and very little contrast. This kind of light is ideal for showing details in fur and feathers.

When Cathy was photographing grizzly bears several years ago, she had typical weather for Coastal Alaska. She prayed for sunshine for five days straight, and day after day dawned dark and wet. Finally, on the last day the sun came out. She had one hour in which to photograph the bears in the sun. The funny thing is, we kept most of her sunny bear shots as an example of how not to photograph bears. In broad sunlight, there was just too much contrast. However, many of the bears she photographed in the rain looked great. The bears look wet, but the detail in their fur is exquisite.

The problem with photographing under overcast conditions is not the quality of the light but the quantity. Sometimes the clouds are just too thick to capture any subject that isn't bolted down, and about the only thing you can do is wait until conditions improve. If there is enough light to shoot, one important thing to remember is to eliminate or minimize the amount of sky. Water is also something you may want to minimize on overcast days because it only reflects the color of the sky. A featureless, gray sky doesn't add much to most photos.

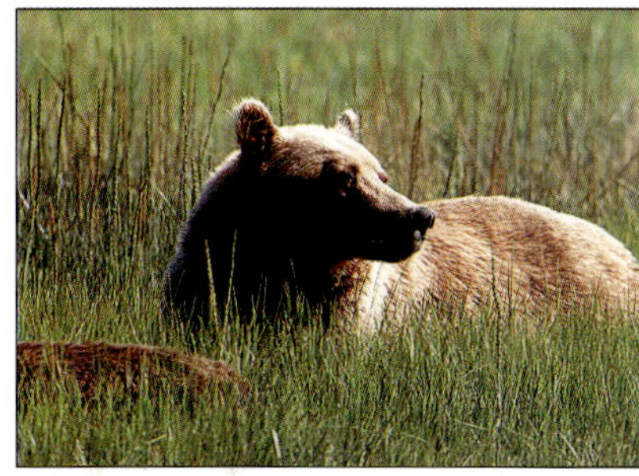

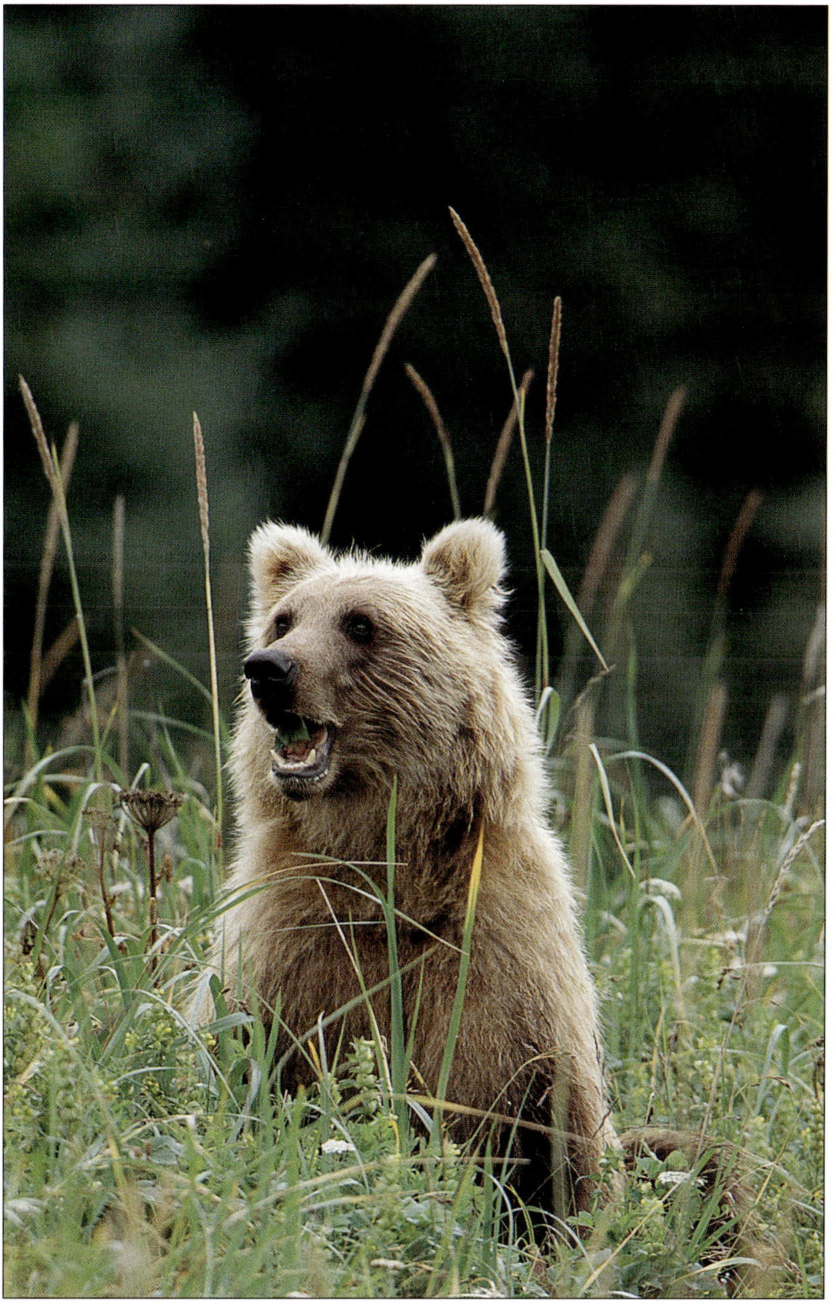

ABOVE—Direct sun often creates too much contrast for acceptable photos. The sunlit parts of these grizzlies are too bright and the shadows are too dark. Lake Clark National Park, Alaska. 500mm lens. **RIGHT**—Even though this grizzly was photographed in the rain, the details in its fur are wonderful because there is so little contrast under overcast skies. Lake Clark National Park, Alaska. 75–300mm lens.

TWILIGHT

In rare situations, you may end up with creatures that hold still enough to photograph them either before the sun has risen or after the sun has set, and we're not talking about silhouettes against a bright sky here. It makes sense that it would be easier to capture some special images during these times, if only because the light source is not one we're used to seeing in wildlife photos. Unusual light often produces unusual looking photos.

The best twilight results are usually obtained with light-colored subjects because they stand out from their background better than darker species in these low-light conditions. Roosting birds are some of the easiest animals to use this technique with, but we've seen photos of species like lions and leopards that were also taken at twilight. Often colors will show up in these photos that the naked eye never saw. We often try to time these efforts with moonrise or moonset to add another element of interest to the image—as well as another light source.

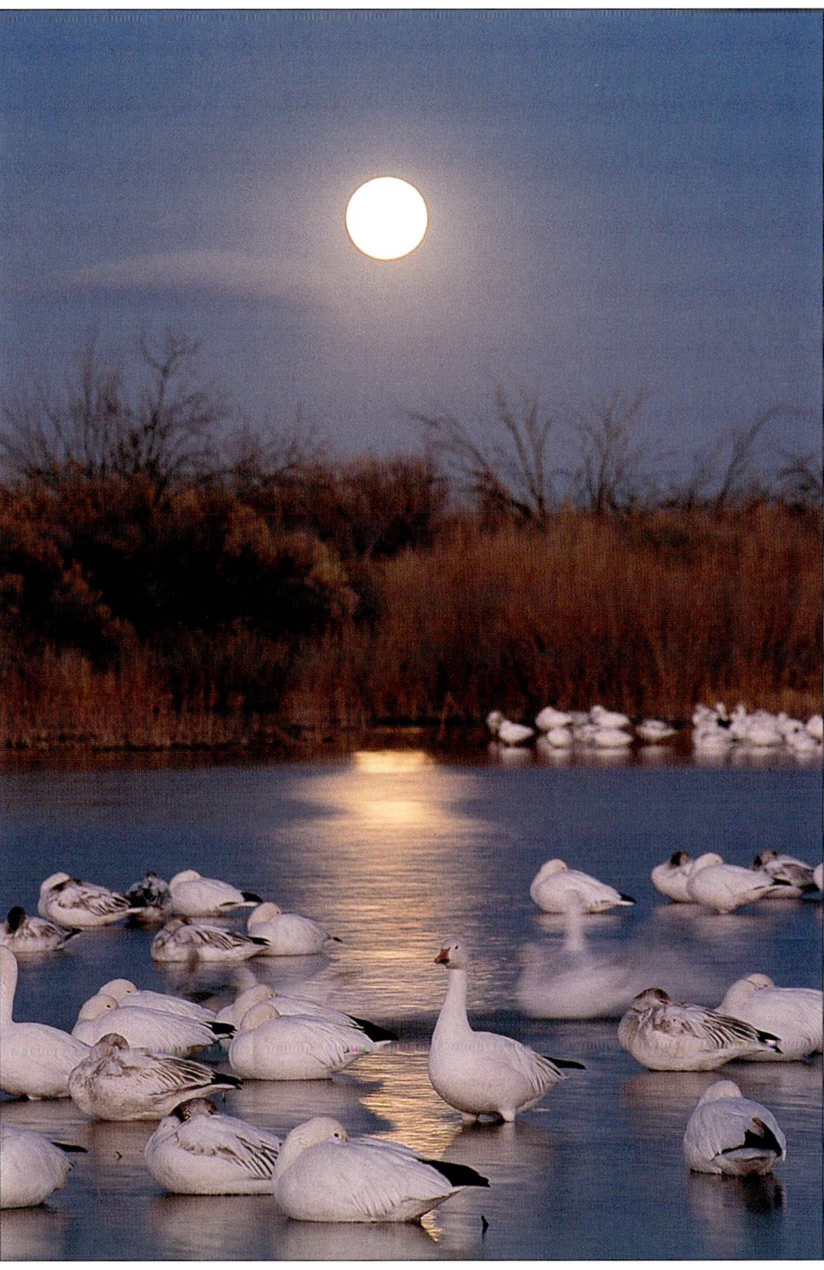

Light-colored subjects, like these snow geese roosting under a rising moon, often seem to glow when the sun dips below the horizon. It makes a wonderful situation to experiment with. Bosque del Apache National Wildlife Refuge, New Mexico. 75–300mm lens.

FILL FLASH

There will be times, probably lots of them, when you have a cooperative subject and the quality of the light is terrible for photography—too much contrast, too dim, whatever. There are already too few times when we have cooperative subjects. We shouldn't have to pass up an opportunity when we find it. A flash can help make up for shortcomings in the quality of the light. There are plenty of times when just a little bit of flash can make the difference between a great shot and one the viewer would not look twice at. And because dedicated flashes make this so easy to do today, there is no rea-

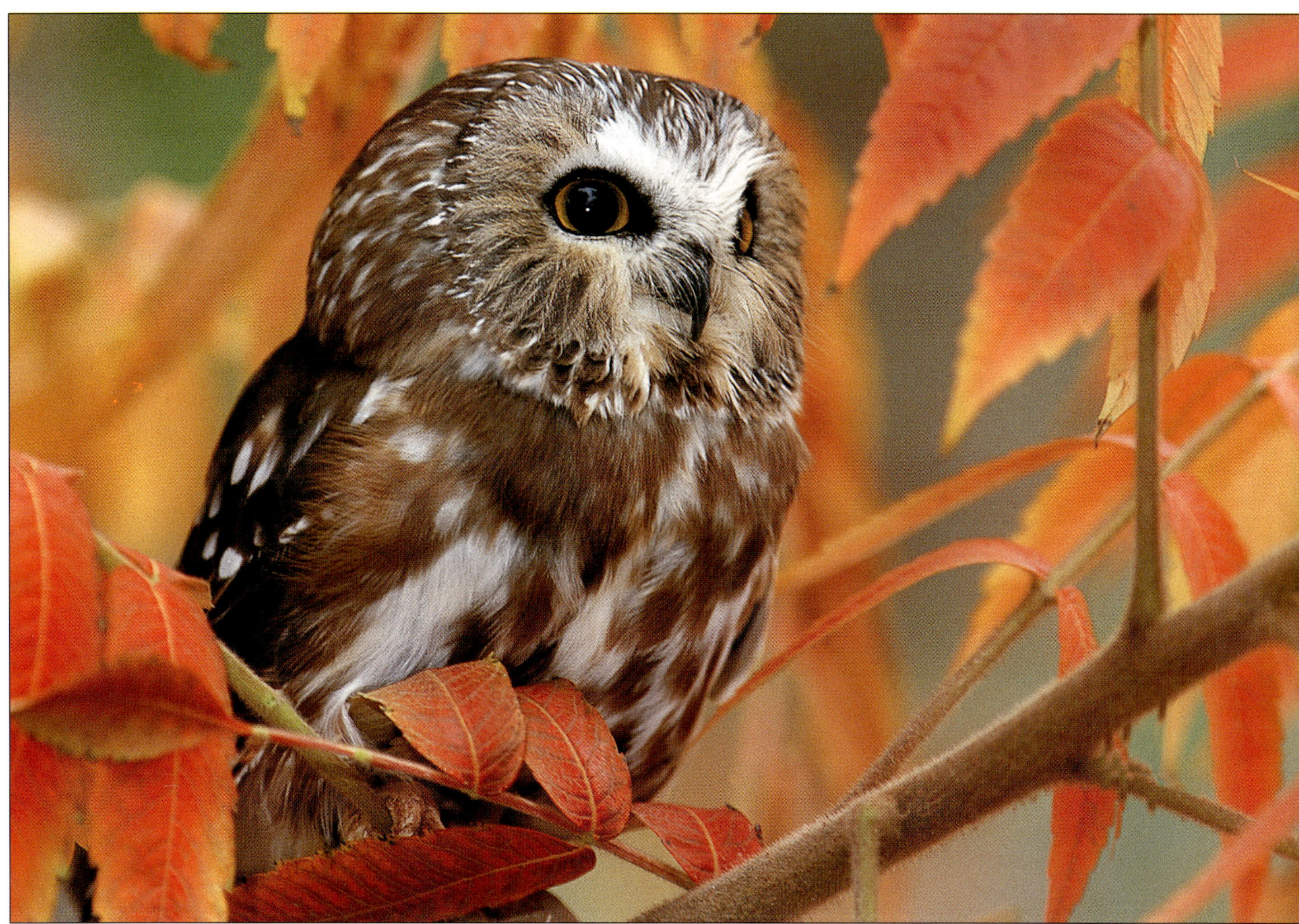

This saw-whet owl was photographed in very low light. A little fill flash helped bring out more color in both the bird and the surrounding foliage. Captive. Larimer County, Colorado. 75–300mm lens with fill flash.

son not to take advantage of it. Flash instruction is worth a book all by itself, but we will touch on the use of fill flash here.

There are several things fill flash can do for you. It can give a nice highlight in the animal's eye, which is especially important when the animal has dark eyes and a dark face. Fill flash can also light up the shadows, eliminating much of the contrast from an image. Fill flash can bring out more of your subject's color in low-light conditions. In these situations, the object is to inject a little light into the scene without ending up with an image that looks like it has obviously been flashed.

Earlier we talked about using high contrast light to create a spotlight effect. Well, many times high contrast light creates a pattern that makes using the spotlight effect pretty much impossible. Often the wrong parts of the animal are shaded or the dappled light is making a paisley design on the scene that's impossible to work with. Some species have a brow ridge that sticks out so far it's hard to get a catchlight in their eyes, even when they're staring straight into the sun. A little flash will light up the shadows enough to see detail, as well as give the desired

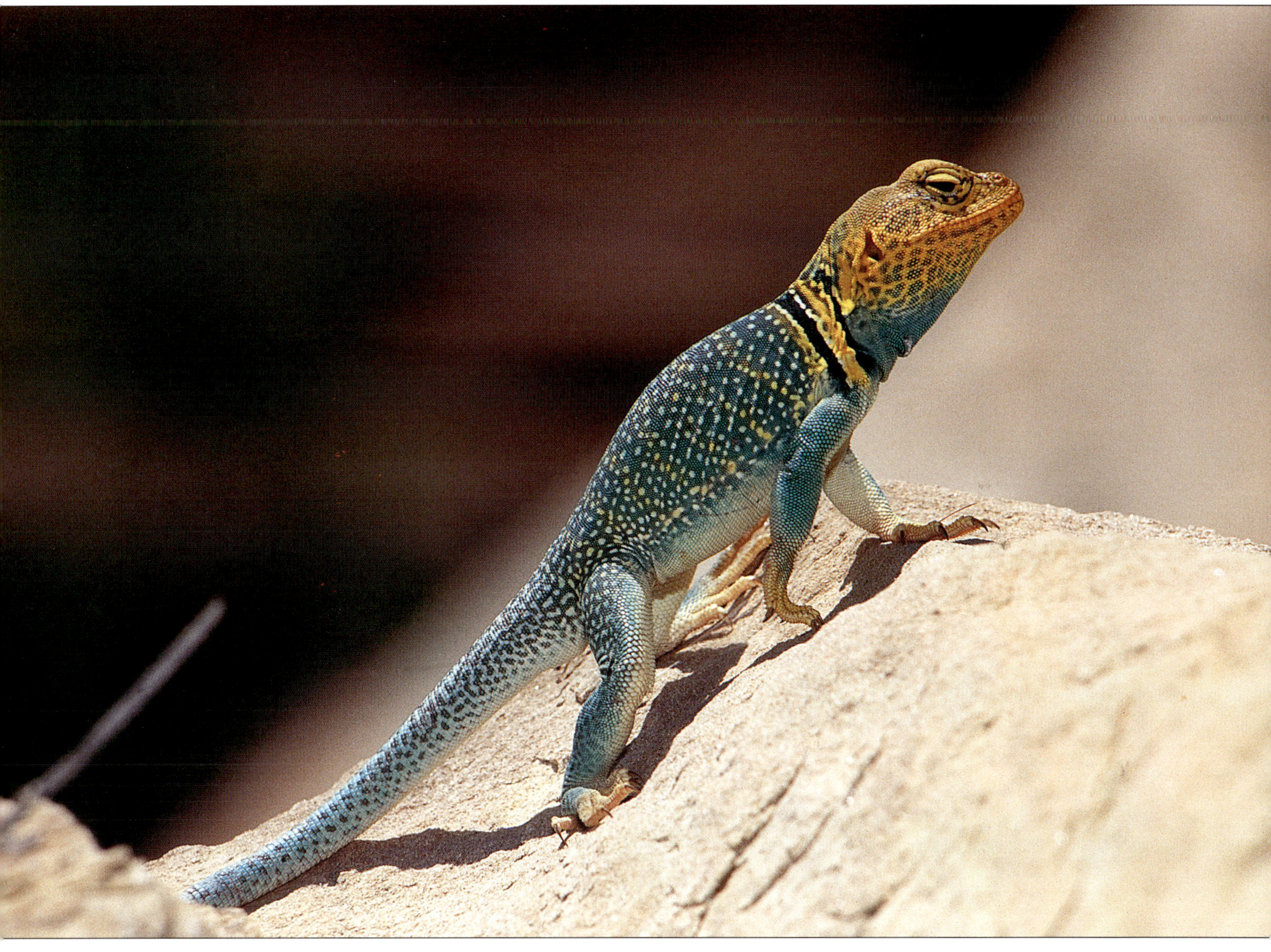

Photographing a subject at midday, like this collared lizard, usually results in images with too much contrast. Fill flash was used here to light up the shadows, giving much more even lighting to the subject. Mesa County, Colorado. 75–300mm lens with extension tubes and fill flash.

catchlight in the subject's eyes, and it will do it without overlighting the rest of the scene.

Dedicated, TTL flashes make determining flash output relatively easy. In most situations, set the flash at –1⅓ stops. This fills in the shadows enough to see detail in them without competing with the main source of light. If you're shooting a bright or light-colored subject, you might want to lower the flash output further, to –1⅔ or –2 stops. If the subject is dark-colored, increase the flash output to –1 or –⅔ stop.

Fill flash can also be used to light up your subject when it would be a silhouette. To light up a silhouette, use the flash anywhere between full power and –2 stops, depending on how much you want your subject illuminated. Just be sure to take your meter reading off the background. In this situation, your subject will obviously look flashed, but the overall effect can still be quite interesting.

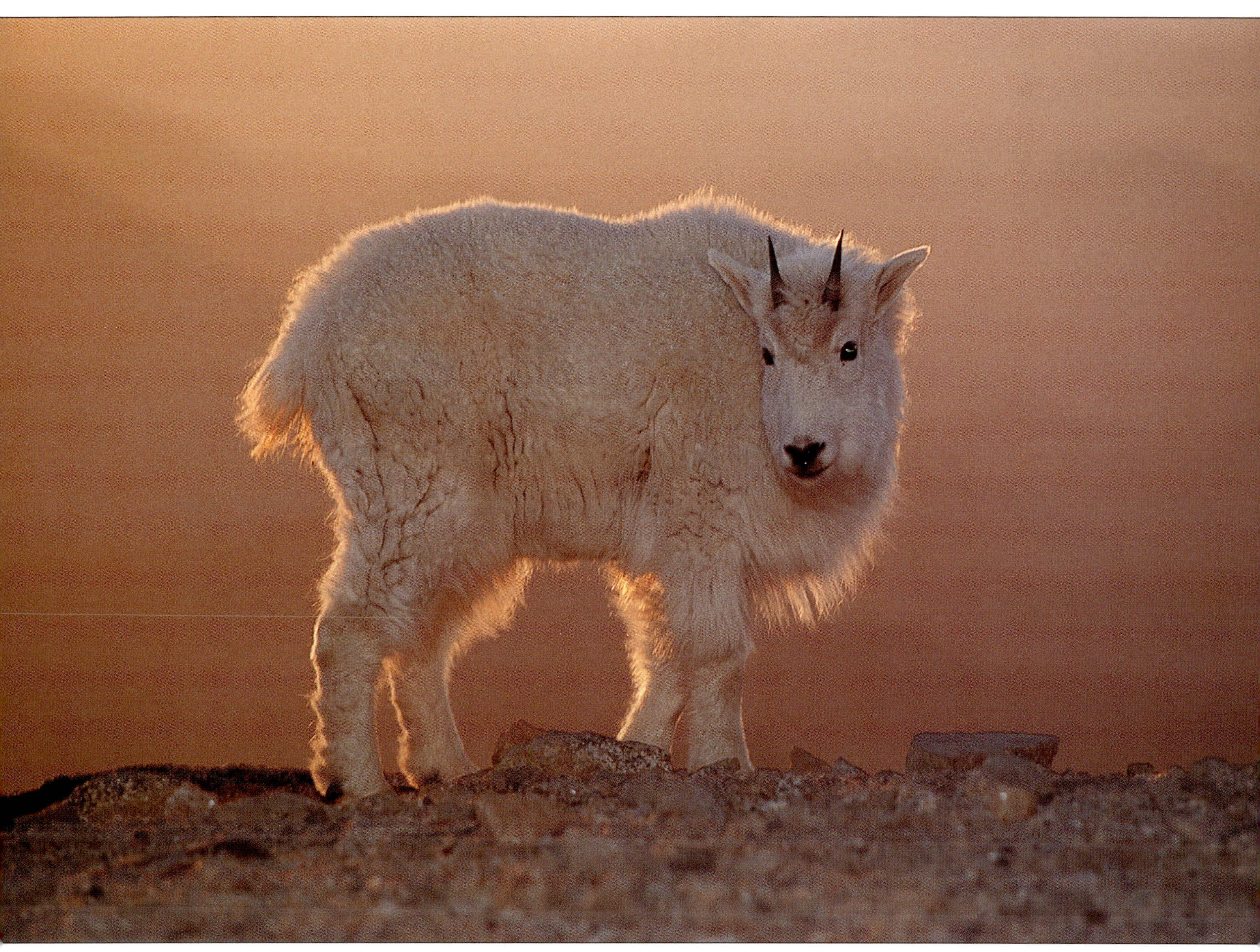

Without using fill flash, this mountain goat would have been just a silhouette at sunrise. Mt. Evans, Colorado. 75–300mm lens with fill flash.

The important thing to remember when choosing the direction of your light source, or choosing whether or not to use a flash, is that light helps create the mood of your image. The quality of the light, the direction of the light, and even the amount of light are often the determining factor in whether the viewer walks past the image or stops and says, "Ooh, nice picture." Front light is a great choice when your subject has either behavior or additional attractive picture elements working with it. However, when your subject has to stand unsupported in the image, just changing the direction of the light can be enough to take the photo beyond documentation.

4. Where Do I Put the Animal?

The question is not what you look at, but what you see.
—Henry David Thoreau

We were told to expect lots of collared peccaries, or "javelina," on a visit to Big Bend National Park in Texas, and we were anticipating adding lots of javelina photos to our files. Our sources were correct. The animals were quite common around the three campgrounds we stayed in. Not only did we see plenty of javelina at close range, but the weather was perfect. Warm, blue-sky days gave us lots of light to stop the nervous little creatures in mid-step. We came home with less than a roll of javelina photos that we were willing to admit were ours.

The problem wasn't the number of subjects or their fear of photographers. The problem was the habitat the animals called home. We either had javelina posing near tents, trailers, water spigots, roads, mowed lawns, and restrooms, or we were trying to focus on them in some of the densest, thorniest brush we had ever seen. It didn't matter that the animals were close and very tolerant. Capturing strong images of the animals in this environment took lots of time, and for every photo we kept there were lots that went into the trash.

Most wildlife photographers are aware that simple images are usually stronger images. Incorporating simplicity into wildlife photos, however, can be extremely difficult. Perhaps you've noticed that most of the animals you want to photograph seem to spend their entire lives buried

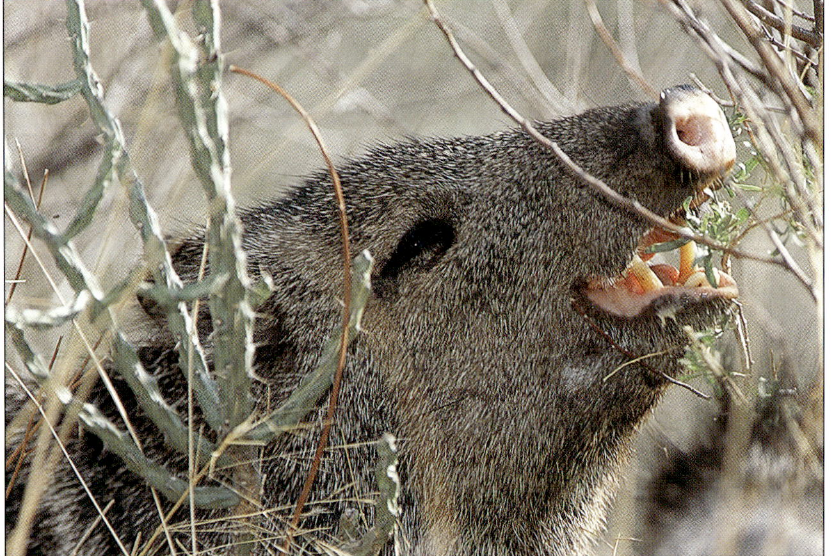

Many species, like this javelina, spend lots of time in a very cluttered environment. All the photographer can do is watch the subject through a long lens, hoping for a chance to compose a strong image. Big Bend National Park, Texas. 500mm lens.

in the messiest collection of brambles and twigs imaginable, making it extremely difficult to create decent images. Sure, there are species that prefer open areas—shorebirds on the beach, mountain goats above timberline—but the lion's share of the earth's fauna seems to like lots of cover.

Actually, it's only natural that most animals prefer messy environments. Many of them are prey species, and they're doing their best to hide from creatures that will eat them. The creatures that are trying to eat them also spend most of their time in the same messy environment, because that's where their prey is found.

Doesn't seem fair, does it? How are wildlife photographers supposed to obtain those award-winning shots if their subjects never pose within a frame of colorful flowers or autumn leaves? It ain't easy, and that's what makes this craft so challenging—and so rewarding when everything does come together.

THAT'S NOT HOW IT LOOKED

When beginning wildlife photographers pick up their exposed film, they are usually quite surprised by images that show a rather untidy environment surrounding a subject that is much smaller than they remembered. That's not how they saw the subject in their viewfinder. When I looked through the viewfinder at the elk calf that started my obsession with wildlife photography, all I saw was the elk calf. In the resulting images, the elk calf actually took up less than half the frame. The rest of the image was filled with clutter that detracted from my center of interest.

Composition is the end result of trying to create order out of chaos.

Composition is the end result of trying to create order out of chaos, and that is what we do whenever we look at any scene. Whenever we open our eyes, our mind automatically overlooks the dross in the view and focuses on only what it thinks is interesting or visually stimulating. Think about my elk calf photo. The animal takes up only a small fraction of the frame, and yet when I looked through the viewfinder, all I could see was the elk calf. It takes a considerable amount of practice to see all of the elements in a scene, the ones you want to leave out as well as the ones you want your viewers to see. Composing an image is as much about what you exclude as it is what you include.

At first glance, painting and photography appear to be very similar, but they are creative opposites. A painter begins with an empty canvas and adds only the elements that support the central theme. A photographer usually starts with an incredibly full canvas and tries to subtract the elements that don't support the theme. However, even though

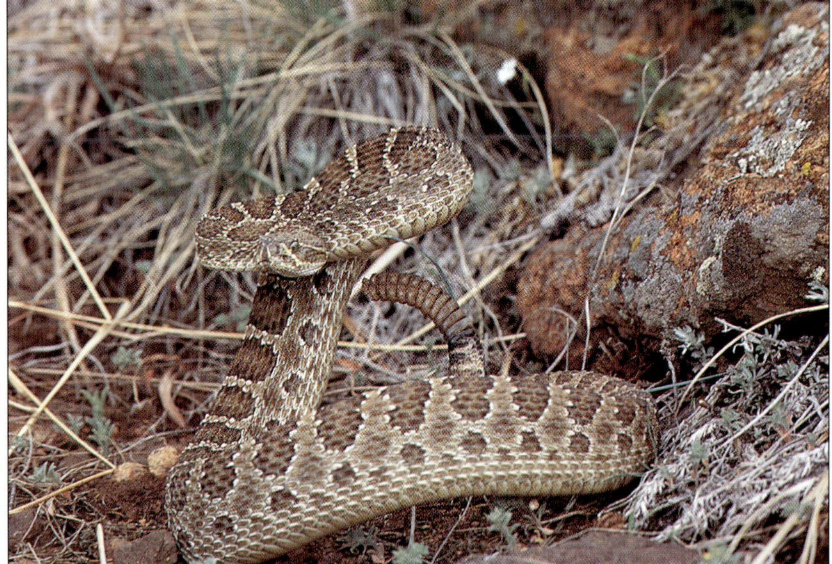

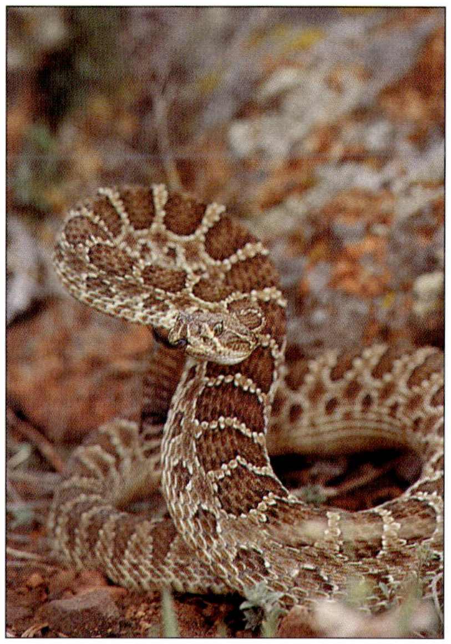

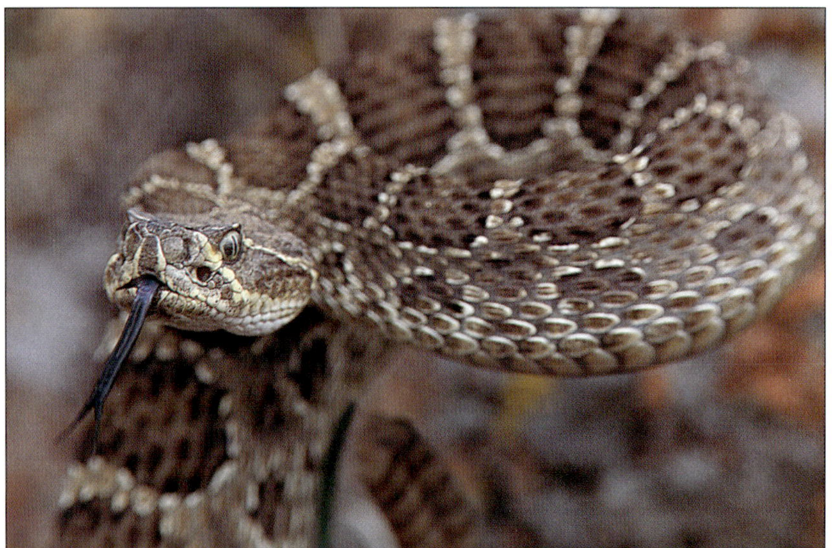

TOP LEFT—This shot of a prairie rattlesnake includes some elements that do absolutely nothing to strengthen the image. Jefferson County, Colorado. 75–300mm lens and fill flash. ABOVE—This shot is better because we have eliminated some of the distracting elements, but it could still be better. Jefferson County, Colorado. 75–300mm lens and fill flash. BOTTOM LEFT—This photo is stronger still. All the distracting elements have been eliminated, and the image still gives the viewer as much information as the previous ones. FYI—We did not approach this snake very closely. This photo was just taken with a longer lens. Jefferson County, Colorado. 300mm lens with 2x teleconverter and fill flash.

photography and painting take opposite approaches to creating an image, the principles that determine the strength of the picture are the same for both, and it is important to know what these principles are.

Ansel Adams said, "The so-called rules of photographic composition are, in my opinion, invalid, irrelevant and immaterial." So why do we need to learn them? It's a good idea to know what the rules are before you go around breaking them, and you should have a darn good reason for breaking them when you do. In spite of his rebellious talk, even Ansel Adams obeyed the rules of photographic composition most of the time.

Unfortunately, the same rules of composition apply to both scenic photography and wildlife photography. Unfortunate because scenic photographers have so much more freedom in changing perspectives and waiting for better light compared with their wildlife counterparts.

When you're photographing an animal, especially if it's a wild subject, you're usually very limited as to how much you can move, and you don't dare wait for the light to change. Your subject will almost assuredly be gone long before that. How often does a scenic photographer have to worry about his subject running away?

COMPOSING WILDLIFE IMAGES

Wildlife photography often happens so quickly and involves such instantaneous decisions that composing an image is almost a subconscious act. How can you possibly compose an image as your subject is moving through the forest, searching around shrubs and circling trees, maybe sticking its face into a patch of particularly tasty vegetation to grab a bite or two? Well, autofocus systems make it both easier and harder to create a great composition.

Autofocus makes composition easier because focusing is so much faster and surer (as long as no pesky twigs are between you and your subject). On the other hand, composing an image is harder with autofocus because we're forced to keep a focusing element on a moving subject's face, which limits where we can put the subject in the frame. Some of the newer cameras have dozens of focusing elements to choose from, and that goes a long way toward correcting this problem, but it still occurs. Despite its drawbacks, Cathy and I still use autofocus whenever we can. It helps to make up for our aging eyes and fogged glasses.

When your subject is moving through a messy environment, all you can do is follow the animal with your lens, constantly refocusing and recomposing, trying to push the shutter button when it appears the elements are working together. Many times you'll be too late pushing the

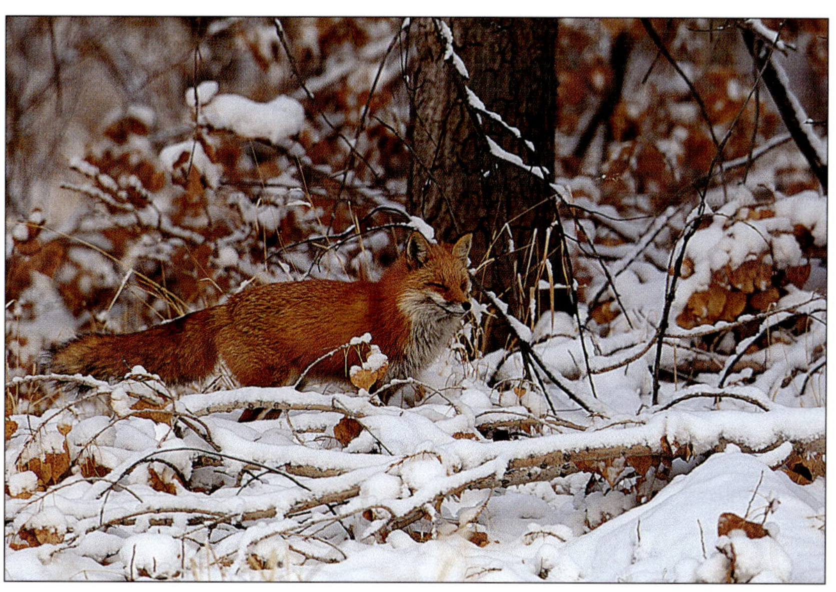

This fox almost left its messy habitat enough for a clean shot. The resulting image is still a good one for showing how well a red fox blends in with snow-dappled autumn leaves. Jefferson County, Colorado. 500mm lens.

button, and your subject will have messed up your wonderful composition. Many times there will be some element you overlooked that definitely detracts from the strength of the composition.

Now, it's not always this difficult, and occasionally animals do cooperate with the photographer. Roosting birds, basking elephant seals, coiled snakes—some subjects will allow the photographer considerable leeway in composing photos, but there are usually problems. The surrounding vegetation, rocks, or even other animals often intrude on your image, detracting from it. And knowing the rules of composition will make it easier to eliminate these distracting elements or at least minimize them.

Your photo should have at least one obvious visual center of interest, and in a wildlife photo your animal subject should be one of those centers of interest. This is where you want your viewer to be looking. Any element that does not support or help lead the viewer's eye to your center of interest should be eliminated or minimized. And none of the supporting elements should be more eye-catching than your center of interest. What makes a visual element more eye-catching? Here are a some general rules you can go by, with the first four being the most important.

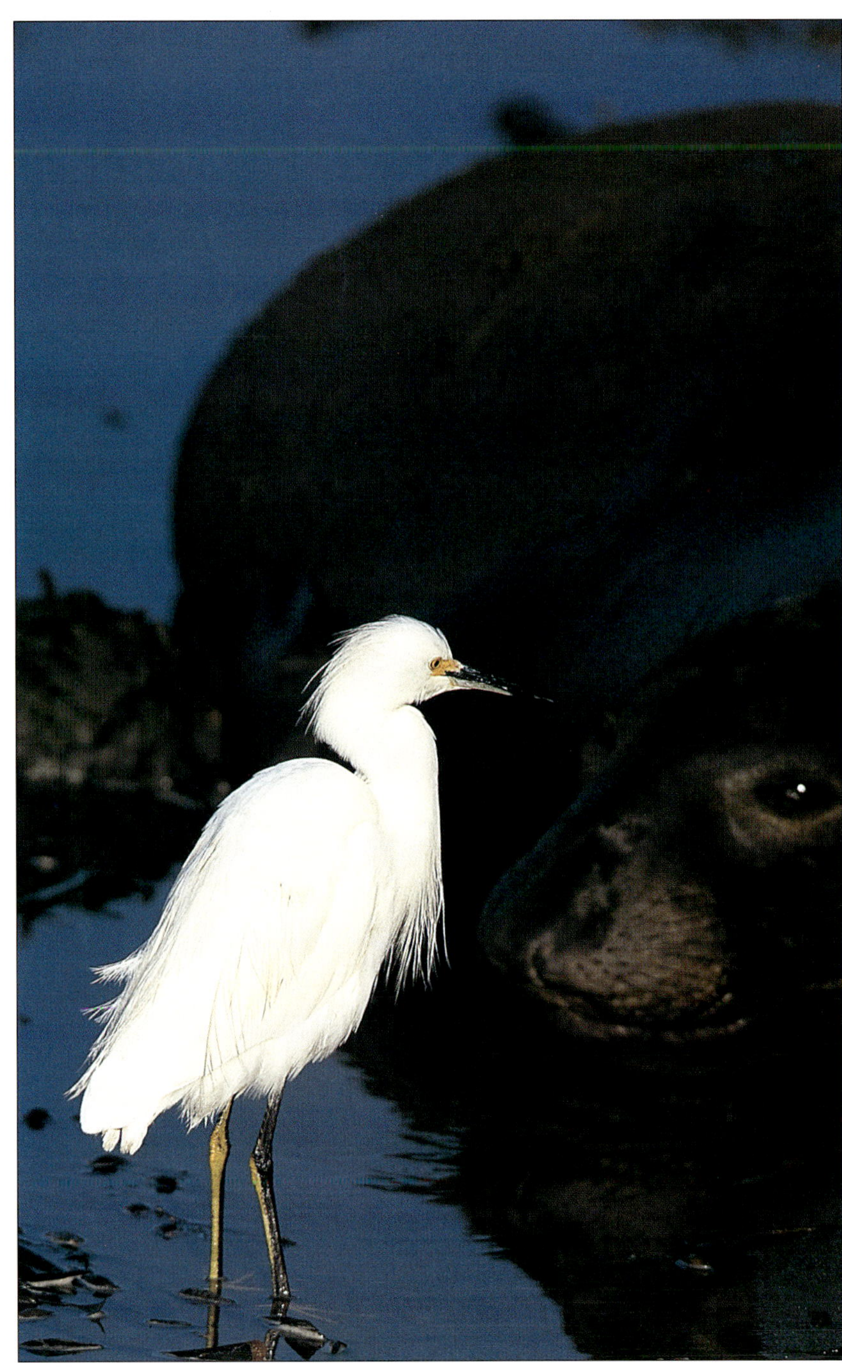

The first thing the viewer sees in this photo is the egret because it's the brightest element. It takes a moment to notice the elephant seal. San Luis Obispo County, California. 500mm lens with 2x teleconverter.

1. Light-colored or bright objects draw more attention than dark.
2. Large objects draw more attention than small.
3. Warmer colors (red, orange, yellow) are more eye-catching than cool ones (green, blue, violet).
4. Sharp or in-focus elements stand out more than blurred ones.

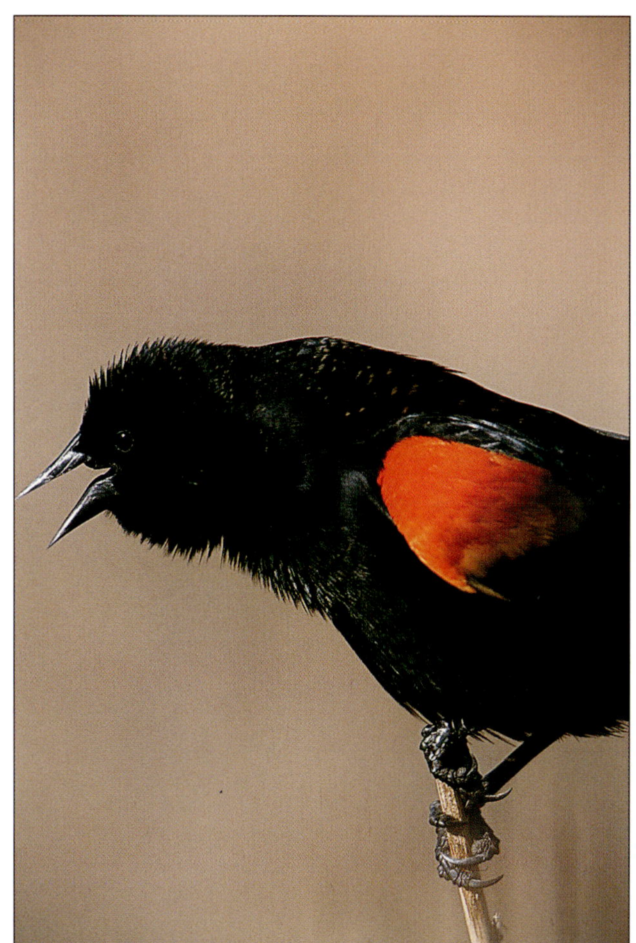

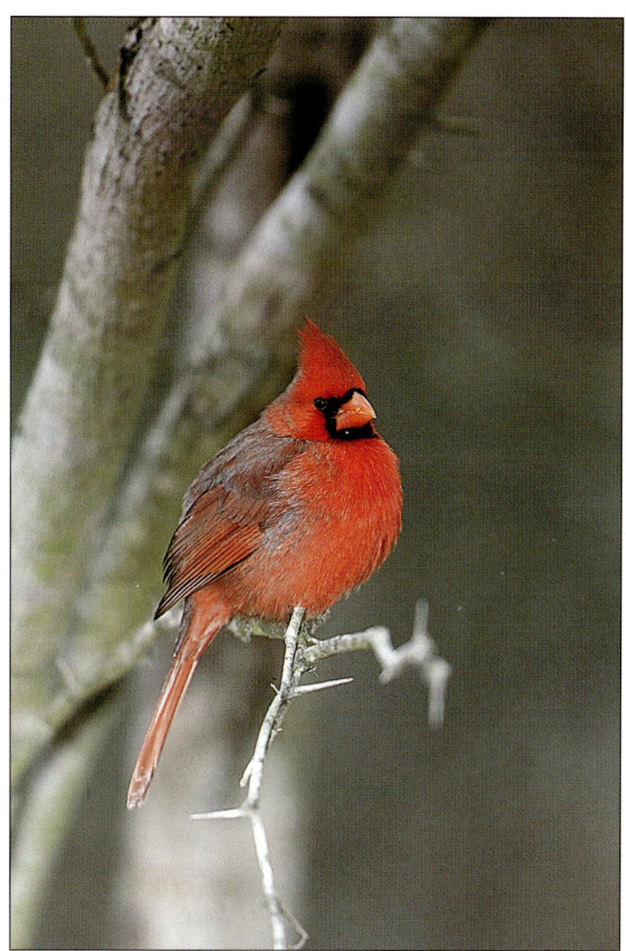

LEFT—If you want someone to notice your center of interest, make it large. Making this red-winged blackbird large not only draws the viewers' attention, it allows them to see details they would not otherwise be able to. Jefferson County, Colorado. 500mm lens with 2x. RIGHT—Warm-colored species, like cardinals, make wonderful subjects because they automatically draw the viewer's attention. Choke Canyon State Park, Texas. 500mm lens with extension tubes and fill flash.

This Forster's tern roosting in a flock of royal terns shows how an object that is in focus stands out much better than out-of-focus elements do. It also shows that differences stand out more than similarities (see rule number 5). The Forster's tern is smaller and has a different colored bill and legs than the royal terns around it. Because of this, it would draw the viewers' attention even if all of the birds were in focus. Sanibel Island, Florida. 500mm lens with 1.4x teleconverter.

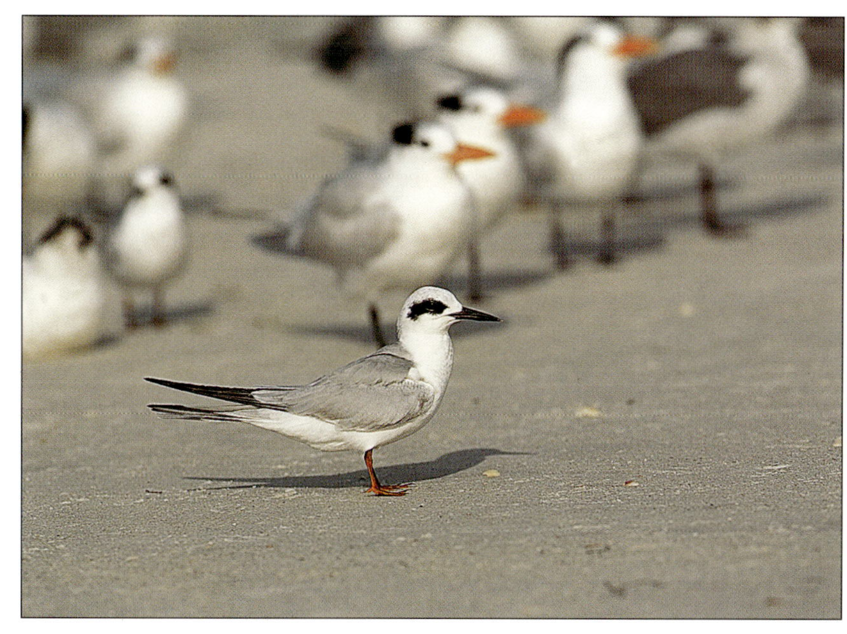

5. Difference stands out more than similarity or conformity. (This is a good one to overlook if you want to show an animal's camouflage at work.)
6. Diagonal lines are stronger than horizontal or vertical lines.
7. Rough draws more attention than smooth.
8. Jagged lines draw more attention than curved ones.

How are you supposed to remember all of these things as you're following an animal with your lens? Don't worry. Many of them will be very obvious as you look through your viewfinder, and you will handle them subconsciously. Some you only learn through lots of trial and error. With most wildlife photos there's only so much the subject will allow you to do compositionally

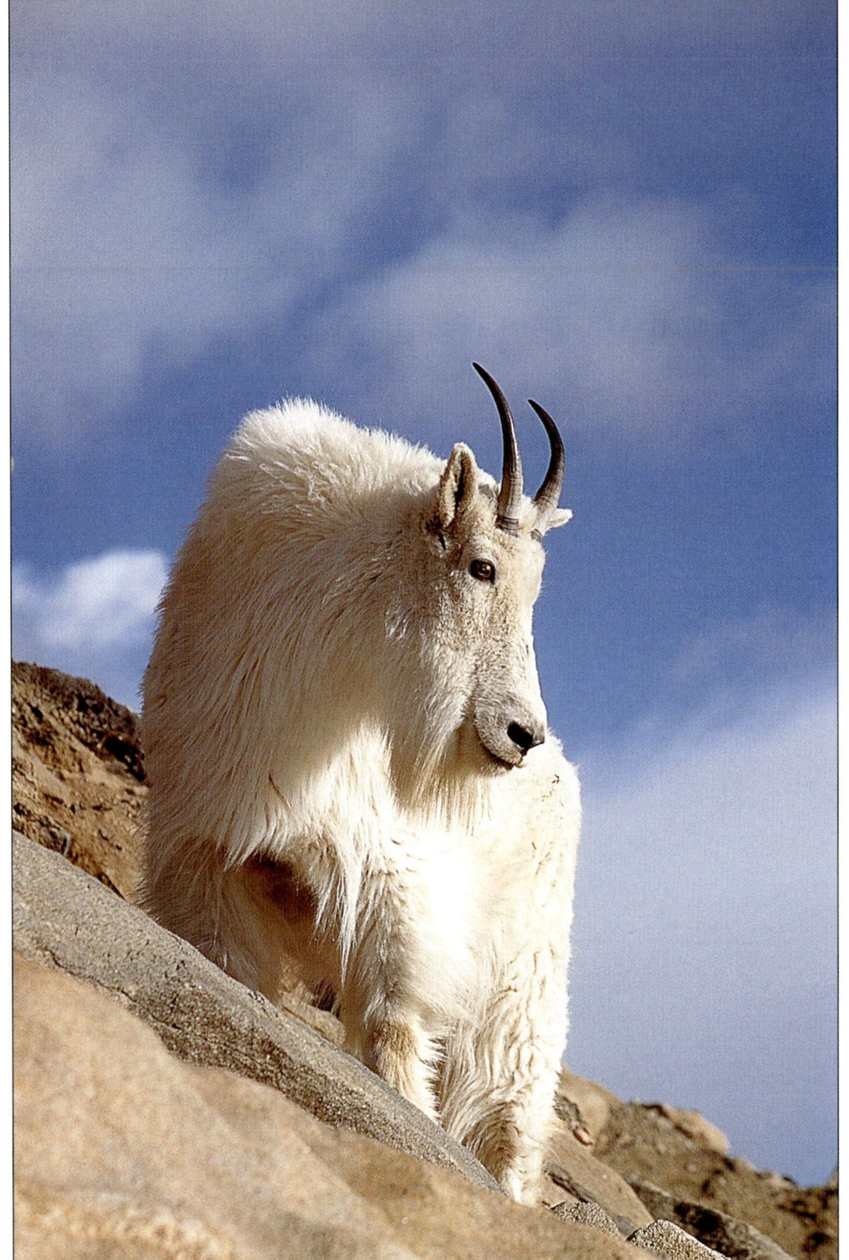

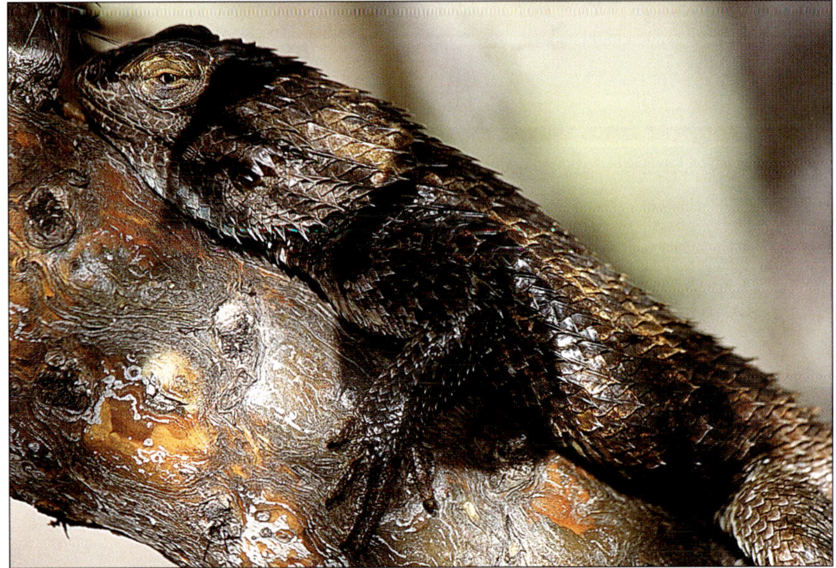

TOP—If this mountain goat had been standing on level ground it would have been a documentary image. The fact that the ground is tilted at a crazy angle is what makes this photo interesting. Mt. Evans, Colorado. 500mm lens. BOTTOM—This desert spiny lizard would be pretty well-camouflaged on this cholla cactus branch if not for the fact that its skin is rougher than that of the cactus. The rough skin helps attract the viewer's attention. Pima County, Arizona. 75–300mm lens with extension tubes and fill flash.

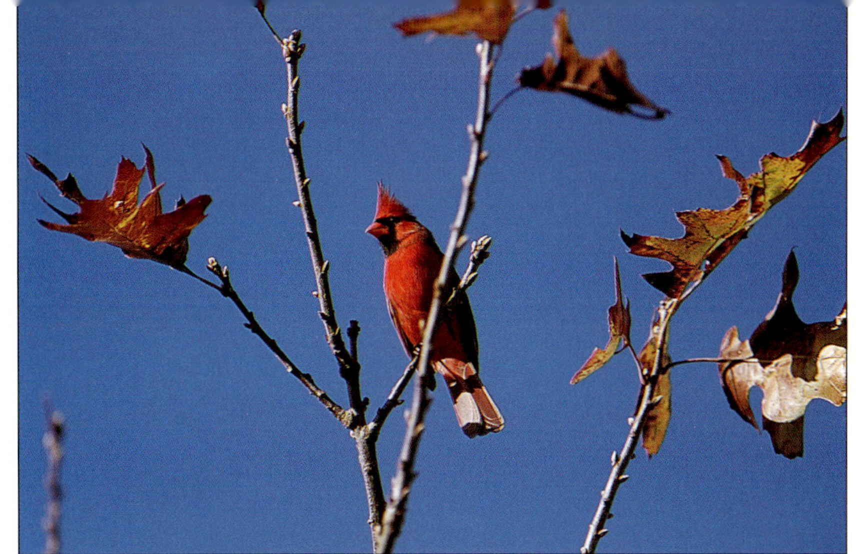

anyway. Sometimes the animal will let you change your perspective to put a less distracting background behind the subject, or maybe frame it with some attractive foliage. Usually, though, if you can just eliminate the bright spots and strong lines that draw attention away from the center of interest, you're doing well.

PLACING THE CENTER OF INTEREST

There are, however, several things you *can* control in almost any photo. With the exception of situations in which the subject is moving like a bat out of hell, you can control where the center of interest is placed within the picture, how much room your subject has to move within the image, and the depth of field. When the subject is running, or flying, or slithering quickly, you

TOP—Placing a small subject in the middle of your frame creates an uninteresting composition. Even a cardinal and a frame of autumn leaves are not enough to make this a strong image. Well-fleet Bay Wildlife Sanctuary, Massachusetts. 300mm lens with 1.4x teleconverter. BOTTOM—Although this cardinal is smaller in the frame, the image is stronger because the center of interest is at one of the power points, and most viewers don't expect to see a cardinal on a saguaro cactus. Pima County, Arizona. 300mm lens with 2x teleconverter.

just have to give it the old college try, hope for the best, and see where the subject ends up in the image.

If the creature is standing still or moving at a more sedate pace, you can control where you put it in the image. Part of the placement of your center of interest will include the possibility of framing it. Framing the center of interest with other picture elements is something that cannot be controlled in every photo, but when it can, it definitely focuses the viewers' attention on your subject.

Asymmetry is usually more pleasing to the human eye than symmetry.

As far as where you put your center of interest, some spots are definitely stronger than others. The center of the image is the first place we look for the center of interest, and if we find it there, we're a little disappointed. It spite of its name, we don't like to see the center of interest in the center of the picture. Our brains actually do like to work at least a little, and they get bored if the game is over too quickly.

Asymmetry is usually more pleasing to the human eye than symmetry. Because of this, making a bull's-eye out of your subject by placing it dead in the middle of the picture is usually the weakest location. This is definitely something to watch out for when using autofocus. You can find the strongest places to put your center of interest by using the Rule of Thirds. The Rule of Thirds is a basic rule of composition, and it is covered in most beginning nature photography guidebooks. Using this rule, we divide the image into thirds both horizontally and vertically, and the four points where the lines intersect are called "power points." These are the strongest places to put your center of interest.

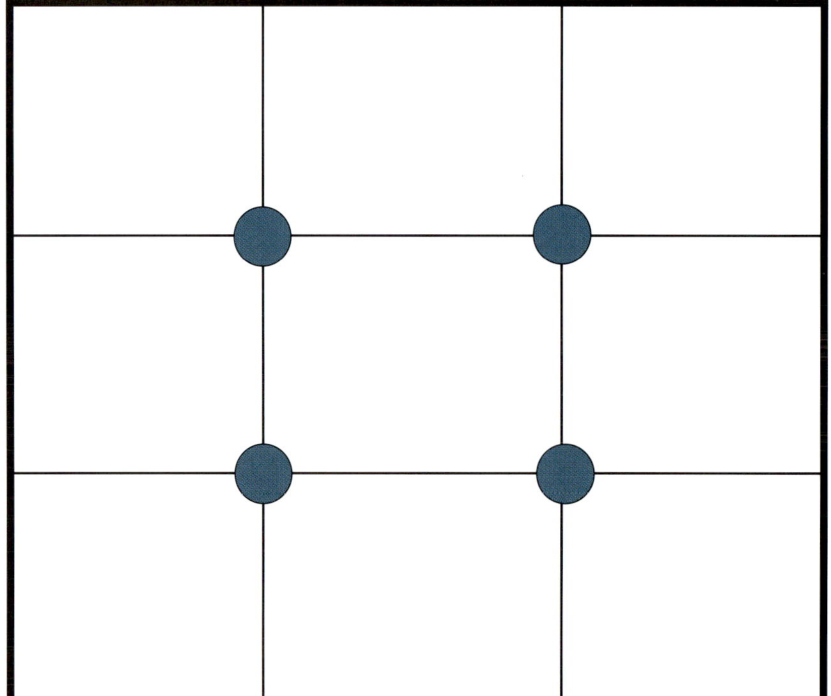

The Rule of Thirds grid with the powerpoints marked in blue.

Some photographers maintain that the weaker your center of interest, the closer to the middle you should put it. Cathy and I disagree. Very seldom is the middle the strongest location. The weaker your center of interest, the closer to one of the power points it should be.

FRAMING THE CENTER OF INTEREST

One method of highlighting your center of interest, especially in a cluttered environment, involves the use of picture elements to frame your subject. Because framing your subject makes it so much easier to find,

Putting a frame around your subject is a great way to get your viewers' attention. If the frame is too obvious, though, it doesn't hold the viewers' interest for long. In this image of a mountain lion, we used a combination of natural features to subtly frame the subject. Captive. Spanish River, Ontario, Canada. 500mm lens.

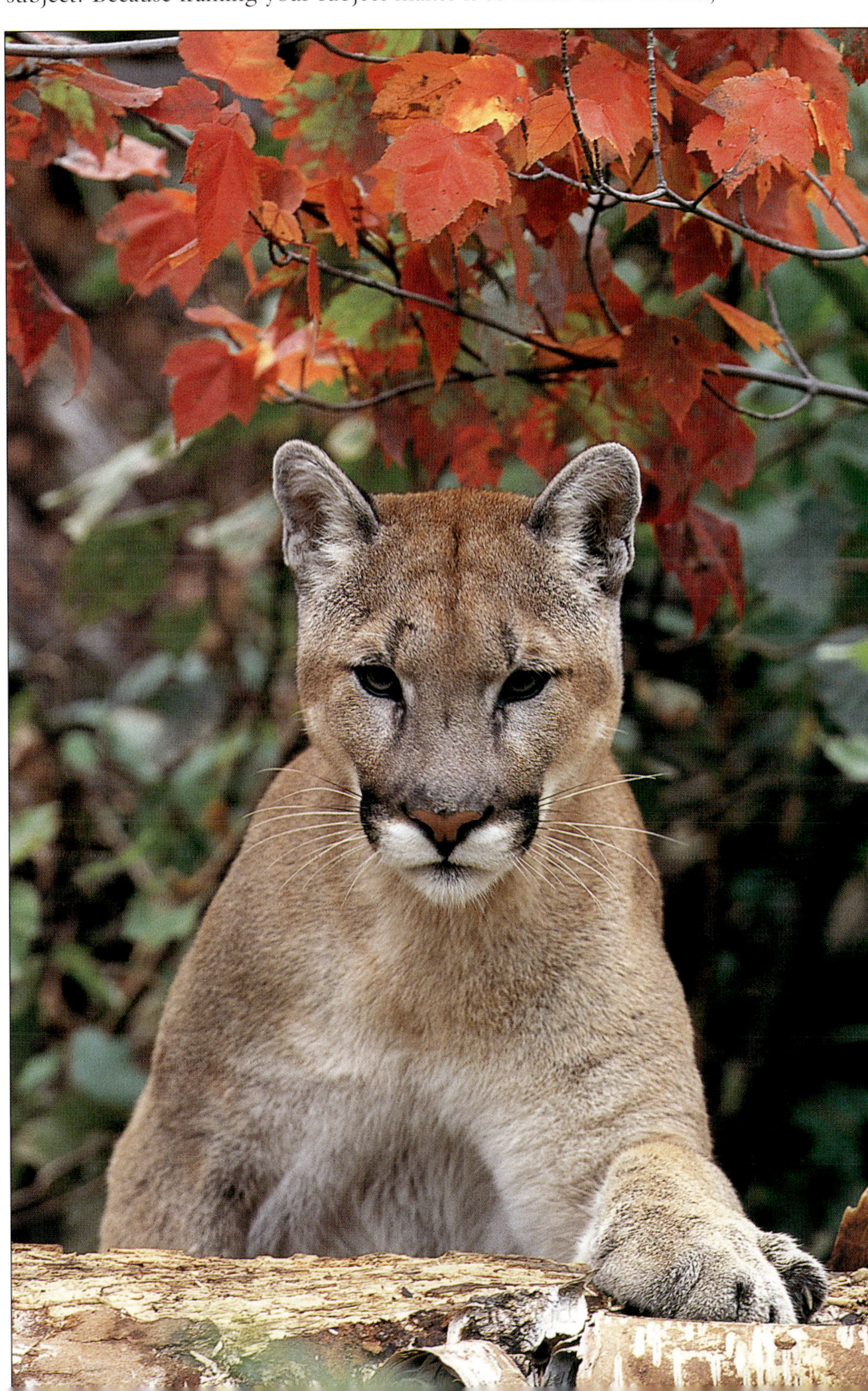

avoid putting it dead center in the picture, where the viewer automatically looks anyway. Subtle frames often work more effectively than obvious ones. Using four branches, like the frame around a painting, to frame your subject, will indeed make it stand out. It makes the center of interest so obvious, though, it's similar to beating your viewer over the head with a club. Make the viewer's brain wake up and work a little. Maybe use some leaves on one side, a dead log on another, and a range of mountains on another. Let a variety of elements in the habitat you are photographing work for you.

DOES YOUR SUBJECT HAVE ROOM TO MOVE?

Give your subject adequate room to move within the picture. It's usually better to chop off the rear of the animal and still give it room to move into the frame than it is to include the entire animal but have its nose almost touching the border of the photo. In the same vein, having your subject looking into the picture rather than out of it is also a much stronger composition. If the animal is looking left, put it on the right side of the image. If it is looking right, put it on the left side.

Give your subject adequate room to move within the picture.

You can use the direction your subject is moving to offset the negative effect of putting your center of interest in the center of the picture.

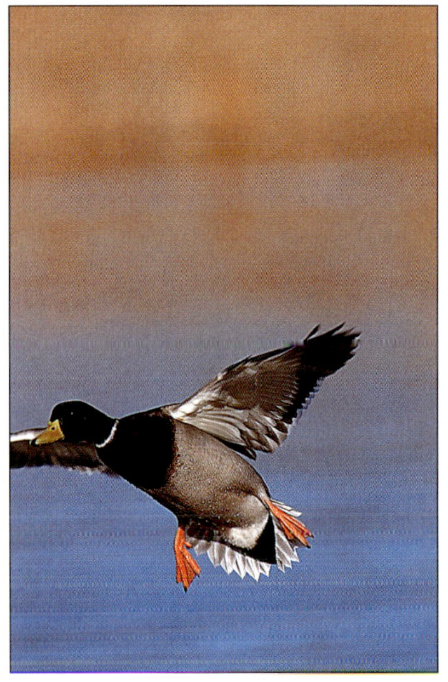

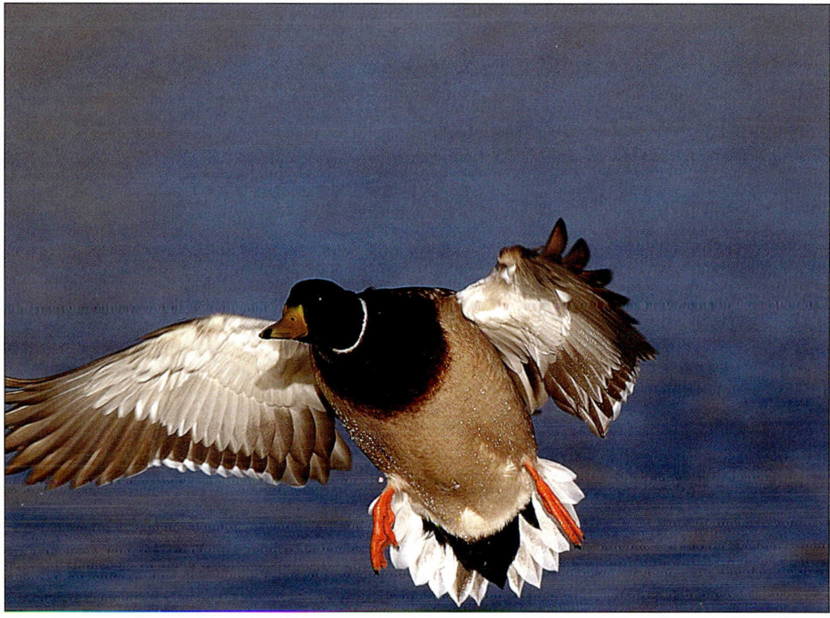

LEFT—In this image, the mallard drake hasn't been given adequate room to move within the frame. This composition draws the viewers' attention to the duck's destination, which is outside the picture. Jefferson County, Colorado. 500mm lens. RIGHT—Give your subject room to move within the frame. This mallard drake has plenty of room to move in the direction it is flying, and viewers have no reason to take their attention from the subject. Perhaps the previous image would have worked as well as this one if we had taken it as a horizontal shot too. Jefferson County, Colorado. 500mm lens.

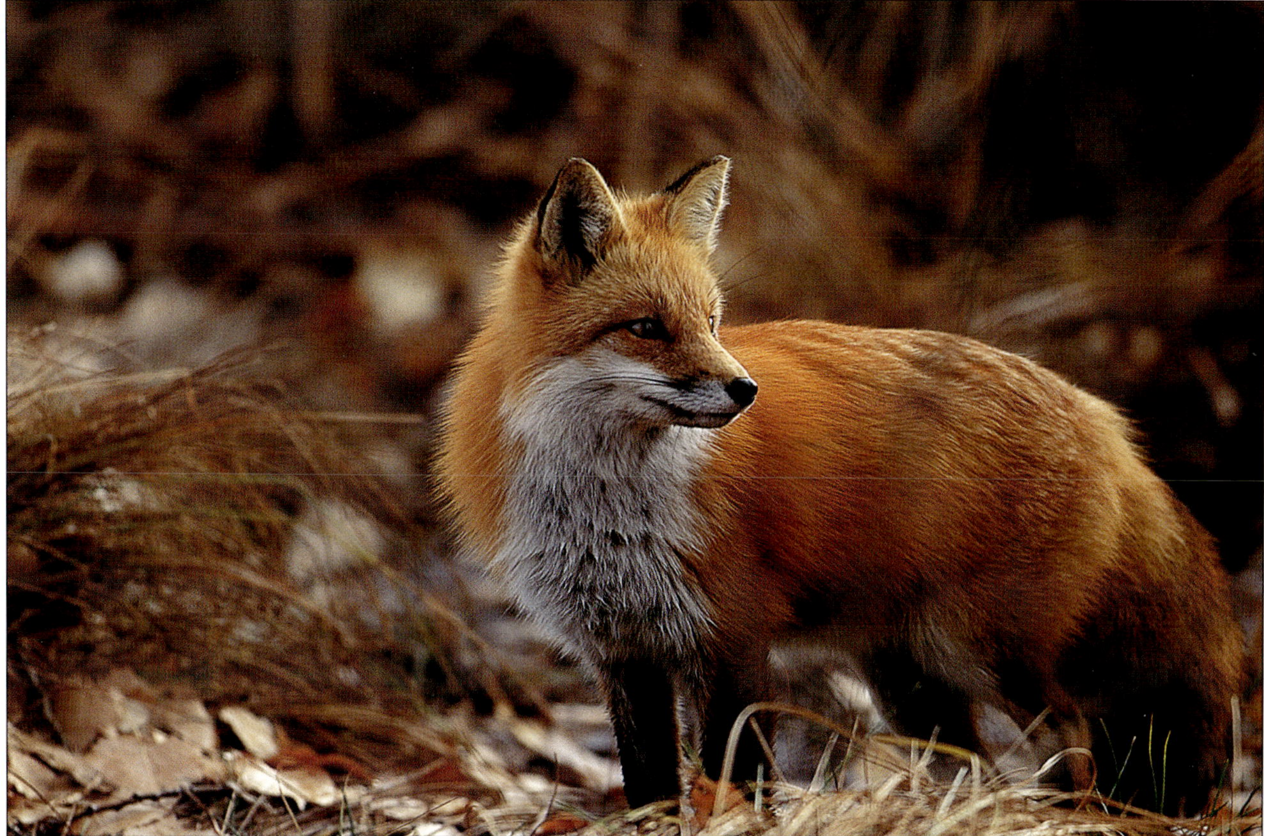

Even though this red fox's head is in the middle of the frame, the animal's body is off to one side. This makes the image asymmetrical and minimizes the bull's–eye effect. Jefferson County, Colorado. 500mm lens.

When you have a subject that appears to be moving through your image, you can often get away with placing the animal's head in the center of the picture. Having the rest of the animal's body on one side of the picture's center makes the image asymmetrical and minimizes the bull's-eye effect.

LOOK YOUR SUBJECT IN THE EYE

Please don't harass wild animals in an attempt to make them look at you.

Another compositional element you can often control is eye contact. Viewers often make more of a connection with the subject if the creature appears to be looking at them. This makes it look like the subject is interested in them. When the subject is looking directly into the lens, the viewers almost become a part of the resulting image. Please don't harass wild animals in an attempt to make them look at you. Be patient. Unless you're in a blind, the subject almost certainly knows you're there, and it will look at you from time to time to check up on you.

Knowing something about the animal's behavior can help you capture eye contact. Cathy and I have found this to be true even when we photograph zoo animals. Watch the big cats when little children show

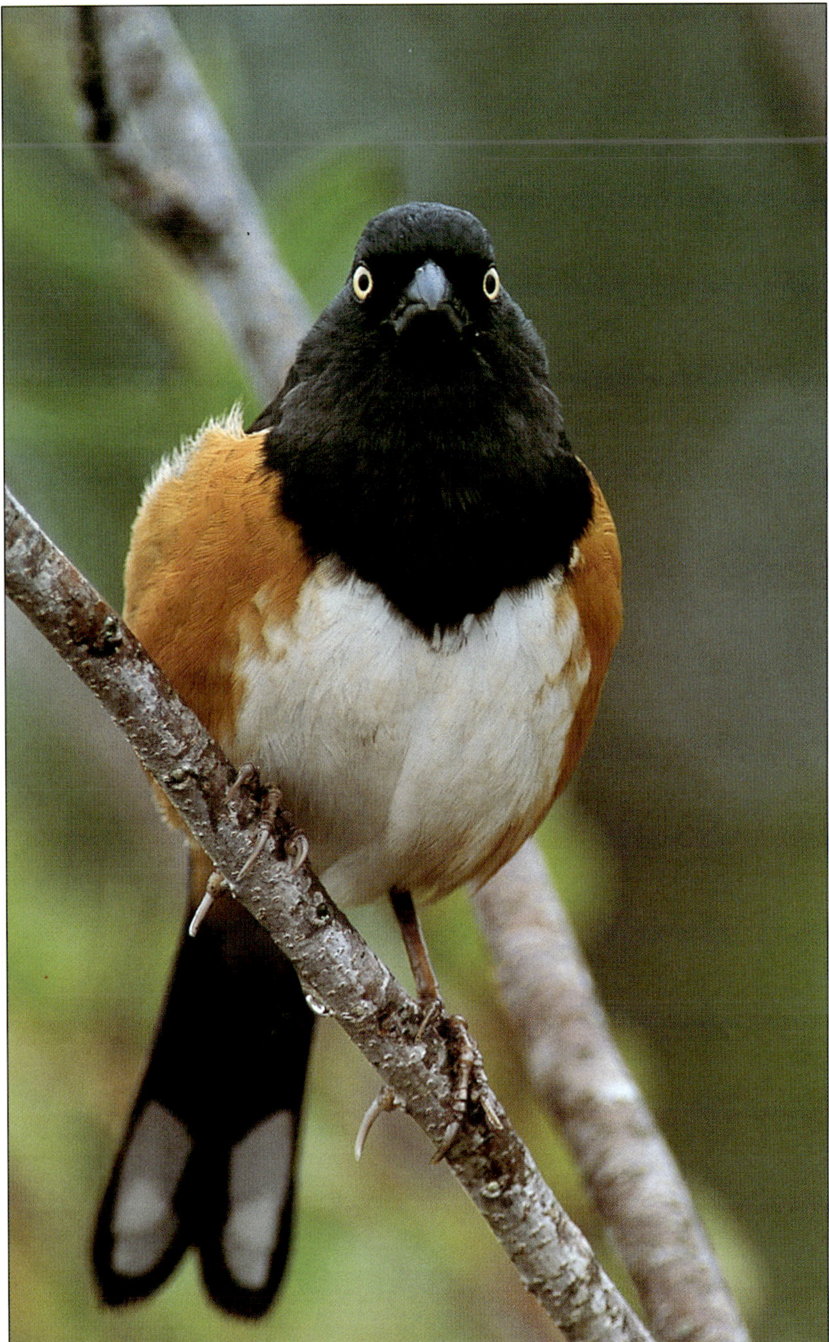

Be patient with your subject. Creatures like this rufous-sided towhee will look up from time to time to check out its surroundings. At these times the alert photographer can create images in which the viewer can make eye contact with your subject. Polk County, Florida. 300mm lens with 2x teleconverter and fill flash.

up. They often perk right up at the sight of these bite-size little morsels, and we prepare to photograph when we hear children approaching.

HOW MUCH DEPTH OF FIELD DO YOU WANT?

At this level of wildlife photography you should know how aperture controls the amount of depth of field in your image. The wider the aperture, the less depth of field in the image. The smaller the aperture, the more depth of field in the image. A popular misconception is that telephoto lenses have less depth of field than normal or wide angle lens-

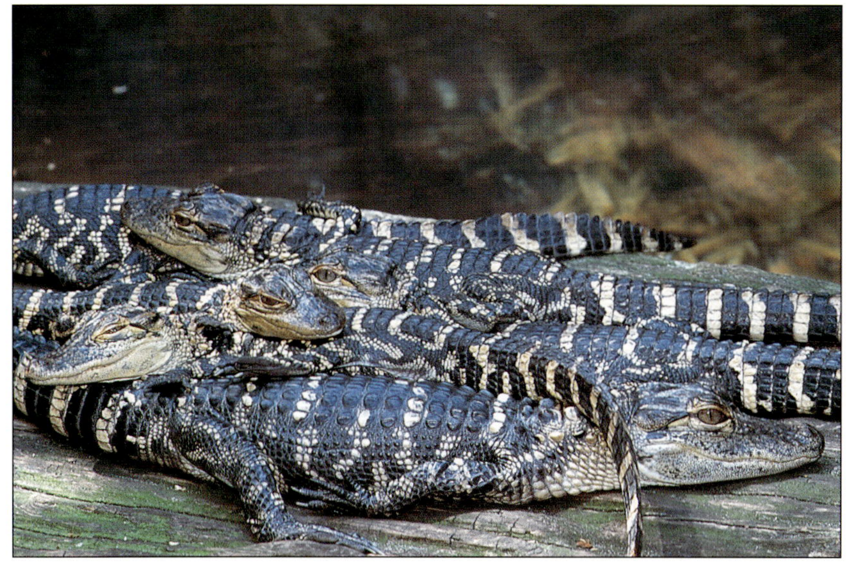

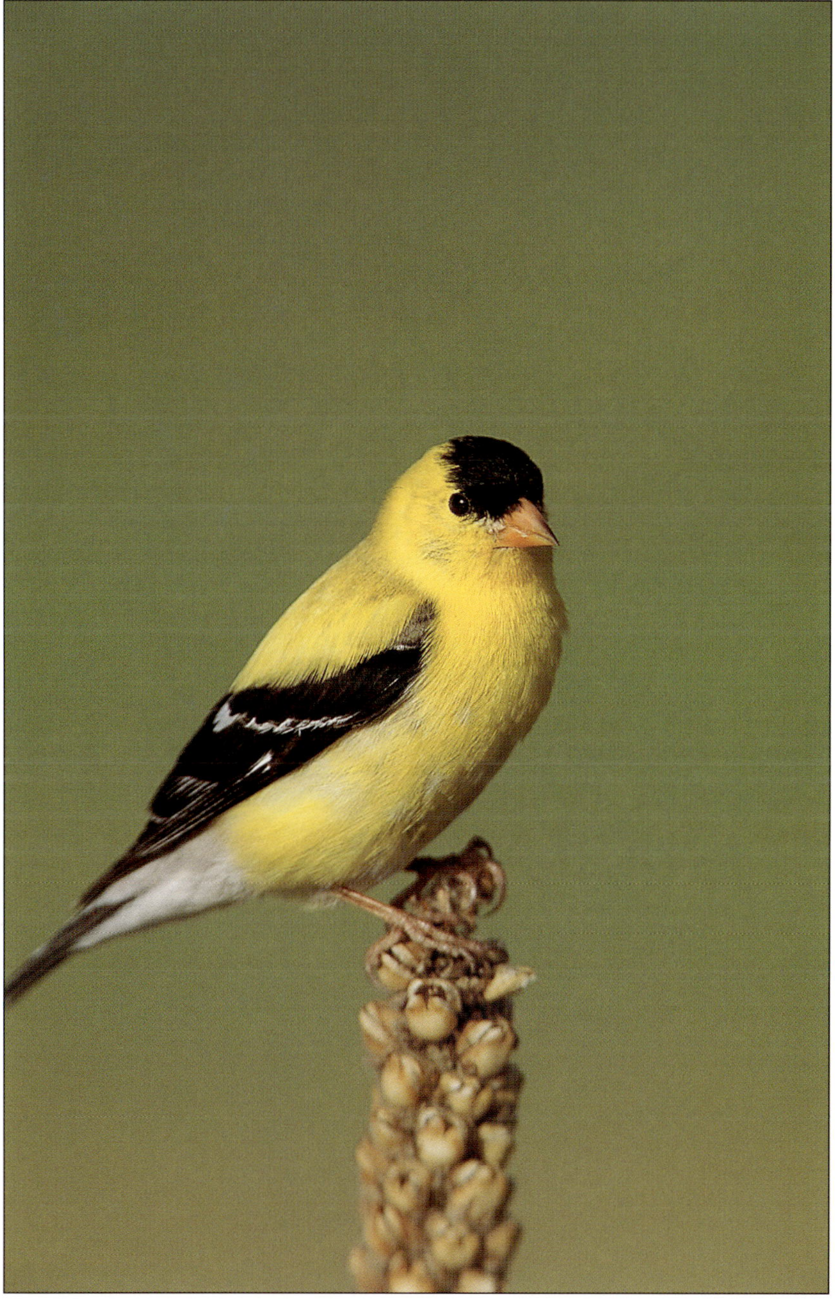

TOP—When photographing groups of animals, you usually want lots of depth of field. The more individuals in the group that are in focus, the better. This photo was taken at f22, and some of the baby alligators are still not in focus. Captive. Alligator Farm, St. Augustine, Florida. 300mm lens with 1.4x teleconverter, extension tubes, and fill flash. BOTTOM—To create strong images of subjects in a cluttered environment, you often want just enough depth of field for only your subject to be in focus while everything else blurs out. That technique was used in this image of an American goldfinch. It helps that the background was quite a distance behind the bird. Arapahoe County, Colorado. 500mm lens with 1.4x teleconverter.

es do. This is not very accurate. The size of the subject in the image affects the amount of depth of field much more than the length of the lens does. The larger the subject appears in the image, the less depth of field you will have at a given aperture. Whether you make the subject huge with a 28mm lens or a 600mm lens makes very little difference as far as depth of field is concerned.

Choosing depth of field is usually a compromise of sorts. You want enough depth for the subject to be in focus from at least its eyes to the tip of its nose, but not so much that distracting elements in the background stand out

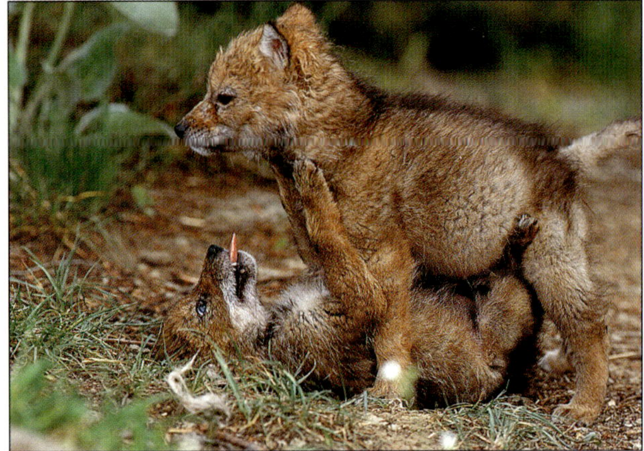

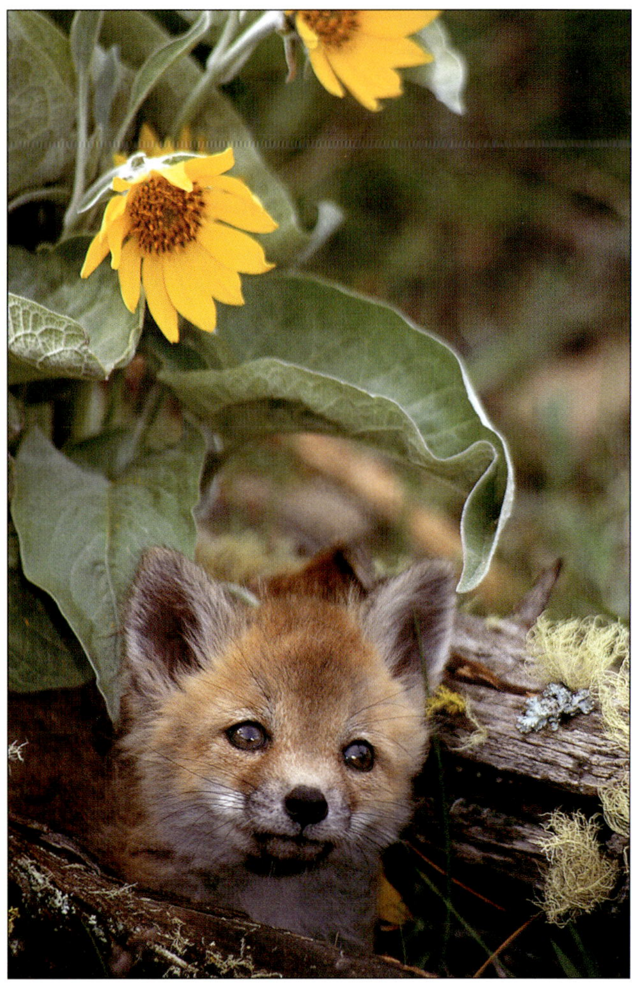

ABOVE—In this photo of wrestling coyote pups, we had to compromise. It would have been ideal to have enough depth of field for both pups to be in focus, but we also wanted to shoot fast enough to stop the action. Here, the action is stopped, and the depth of field is adequate. Captive. Bridger Mountains, Montana. 75–300mm lens with fill flash. RIGHT—Here we also have more than one center of interest. Although the balsamroot blossoms are much brighter than the fox pup, they don't overpower it because the pup is so much larger in the image. Captive. Bridger Mountains, Montana. 75–300mm lens with fill flash.

clearly. When your subject is the only center of interest, using a very shallow depth of field to totally blur out the background until it is only a wash of color makes a particularly pleasing image. If your subject is the only object in the image that is anywhere near in focus, the viewer's attention is drawn to it as if it were in a spotlight.

When you create an image with more than one center of interest, ideally you should close your aperture down to get enough depth of field for every center of interest to be in focus. Suppose you have a red fox pup resting beneath a balsamroot blossom or two coyote pups playing. Both centers of interest should be in focus, or the out of focus one will lose importance and may become more of a distraction than a supporting element.

When you have more than one center of interest, you also need to strive for balance in the image. You don't want one center of interest to be visually stronger than the other, and there are a number of ways to balance them. The easiest way is to keep them close to the same size, brightness, and color. This method was used in the photo of the coyote pups. In the photo of the fox pup and balsamroot flowers, we have a

You don't want one center of interest to be visually stronger than the other.

larger center of interest balanced by one that is smaller but brighter and warmer colored. You can even use two or more small centers of interest to balance a large one, although this is very difficult composition to pull off in wildlife photography. The subjects are usually just too active.

The central theme of this photo is not the mountain lion but a concept that is evoked by the relationship between the mountain lion and its habitat. And every viewer could see a different concept in this image. One possibility is "life in a harsh environment." Notice how the cat is framed by the vegetation and the horizon, and the tracks lead the viewers' eye right where we want them to look. As you can see, there is nothing in this shot that draws the viewers' attention outside the frame. Captive. Bridger Mountains, Montana. 75–300mm lens.

WHAT IS YOUR CENTRAL THEME?

What is the "central theme" of your photo? The central theme can be simply the animal you are photographing, or it can be something much more complicated. If you have more than one definite center of interest, the central theme becomes the relationship between those two elements—the fox pup to the balsamroot blossom or the coyote pups to each other. Such relationships can be used to represent intangible concepts such as loneliness, solitude, serenity, or love, and in such cases, the concept becomes the central theme. Give the viewer an interesting theme to consider and your image is well on its way to the land beyond documentation. Using your subject's size in the image to help create a central theme will be covered more in chapters 5 and 8.

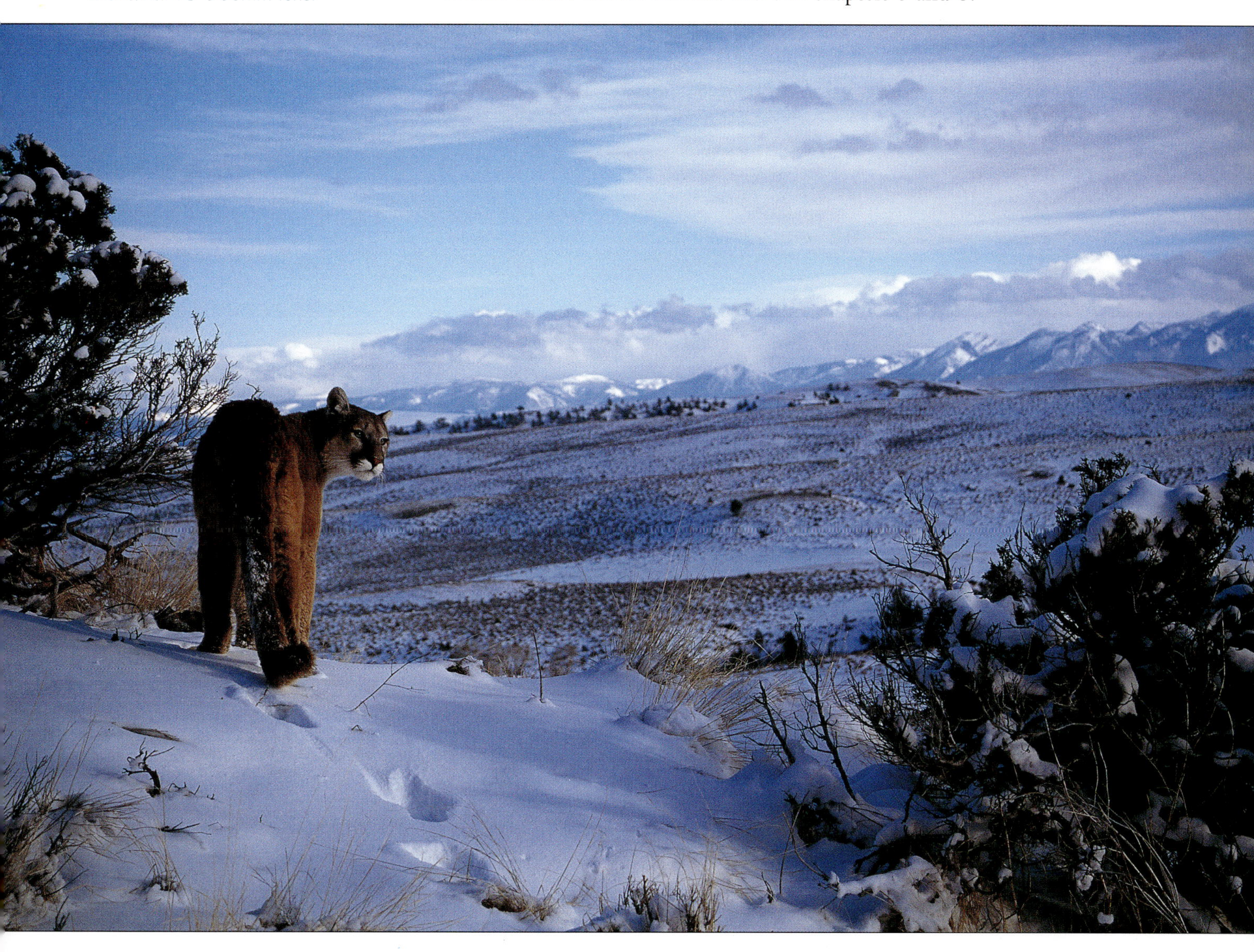

DO YOU HAVE RHYTHM?

Does your photo have a definite pattern of accents and intervals? Each animal, for instance, would be an accent, and the space between the animals would be an interval. If this description fits your image, then rhythm definitely plays a role in its composition. Rhythm can be a strong central theme all by itself, but it can also be difficult to capture in wildlife photography for several reasons. First, it takes more than one subject to create rhythm. Second, you often need lots of depth of field. Every individual need not be tack sharp (although it helps), but they do need to be in focus enough to maintain the rhythm. And third, rhythm implies order. Herds, flocks, pods, and coveys are often anything but orderly. Sometimes, though, the magic works, and rhythm is something to look for when you are photographing groups. For example, rhythm could play an important part in an image showing a line of cranes in flight or a group of goslings walking to the water.

Breaking rhythm is also a good technique for drawing attention to your photo. Remember, difference stands out more than similarity. If you're focusing on a line of sleeping ducks, and one of them lifts its head up to look around, that alert duck is going to draw much more attention than any of the others.

Here we have three back-lit Canada goslings looking like little lightbulbs. Each bird is in the same position, the birds are separated by the same interval, and the rhythm created by this composition is the central theme. Even though only one of the goslings is perfectly sharp, we still have rhythm. Part of the reason for this is each accent is more of a golden glow rather than a count-every-feather portrait. Jefferson County, Colorado. 500mm lens with 1.4x teleconverter.

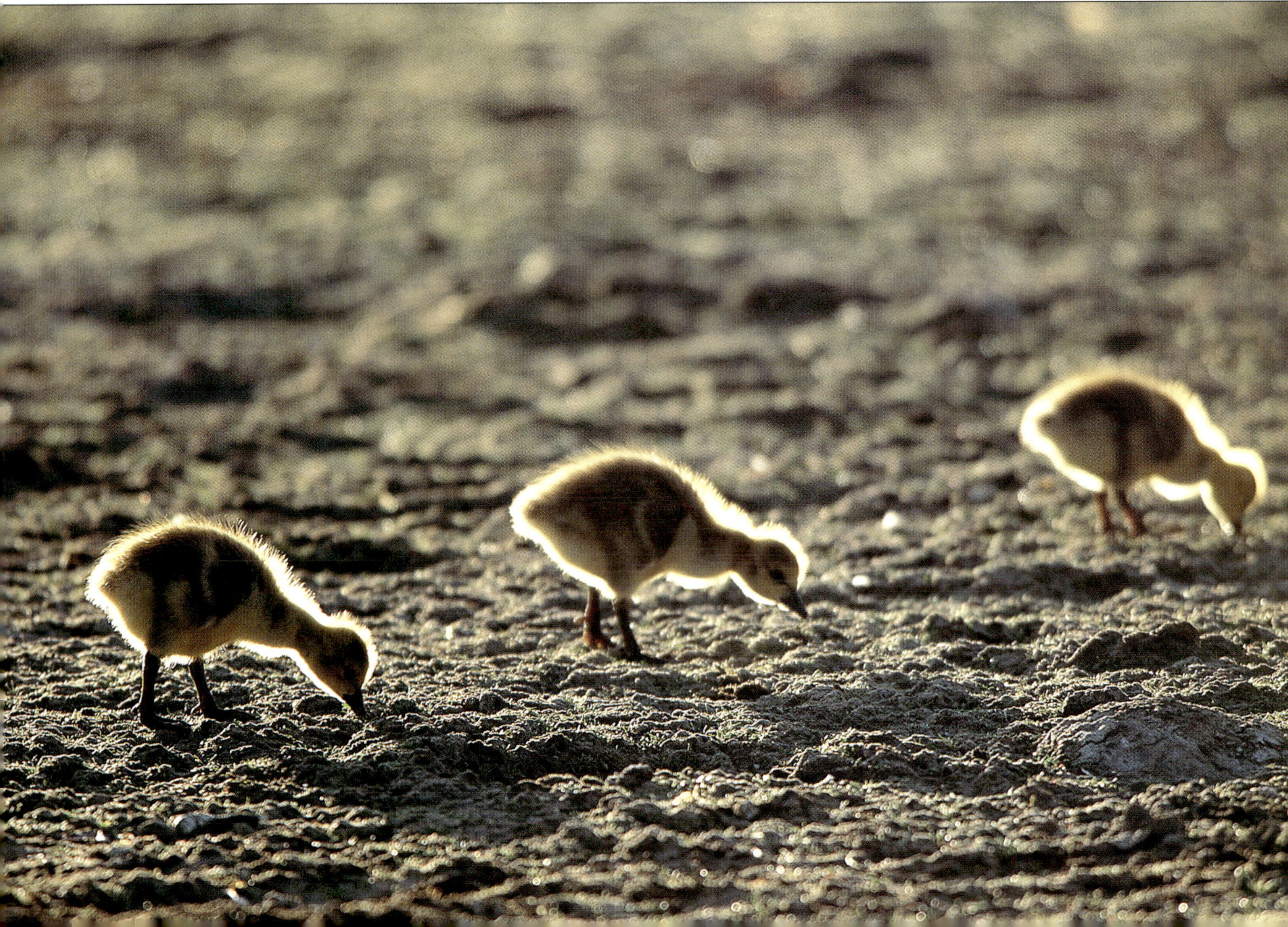

Wildlife photographers often find themselves with the near impossible task of imposing order on a very chaotic environment, and trying to find elements in a mess of brush and brambles that support a center of interest that refuses to stand still. The trick to being successful is noticing all the picture elements in your viewfinder, both the distracting ones you want to eliminate and the supporting ones you want to include. This process will never be easy, but there are a number of techniques, like framing the center of interest, capturing eye contact, balancing more than one center of interest, and the use of rhythm, to help us compose images that go beyond documentation.

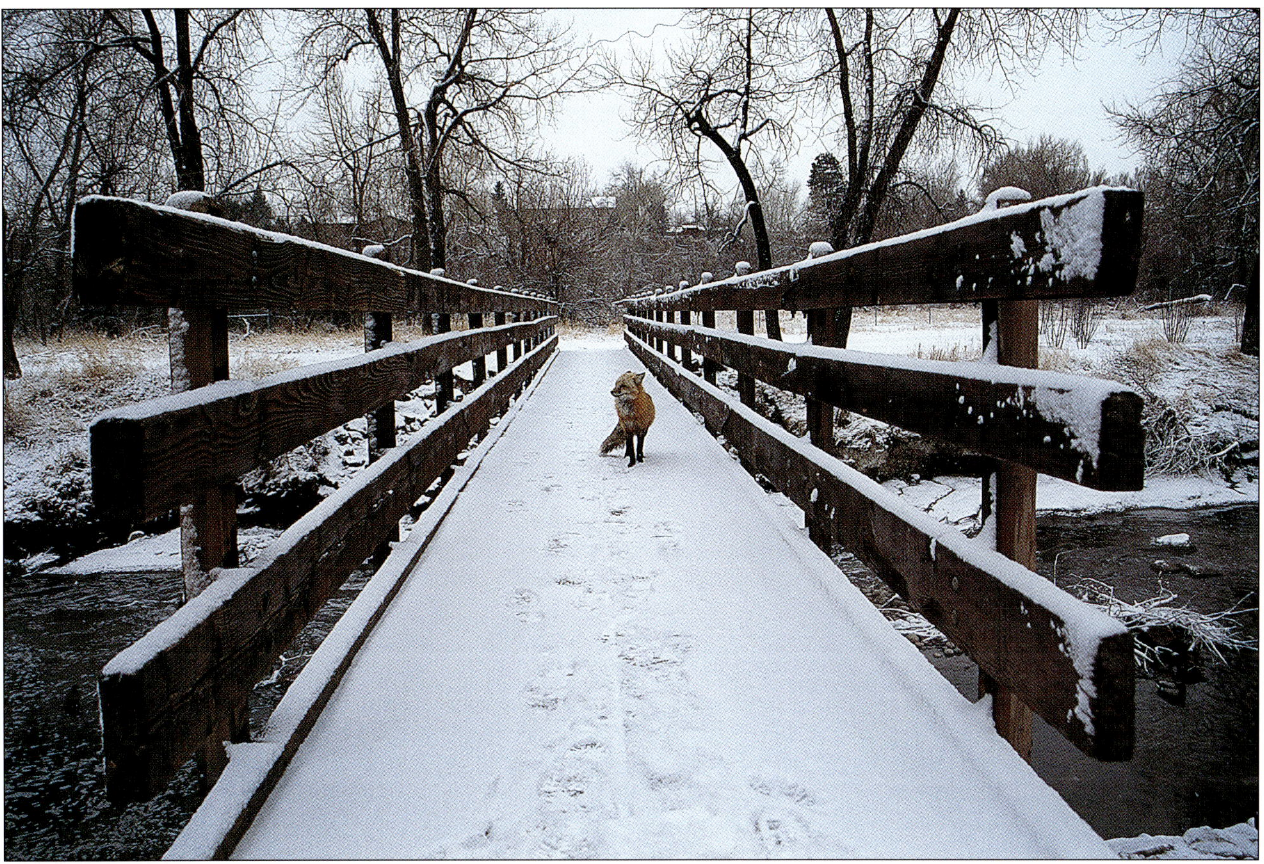

Just to show that rules are made to be broken, here is a photo that works even with the subject placed dead in the center. There are several reasons why this works here. First, the bridge railings and tracks in the snow make strong leading lines guiding the viewer directly to the fox. The use of a wide-angle lens exaggerated these leading lines. Second, because so much of the foreground is empty snow and the background is a leafless forest, it appears that the fox is closer to the top of the image than in the middle. And third, the fox is the only bit of color in this mostly black & white photo, which also draws the viewer's attention. Jefferson County, Colorado. 28–80mm lens.

5. Fine-Tuning Your Composition

Image quality is not the product of a machine, but the person who directs the machine, and there are no limits to imagination and expression.

—Ansel Adams

Many years ago, back when magic was more common on this planet, Cathy and I were driving through Rocky Mountain National Park when one of the finest rainbows we've ever seen appeared. There were several rather unusual things about this rainbow. For one thing, it occurred in early October rather than during the summer rainy season. For another, it appeared first thing in the morning, so not only did we have an incredible rainbow, we had warm, early light, also. But the strangest thing about this rainbow was the herd of elk at the end—almost as rare as a pot of gold.

We couldn't even see the elk at first. As we rounded a curve in the road, though, there was a bull elk rounding up his harem of cows and bugling challenges into the morning. By moving only a few steps, we could have the rainbow come down right on top of them. Well, it was obvious what we needed to do for the strongest image. As least we thought it was obvious. I grabbed the 500mm lens and started composing tight images of the bull elk with the end of the rainbow coming down right on top of him. With a 28–80mm zoom (our only other lens back in those days), Cathy began taking wide shots of a rainbow rising from an elk herd.

Now I was sure that the tight images taken with the 500mm lens would end up being the strongest, but I was wrong. Those shots were too tight, and they did not tell enough of a story. There is only one center of interest in these photos—the bull elk—and that is the central theme in this shot. The other elements, a little bit of the rainbow

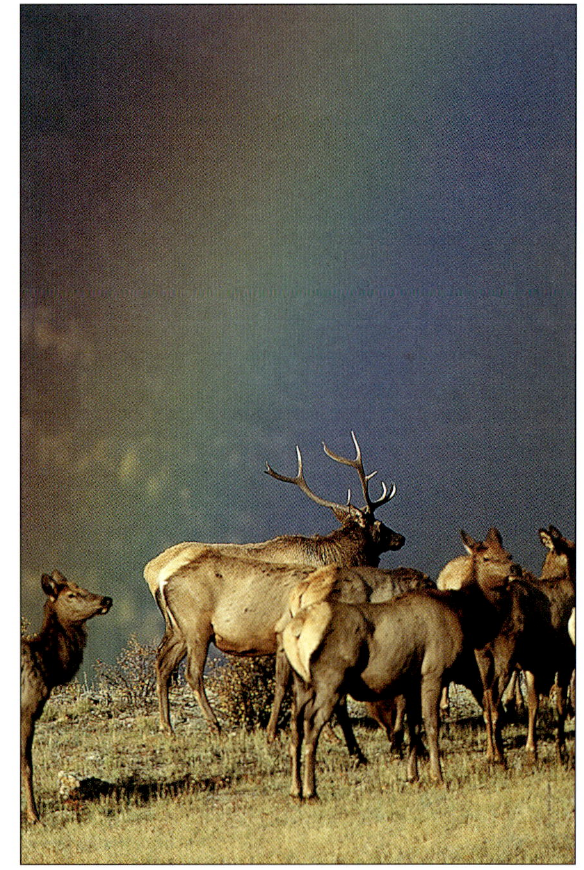

In this tight shot of the rainbow and the elk herd, not enough of the rainbow shows to tell much of a story. The rainbow almost looks like a defect in the film. Also, the cows in the foreground end up being distractions rather than supporting elements because they are out of focus. Rocky Mountain National Park, Colorado. 500mm lens.

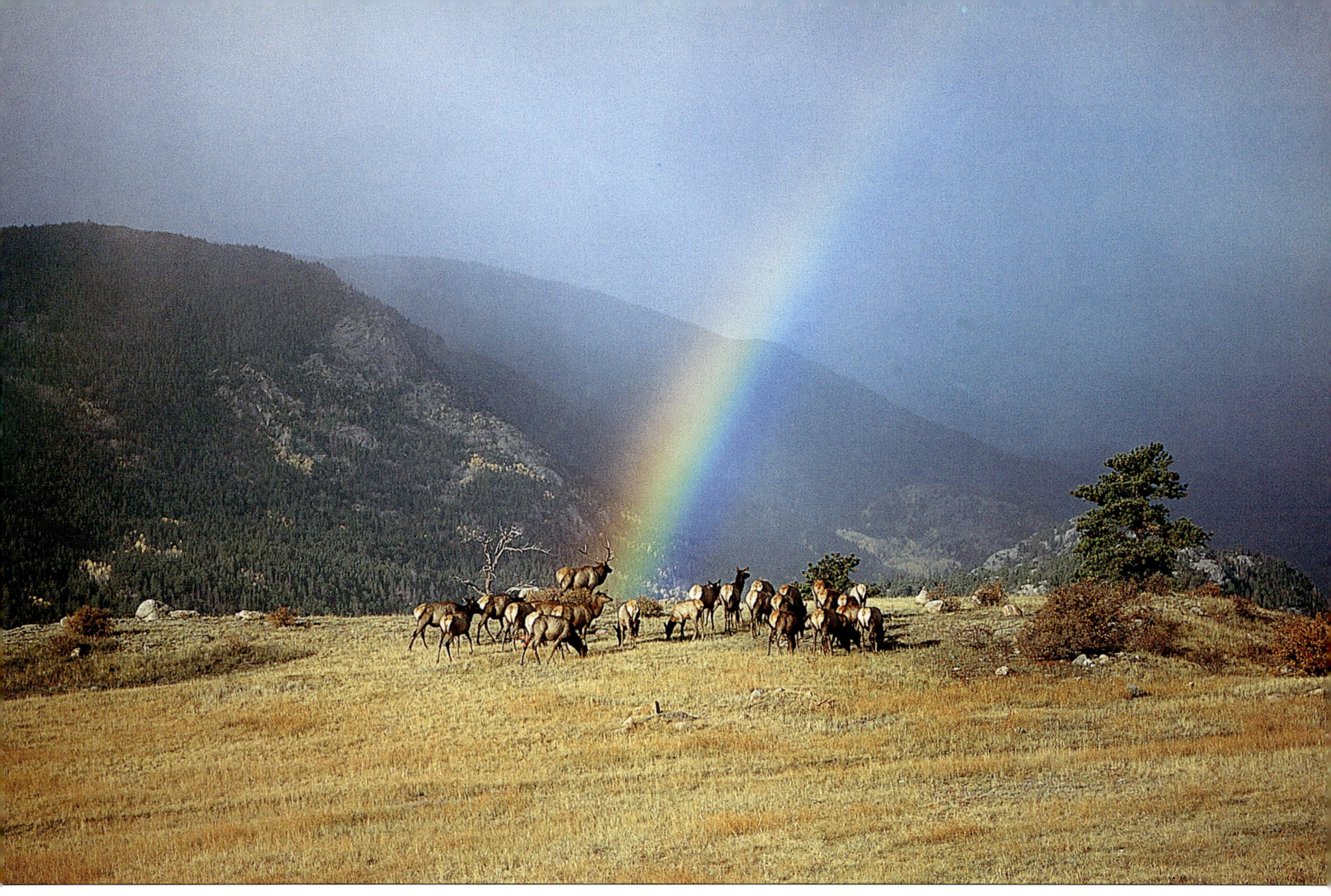

This wide shot showing the entire valley is much stronger. Here the entire elk herd is a center of interest rather than just the bull. Enough of the rainbow shows to give the viewer a better feel for what's going on. Between the elk, the rainbow, and the dark clouds, this image speaks volumes. Rocky Mountain National Park, Colorado. 28–80mm lens.

and a few cow elk, are either too small and indistinct or out of focus. The rainbow could be a supportive element if there was more of it. The cows are actually distracting because they are out of focus. In short, I botched a once-in-a-lifetime opportunity.

Luckily, Cathy was there to back me up. The photos taken at 80mm show a mountain park covered with golden grass, a bull elk guarding his harem, and a brilliant rainbow highlighted against the dark, brooding storm clouds behind. There are two main centers of interest here—the elk herd and the rainbow. These two centers of interest and all the other elements within the photo work together. The rainbow leads the viewer's eye right to the elk herd. The herd stands out well against the bright grass, and the dark hills and clouds make a very nice frame around the herd. The herd is a little too centrally placed in the image, but we feel the other elements are strong enough to make up for it.

In the wider image, the central theme is not the bull elk or even the elk herd, but a concept evoked by the relationship between the herd and its environment. The central theme could be "wilderness" or, with the rainbow falling on the courting elk in the face of the approaching storm, "perseverance," or "live each day as if it were your last." A photo like this can evoke as many different concepts or emotions as there are viewers who look at it, and when an image can do this, it becomes more than the sum of its visual elements. This photo is far more than a mere documentation of the fact that we saw some elk and a rainbow, and that's what Cathy and I want to do with our wildlife photography.

Obtaining great shots is more than just pointing and shooting.

AVOIDING NO-MAN'S LAND

Even with the fanciest, most advanced camera gear, obtaining great shots is more than just pointing and shooting (that's more or less what I did with the tight shots of the elk and the rainbow). And that is why we went to the trouble of learning about composition in the last chapter. It's time to put our knowledge of centers of interest, central

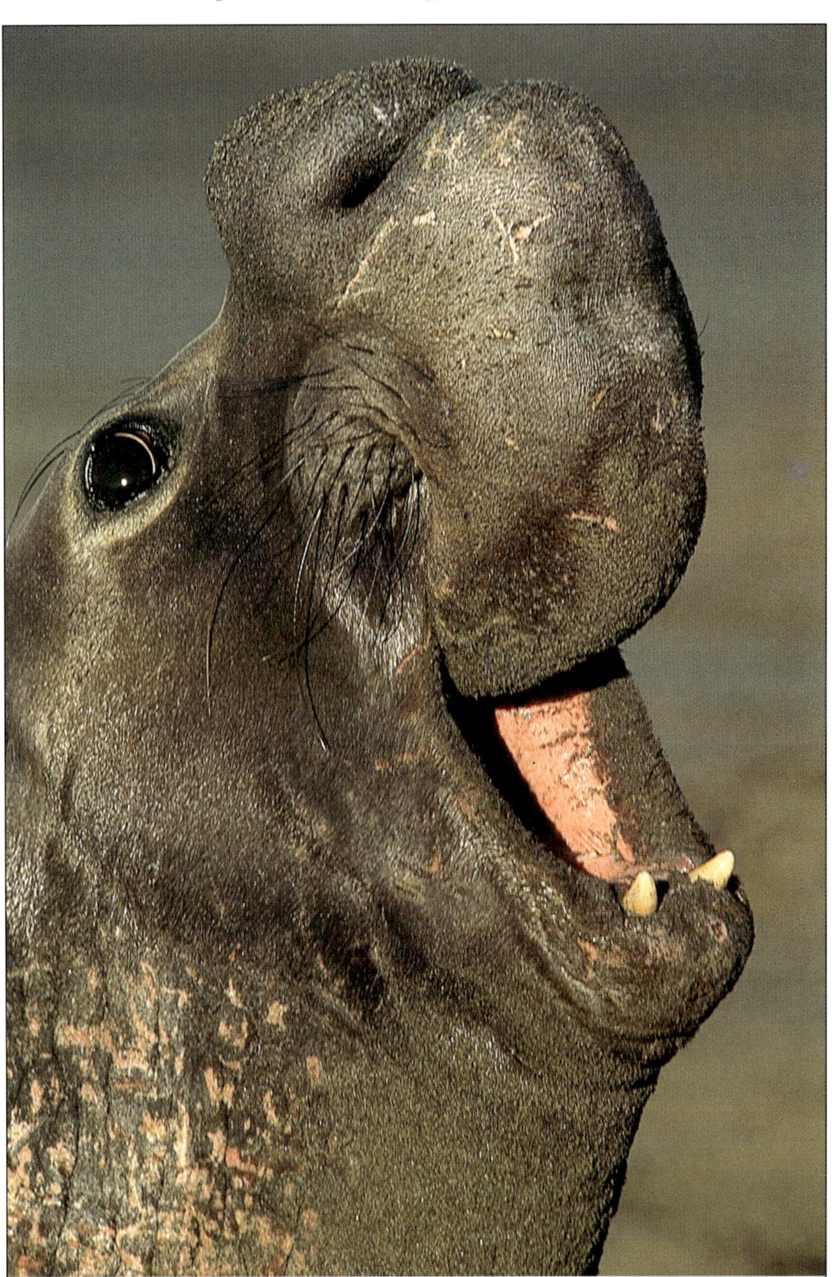

This shot of a northern elephant seal bull bellowing is tight enough to show the viewer some real detail in the animal's face. It gives them a feel for what it must be like to go through life worrying about biting your own nose. San Luis Obispo County, California. 500mm lens with 2x teleconverter.

themes, balance, and rhythm to good use. And the size of the subject in the frame plays a big role in how you compose the image for the strongest effect.

The subject's size also plays a part in whether or not your photo does more than just document that you saw an animal. Documentary photos are often in a "no-man's land" of subject size. They are not tight enough to show any expression or real detail, and they are not wide enough to show much of an environmental relationship. Photos in this no-man's-land usually need interesting behavior or supporting elements of beauty to take them beyond documentary. Shooting either tighter or wider can give your viewer more information to work with, and give them more reason to spend time looking at your image.

The subject's size also plays a part in whether or not your photo does more than just document that you saw an animal.

Art Wolfe and Frans Lanting took opposite approaches to this problem in their books, *The Living Wild* and *Eye to Eye*. In *The Living Wild* (Wildlands Press, 2000), Wolfe includes both tight portraits and wide shots showing the subject's relationship to its environment. The portraits in the book are good, especially considering that almost all of them are of wild subjects, but it is the wide shots that make the book special. Lanting's book, *Eye to Eye: Intimate Encounters with the Animal World* (Taschen Verlag, 1997), does just that—gives the viewer "in-your-face" shots of the animal subjects. Both books, though, are filled with images that are more than just documentary.

SHOOTING TIGHT

We'll start with photographing your subject tight because it's much easier to go beyond documentation with a tight shot than it is with a wide shot. Composition in general is easier around a tightly cropped subject. In fact, the tighter the shot or the more of your frame the subject takes up, the less it is affected by the rules of composition. Let's say you're photographing a red fox. If you can fill the frame with the fox's head, there's not a lot more you can do to compose the image.

You can't move the subject around or you start chopping off important pieces of its face for no good reason, and you can't include any other elements without obscuring some of the fox. If only one of your subject's eyes is visible, you might want to keep it off center. If both eyes are visible, then it doesn't matter because even if one eye is dead center, more than half of the creature's face will be on one side of the picture. This maintains the picture's asymmetry and minimizes the bull's-eye effect.

A word of caution about shooting these tight photos. They require a very long lens and/or a very tolerant subject. The subject may be tol-

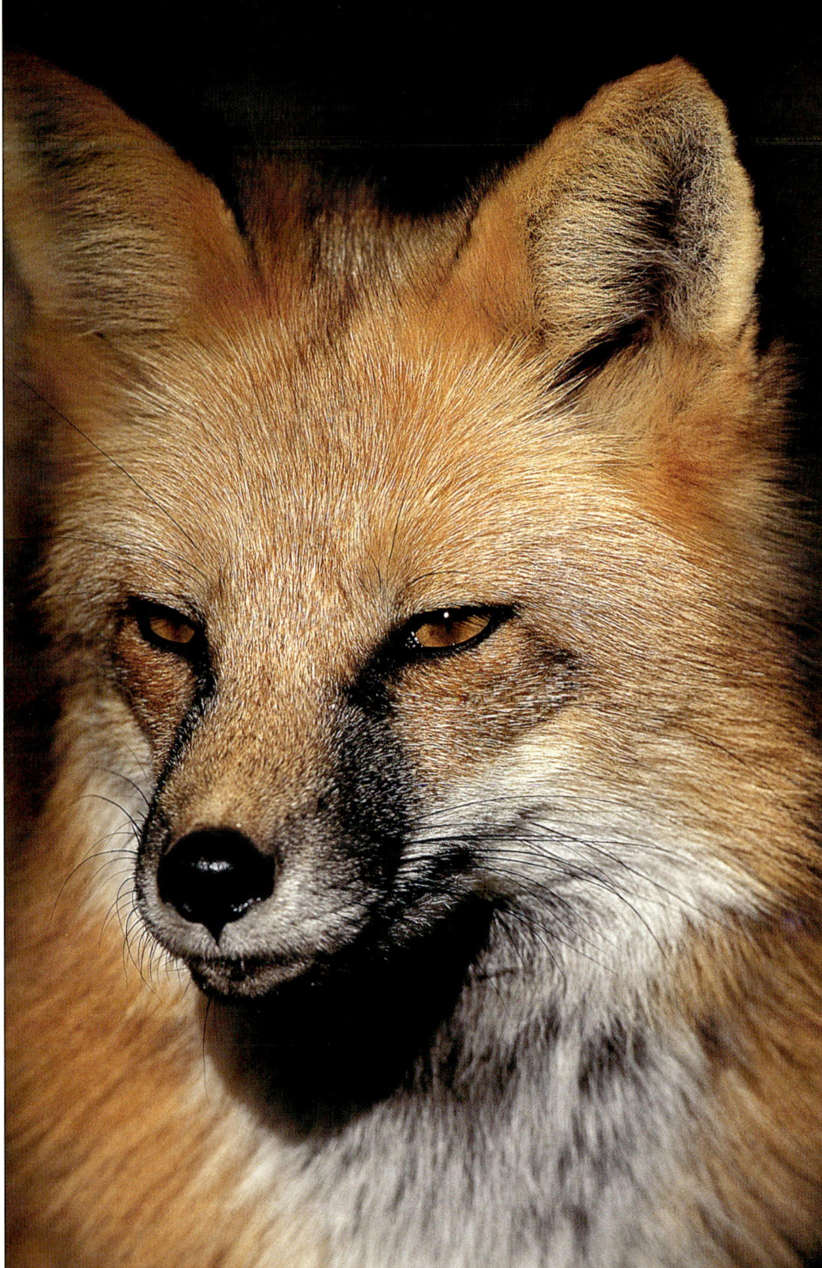

There's not a lot more a photographer can do to compose a fox image that is cropped this tightly. Jefferson County, Colorado. 500mm lens.

erant because it's unaware of your presence, or it may just not mind humans at close distances. Whatever the reason, though, be aware of your subject's reaction to your presence. Some animals don't have the luxury of being able to escape our scrutiny when they want to, especially young animals that are still bound to the den or nest. It's easy to harass your subject to the point that it's threatened, and no photo is worth that. Know your subject's body language and pay attention to it. If the animal is paying attention to you rather than attending to its normal activities, or if the parents seem to be staying away from the young ones longer than they should, back off and give the creatures a break.

If you're lucky and persistent enough to find a suitable subject, keep in mind what we're trying to do with these close-ups. We're obviously not going to capture much in the way of behavior in most instances. We're trying to create an image that goes beyond documentation by showing the viewer the texture, expression, and beauty of the animal's face. We're trying to show them details that they probably would never see in any other way.

SHOOTING WIDE

We can also use the other extreme and make the subject small in the frame to go beyond documentation. If you choose to approach the image this way, ask yourself if you are making the subject small just because you can't get any closer and don't have a larger lens, or are you making it small to show the viewer something of artistic or scientific interest? If you're using your longest lens and the subject is still small in the frame, there's a good chance you just can't get any closer to the subject. If you find yourself grabbing for a shorter lens, it sounds more like an attempt to fulfill an artistic vision. Or you may be just grabbing the wrong lens, and you probably won't know until you see the results.

When photographing groups of animals, often the individual creatures are small in your frame, but your subject or center of interest is

In this photo of snow geese at sunrise, no individual goose is a center of interest. Instead the entire flock is a center of interest and the rising sun is a secondary center of interest. The goal is to keep the viewer's attention balanced between these elements. Bosque del Apache National Wildlife Refuge, New Mexico. 28–80mm lens.

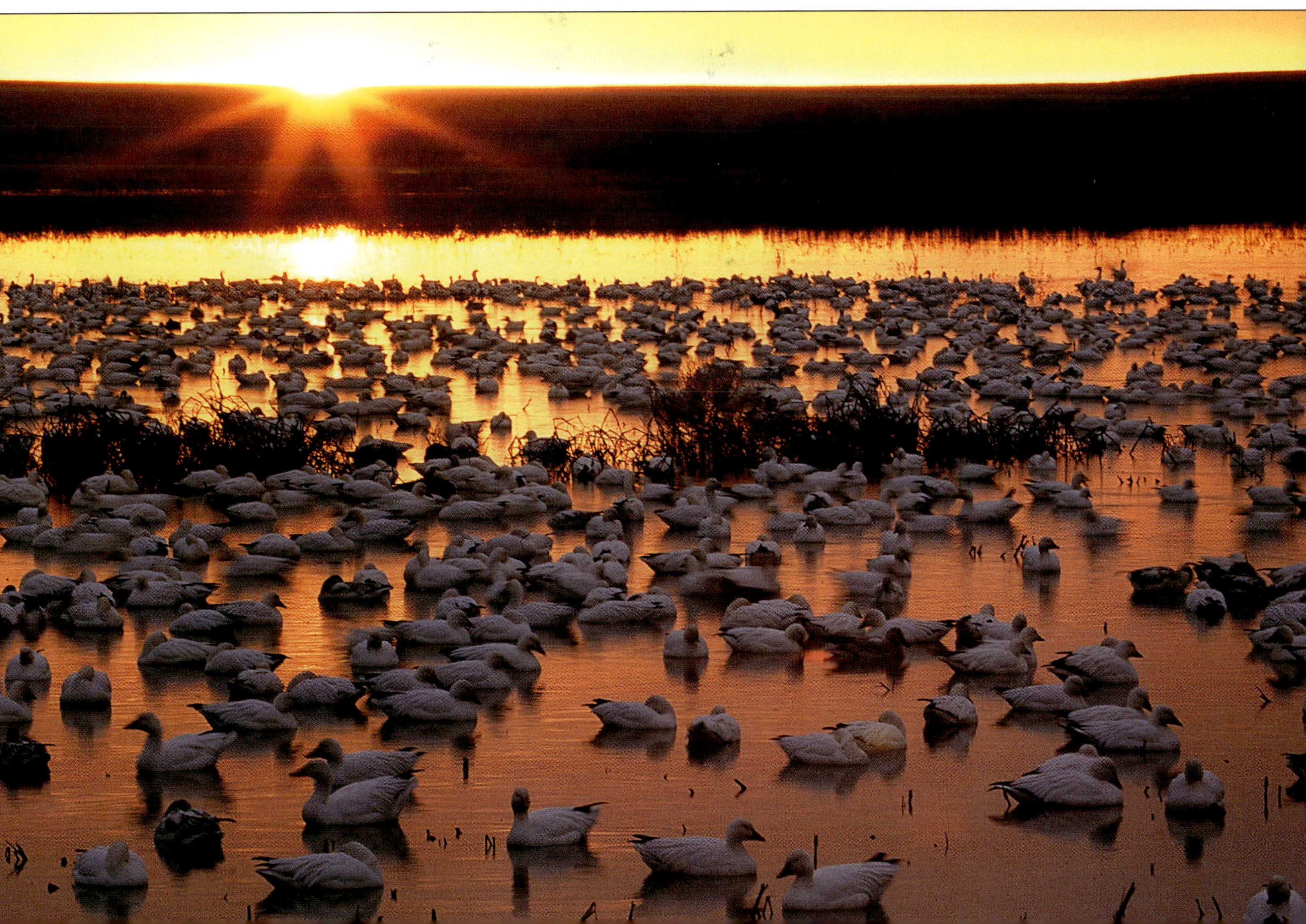

large, since the center of interest is not an individual but an entire flock or herd. Your central theme then revolves around not a particular animal, but the relationship between the group and its environment. For these images to be effective, the animals must be grouped together tight enough for the group to be considered a single subject, but not so tight that the individuals obscure each other or blend together.

It's been said that short lenses are not much good for wildlife photography. This is a gross generalization. It is true that you will probably have more opportunities with longer lenses, but a super telephoto does not guarantee the strongest photos. Cathy did much better with a 28–80mm zoom on the elk at the end of the rainbow than I did with a 500mm. Shorter lenses often play a role when you're trying to show the animal's relationship to its environment. In these situations, though, the smaller the subject is in the image, the more important composition is. You can't get away with keeping your center focusing element on the subject's eye like you can when you're just photographing its head.

There's something particularly appealing, though, about a successful image with a small animal subject. Anyone with a long lens and a tolerant subject can capture a face shot. Creating a strong image with a small subject takes

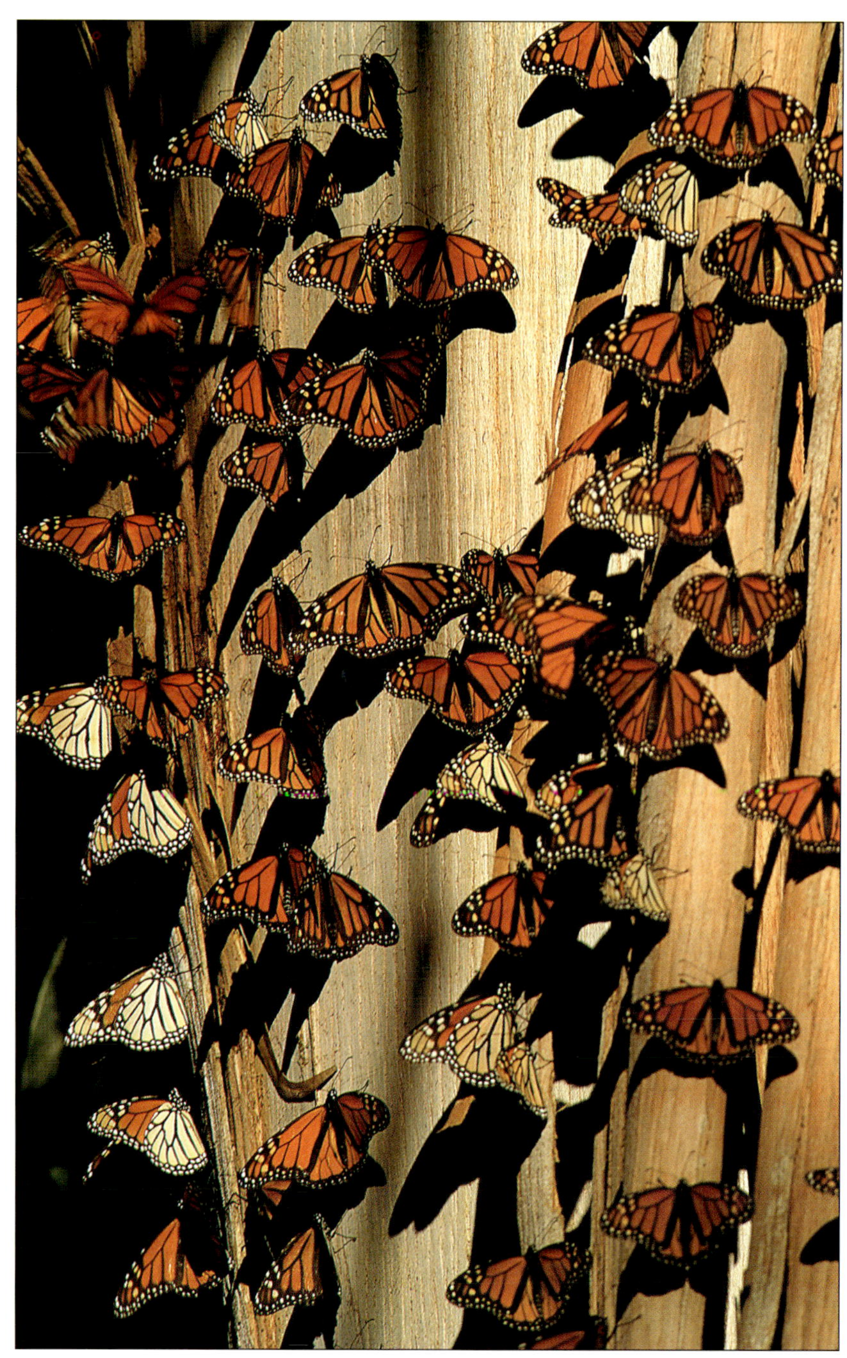

The center of interest in this photo of wintering monarch butterflies is the pattern the sunlit butterflies create against the dark background, and the central theme is the butterflies' relationship with the eucalyptus tree. Pismo Beach, California. 500mm lens with 2x teleconverter.

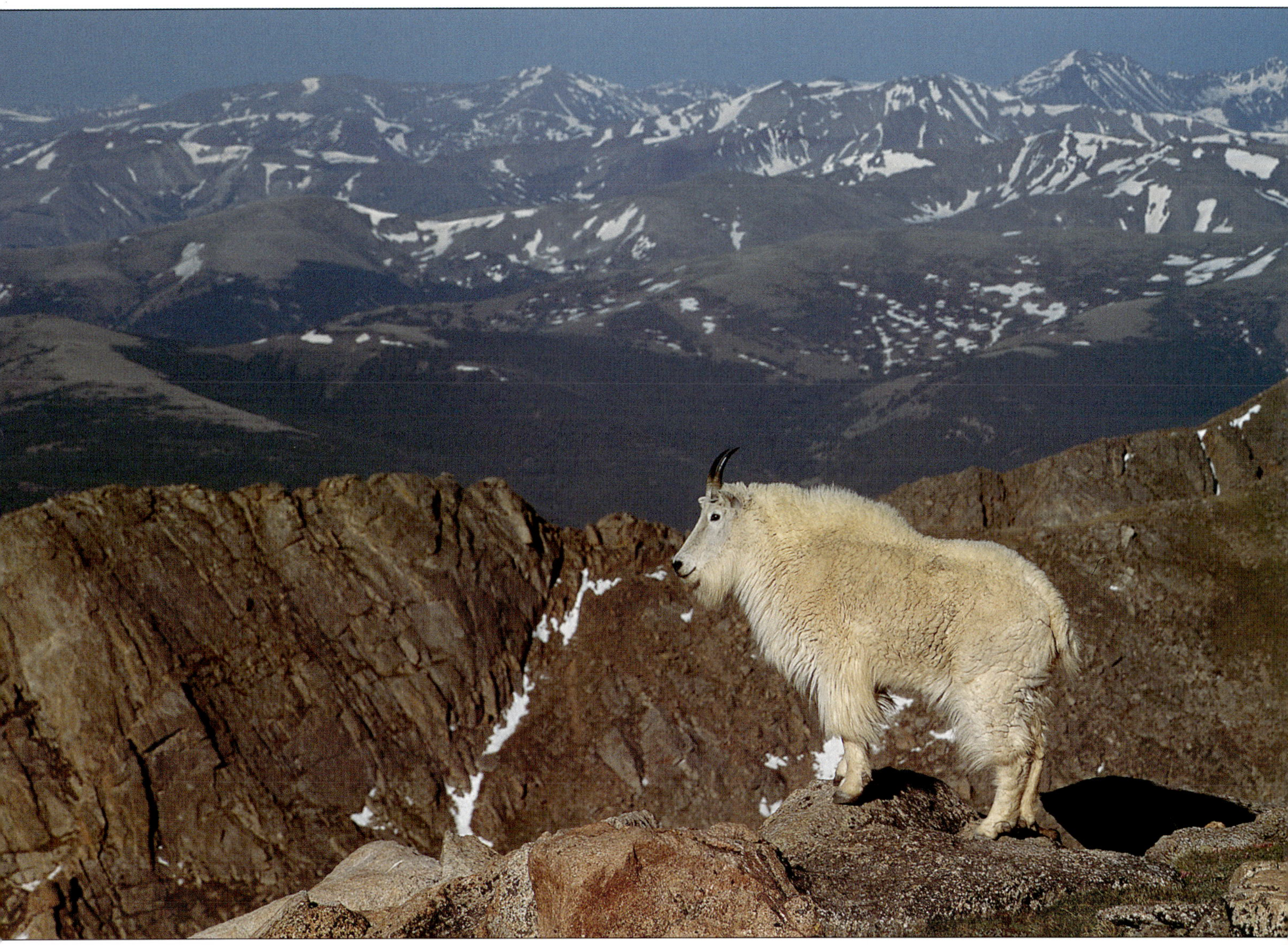

The relationship between this mountain goat and its alpine habitat is clearly seen in this photo. A tight shot of the animal would not have given the viewer this information. Mt. Evans, Colorado. 75–300mm lens.

some artistic talent and vision (which can be developed and improved). In this situation, we're trying to accomplish a couple of things. The first is the creation of a strong scenic shot out of a wildlife photo. The second is an image that shows the creature's relationship to its environment. If the image works, not only do we have a landscape photo with a bit of life injected into it, but we have an image of some scientific interest because it shows where this animal lives.

PROBLEMS AND SOLUTIONS

Keep in mind that it is definitely more difficult to compose a strong image around a small subject. Remember what we learned in the last chapter. Big draws more attention than small. Unless the subject is prominent and easily visible, you're going to end up with a photo in which no one even notices the animal. So what can you do to make your subject easily visible even though it's relatively small? Doing something to make it stand out from the background is a good start, maybe placing a dark subject against a light background or a light subject against a dark background. Also warm-colored animals, like cardinals, will stand out against almost anything but a fire truck.

It's very important to keep the overall image simple when the subject is small. With a complicated scene, the viewer may lose the subject—even if it stands out against its background. Scenes with uniform backgrounds, like snow, prairie grass, or calm water can make a lovely habitat in which to plop down an animal subject. Differences are more eye-catching than conformity, so putting an animal in such a scene almost automatically makes it stand out. You can see that some environments lend themselves to this kind of image much more than others. This would be a tough shot to attempt in a complicated, messy environment like a rainforest—not impossible, but very difficult.

Study Jim Brandenburg's photographs. Many of his best known images feature small animals in an immense landscape. He's an expert at not only making his small subjects stand out, but creating fantastic works of art in which wildlife and landscape work together. Making your animal subject easily visible is just the beginning.

When the subject is small, there needs to be something else of interest in the picture to create a very strong image. A subject that stands out perfectly well in an endless sea of grass may work fine as a scientific study of the creature's habitat, but without another center of interest, the photo will usually come up lacking artistically. Ideally, the viewer's inter-

Even though this wolf is small in the image, it stands out from the background, making it easily visible. If it were in the forest rather than crossing the river, it would not have stood out nearly so well. Captive. Pine County, Minnesota. 75–300mm lens.

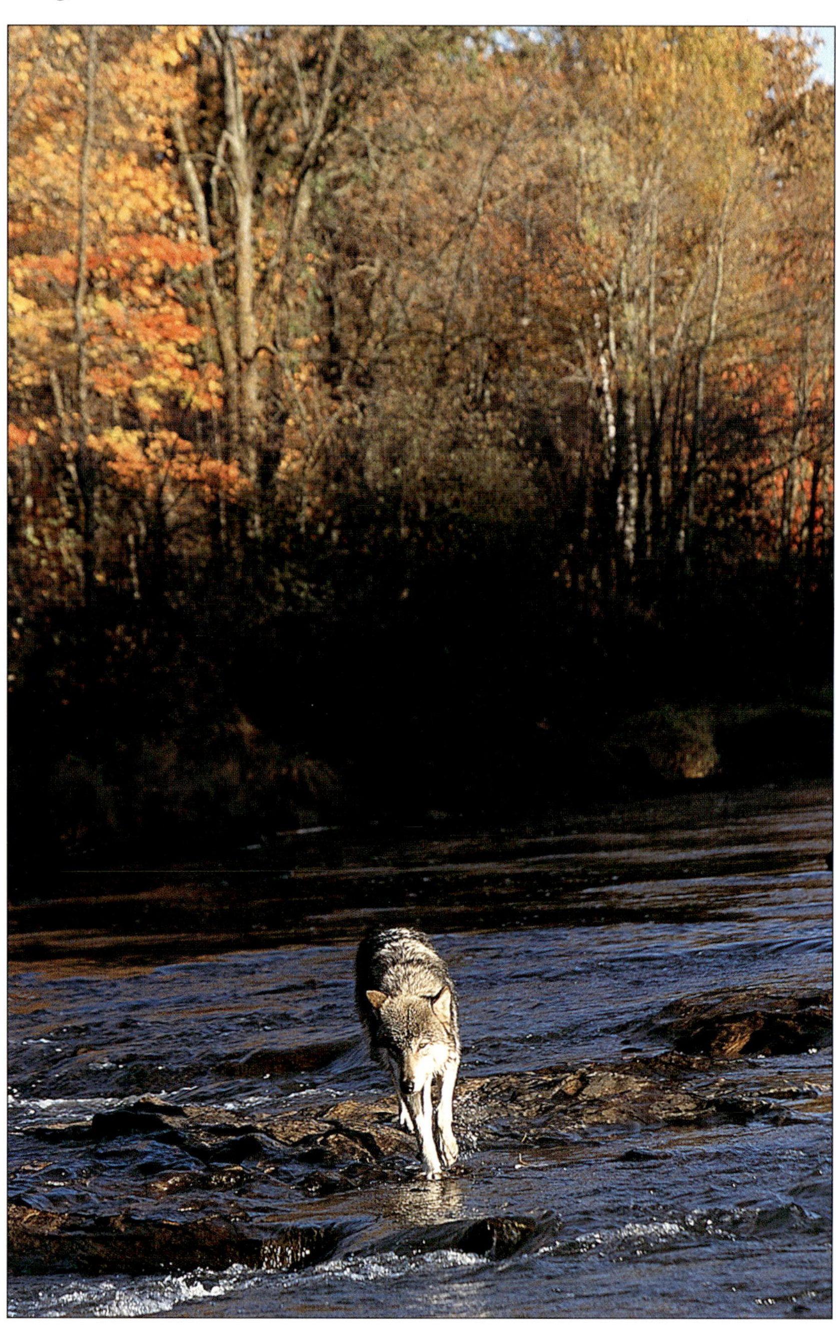

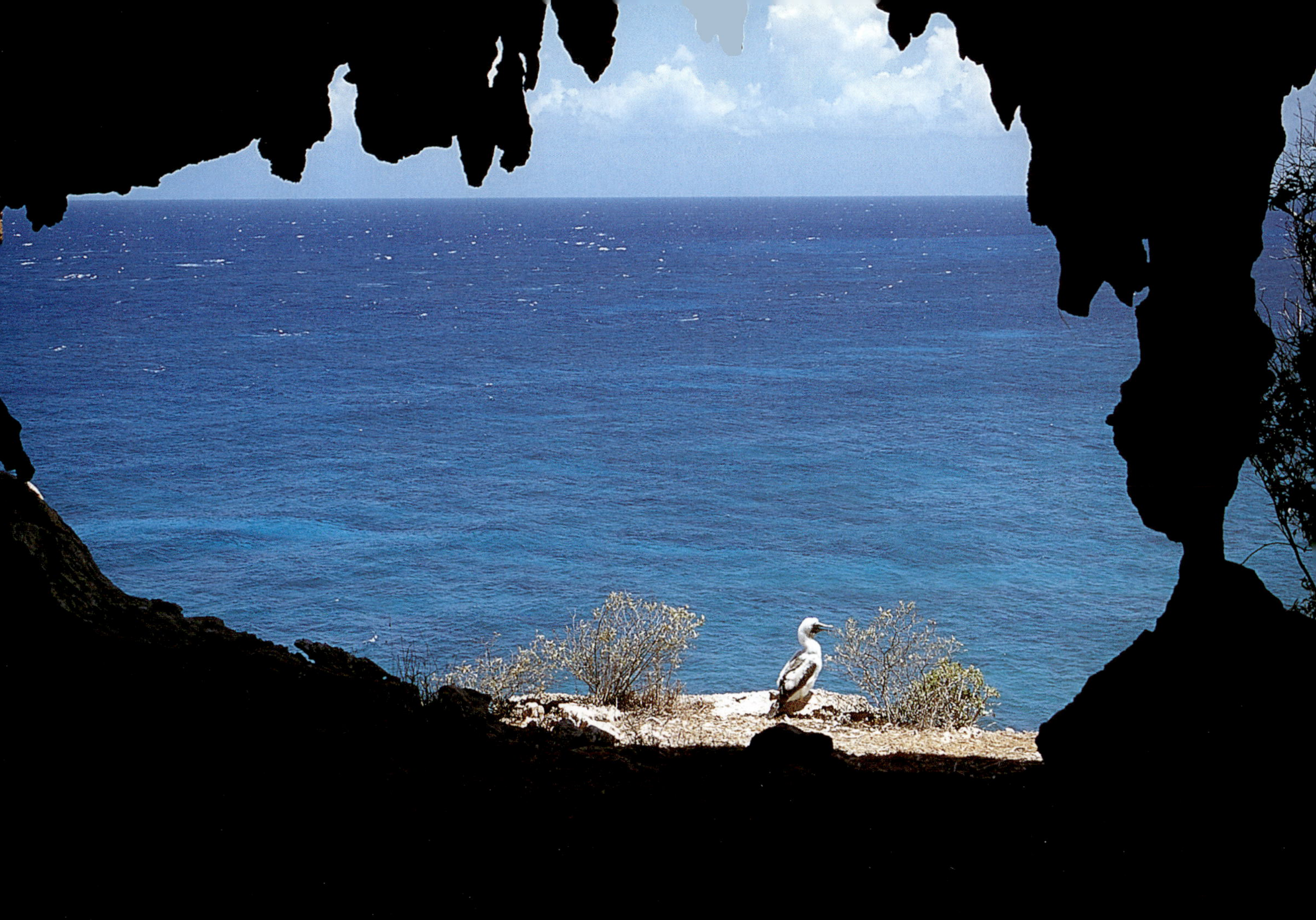

The mouth of the cave where this juvenile brown booby waited for its parents' return makes a good frame, even though it's very obvious. The jagged edge of the cave not only makes the frame more interesting, but each stalactite is pointing down to the bird, keeping the viewers' attention where we want it. Mona Island, Puerto Rico. 28–80mm lens.

est should be kept teetering back and forth between your image's various centers of interest.

This can be done by using picture elements to frame those centers of interest and by using lines that lead toward them—and maybe even connect them. Leading lines can be created in any number of ways. They can be made of shadows, footprints, the horizon, a mountain range, vegetation—the list is endless. Leading lines can even be insinuated. When two subjects are looking at each other, there is a definite imaginary line connecting them. The important thing to remember is that any lines in your image should be pointing into the image rather than leading the viewer's eye out of your picture.

When you're deciding on where to put your subject in the frame, don't forget the Rule of Thirds. The weaker your subject is—and smaller is weaker!—the closer to one of the power points it should be. Very seldom do you want to make a bull's-eye out of your subject by placing it in the middle of the frame.

Keeping your subject small within the picture can help create an image that looks three-dimensional. By placing something of interest in the foreground, the middle ground, and the background of the image, you can literally walk the viewer into the picture. All of these centers of interest must be in focus, but since you automatically have more depth of field with smaller subjects, it's not that much of a problem.

Yes, there are a few things to keep in mind if you're going to go beyond documentation with an image that has a small subject. And no one realizes how difficult it can be more than Cathy and I. How can you possibly go into the field with this kind of shot in mind? You're shooting the scene so wide that it can be almost impossible to keep out competing or distracting elements. There is often little or no leeway in a successful composition. The animal has to move to just the right spot—sometimes it also has to look in just the right direction—before the image works.

Cathy and I rarely go into the field specifically for this kind of shot (or any other kind of shot for that matter). We go after a particular species or habitat with our minds open to the possibilities that might occur. Then if we see an animal in the right scenery, we are at least prepared if it does move to just the right spot.

The size of your subject can play a big role in the strength of your image. Many times the

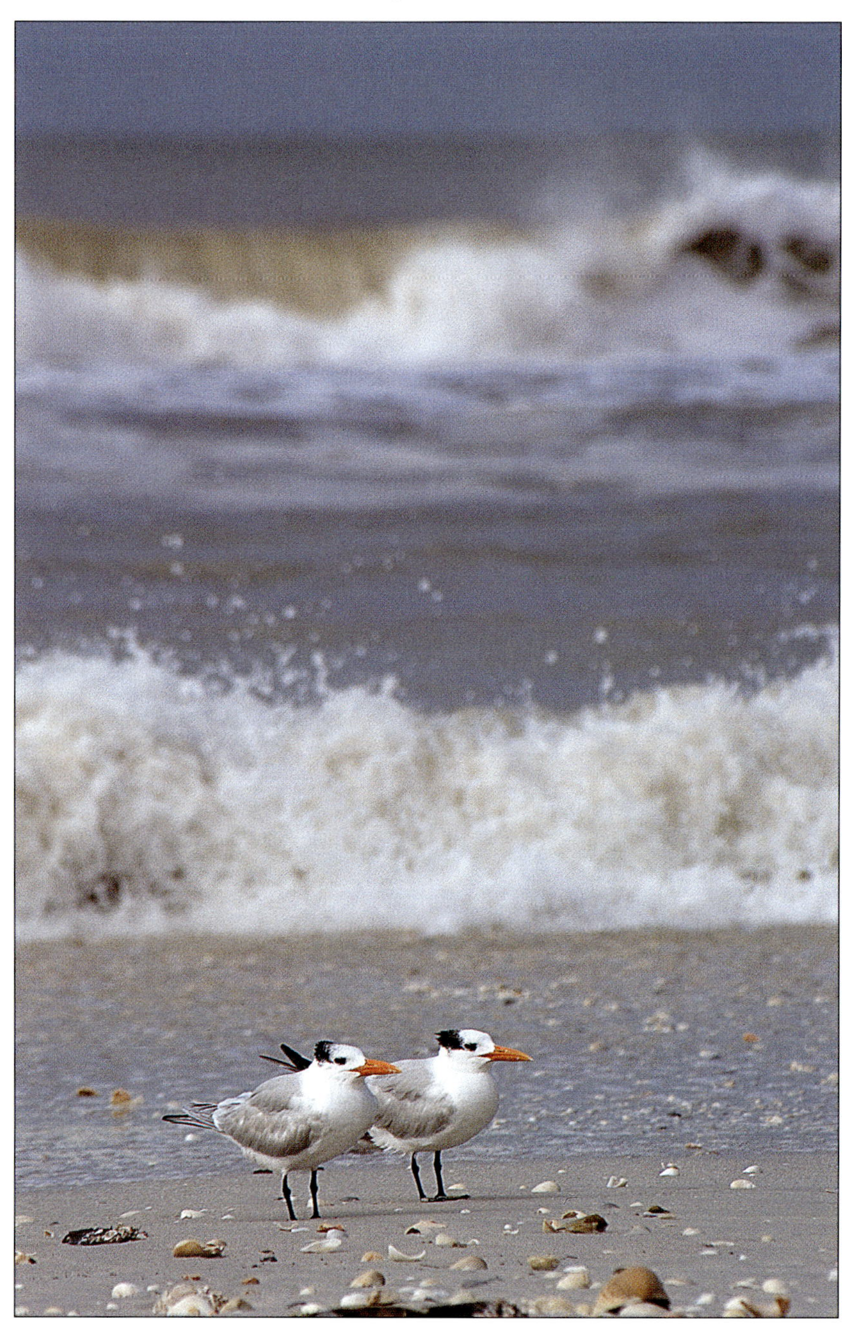

A tight shot of this pair of royal terns would have told the viewer very little about the world they live in. With the waves crashing behind them and the shells at their feet, this image gives the viewer more information. Placing the birds near one of the power points makes the image stronger, and their orange beaks help draw the viewer's attention. Sanibel Island, Florida. 75–300mm lens.

When Cathy and I saw this hermit crab near the beach and the setting sun, we recognized the possibilities. I had to move the crab (I moved it back afterward) into the right spot, and we had to wait for it to feel comfortable enough to stick its legs back out. With the sun setting into the sea, the palm frond, and the beach behind the crab, we not only have an image that tells a good deal about the animal's habitat, we have a scene with a three-dimensional feel. Mona Island, Puerto Rico. 17–35mm lens and fill flash.

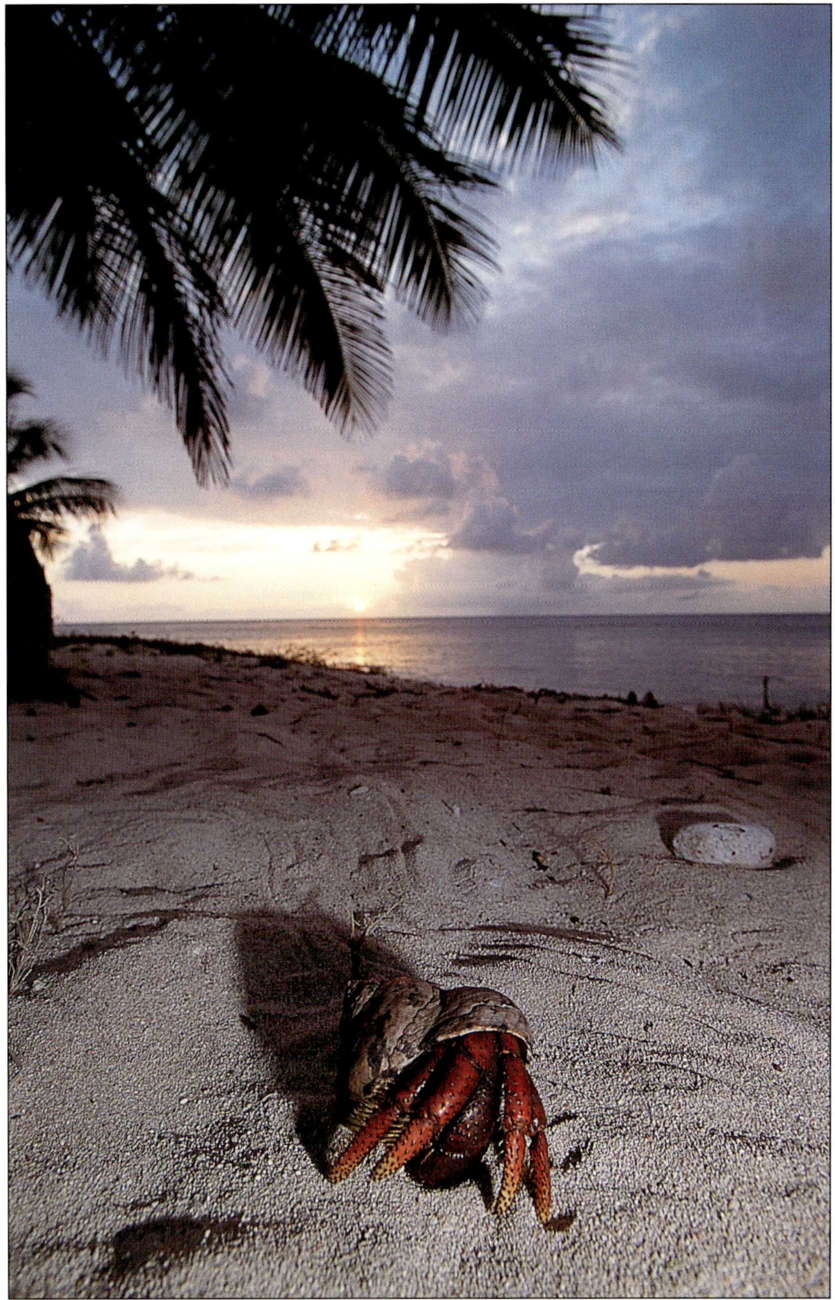

secret to going beyond documentation is either making the subject large enough that we can see interesting, hard-to-notice details, or small enough that we can see its relationship with its environment. A small subject presents more problems compositionwise than a large one, but keeping the subject small can also offer unique possibilities. Learning when to shoot tight and when to shoot wide is a valuable skill for the photographer who wants to stretch his artistic horizons.

6. The Best Perspective

If I were a painter, I would go to nature for all my patterns.
—Thomas Bewick

I suppose perspective is technically part of composition. It's important enough, though, to warrant its own chapter. Few things will influence your viewer's opinion of your subject as much as perspective will. And it's one of the few things you can usually control that will dramatically strengthen or weaken your wildlife images.

A CASE STUDY

A few years ago, we were photographing a fox den that was only twenty feet off a greenbelt walking trail. The pups saw so many people every day they paid little attention to their audience. The last thing a photographer needed was a blind. It was the perfect situation except for one thing: There was a six-foot chain-link fence between us and the foxes.

Because of the fence, another photographer may have just admired them and moved on without taking a photo. The foxes, though, were too cute and too close for us to pass up. Our first attempt involved me trying to balance on top of a stump next to the fence, and it would have worked great, had we wanted only to capture the tops of the foxes' heads.

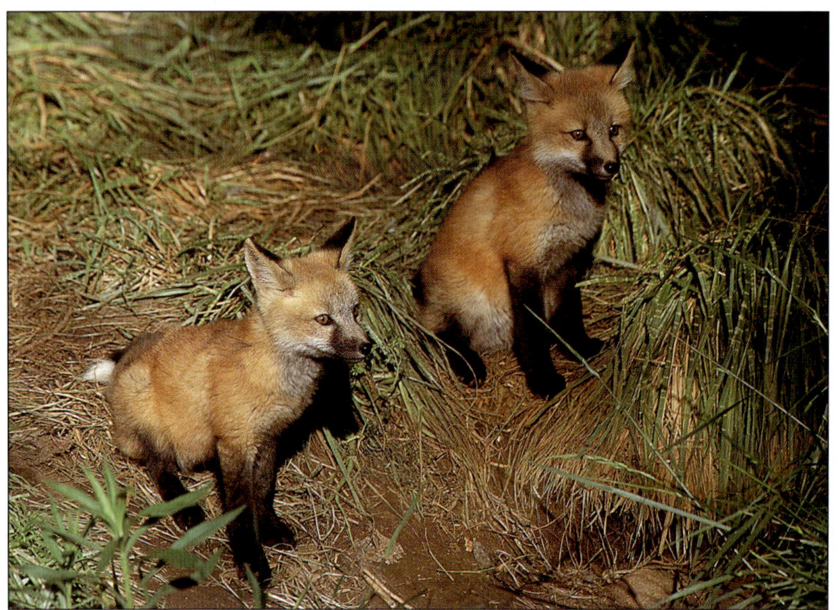

This photo was taken by shooting over a tall fence. It's a decent shot of red fox pups—if we wanted to show the tops of the animals' heads. Shooting down on your subject puts it in a position of lesser importance, and this is rarely what we want to do with our subject. Jefferson County, Colorado. 75–300mm lens.

Even though this photo was taken through a chain-link fence, it's much stronger than the previous one solely because it was taken from the fox pup's height. Jefferson County, Colorado. 75–300mm lens.

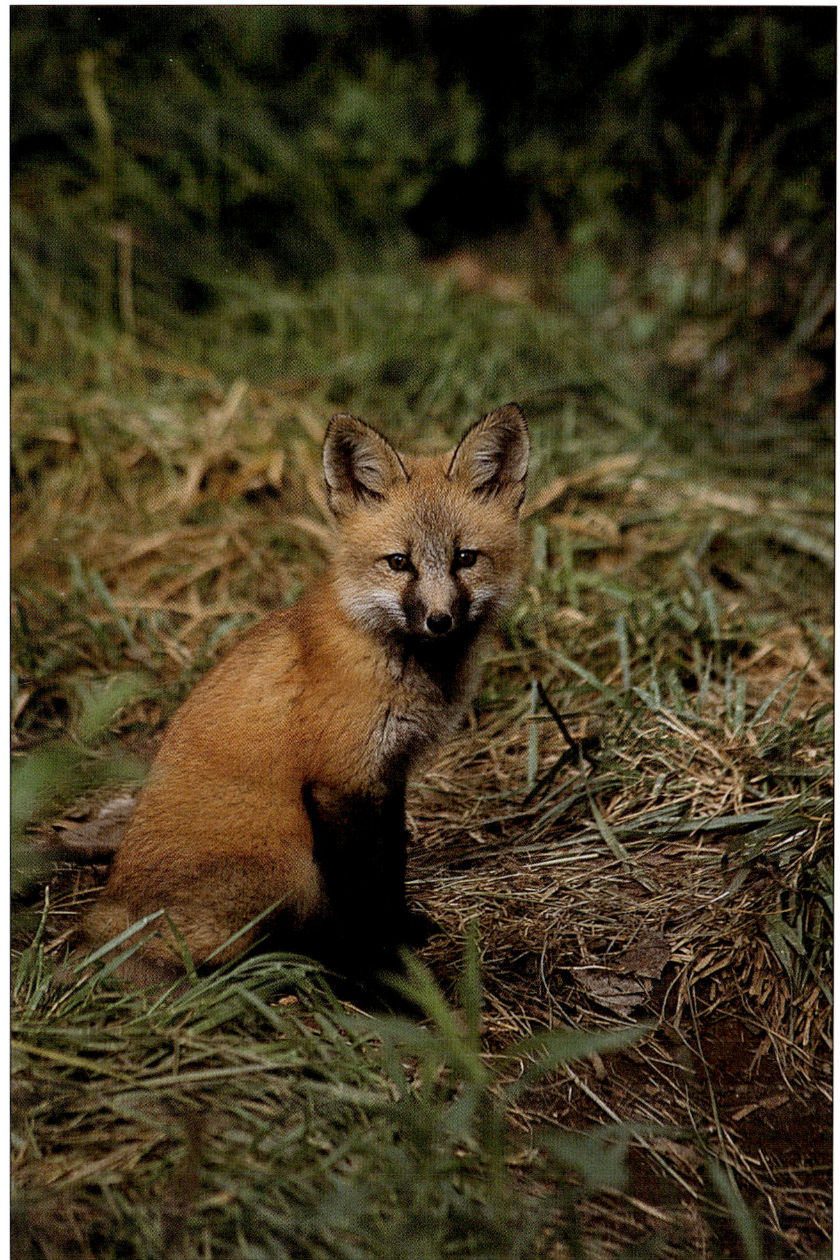

Next we tried shooting through the fence. If we put the lens up against the fence, shot through the holes in the chain link, and used a wide-open aperture for minimum depth of field, the fox pups turned out sharp and the fence blurred out. The downside to this technique was a lack of depth of field. Still the photos shot through the fence were much stronger than the ones taken from the stump, and the only reason is perspective.

PERSPECTIVES ON PERSPECTIVE

Almost every one of the jillions of photos taken over the years were taken from the approximate height of a standing person, between four

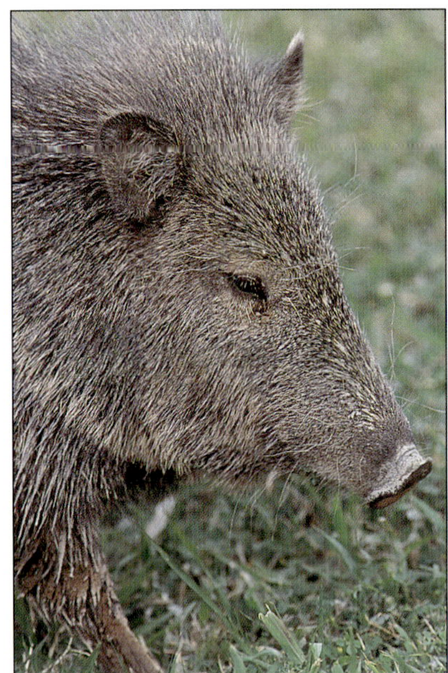

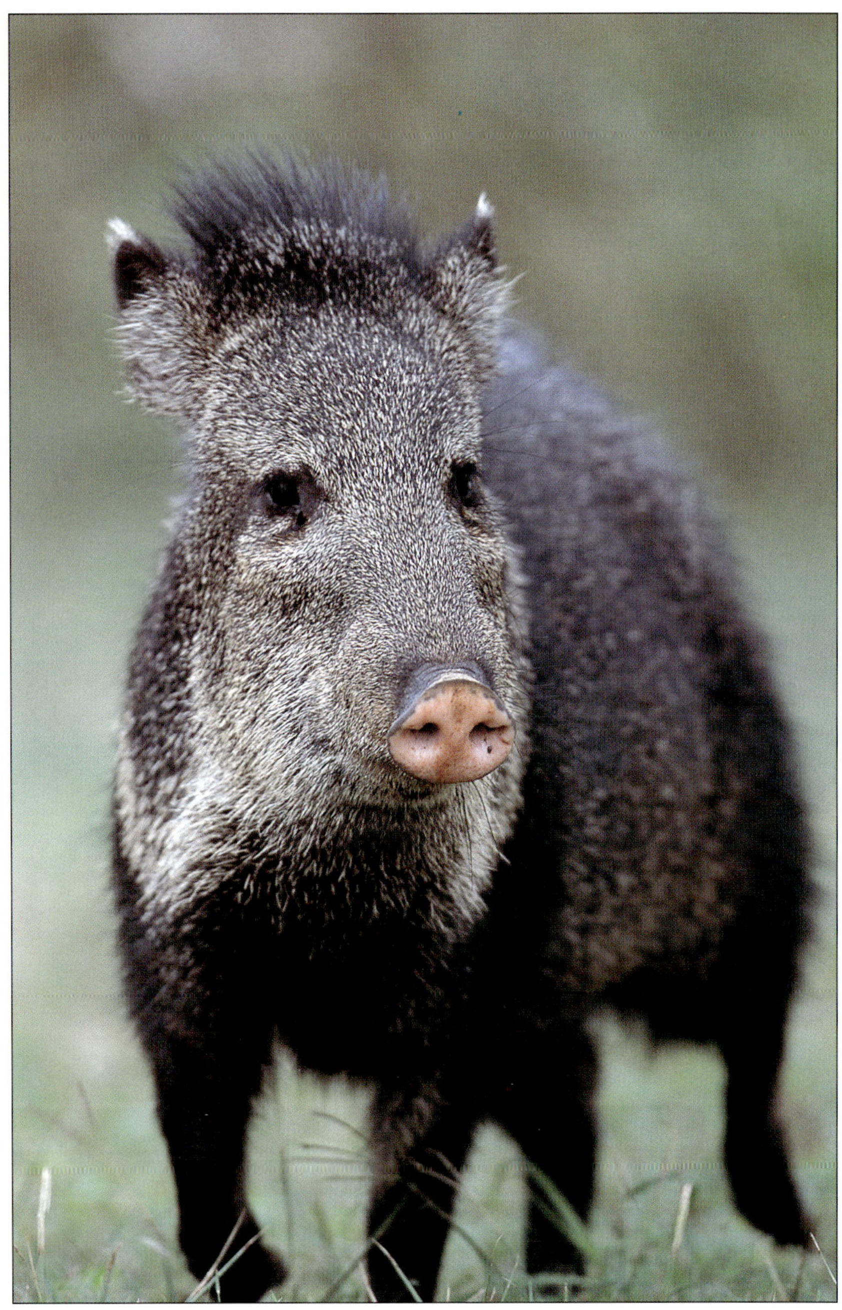

ABOVE—Most photos, like this one of a collared peccary, or javelina, are taken from the height of a standing person. At this height, you're going to be shooting down on most wildlife subjects—not the best composition if you want to go beyond documentation with your images. Big Bend National Park, Texas. 500mm lens. RIGHT—This javelina was photographed from its level, and it's one of the reasons this image is so much stronger than the previous one. Choke Canyon State Park, Texas. 500mm lens.

and six feet above the ground. Let's say, for the sake of argument, that you want to make your photos stand out, and you want them to look different from most of the other photos out there. Should you take them from standing height? Of course not! For one thing, that position is way too comfortable. If parts of you are not in constant pain or you are not in danger of falling (we are not advocating that you risk injury to yourself or damage to your equipment), you should probably be photographing your subject from another position.

Seriously, taking your photos from either substantially higher or lower than standing height will help make the resulting images stand out from the crowd. Showing your viewer a perspective that they don't normally see is a good way to make your photos more interesting. Most people are not accustomed to looking at their world from atop a ladder or while crawling on their belly like a snake. Photos taken from these positions are often unusual enough to make the viewer take a second or even a third look.

WHAT IS YOUR RELATIONSHIP WITH YOUR SUBJECT?

The perspective from which a subject is photographed implies a relationship between the photographer and the subject and, therefore, between the viewer and the subject as well. Shooting down on the subject puts the subject in a position of lesser importance, making it inferior to the photographer. Shooting up at your subject puts it on a pedestal. The subject is in a superior position and you are looking up to it. Which perspective describes the relationship you want to imply with your subject?

Of course we have to be realistic about perspective, also. Shooting up at your subject may put it in a superior position, but, if carried to extremes, it distorts the image as well as showing what is probably not the most attractive view of an animal. In most situations, making your subject as strong as possible means photographing the creature from its level.

Shooting at your subject's level also serves another purpose: It makes it easier to blur out the background because the subject and the back-

The farther away the background is, the easier it is to blur out distracting elements. This is one more reason to photograph the subject from its level.

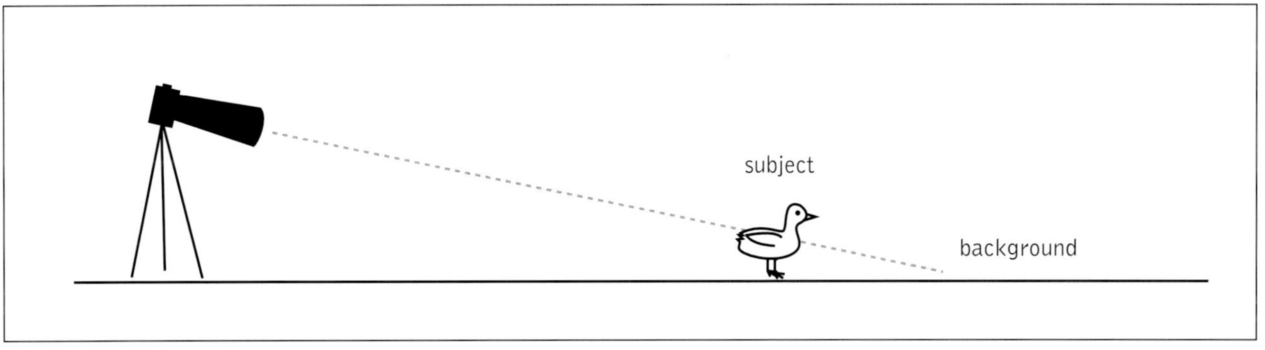

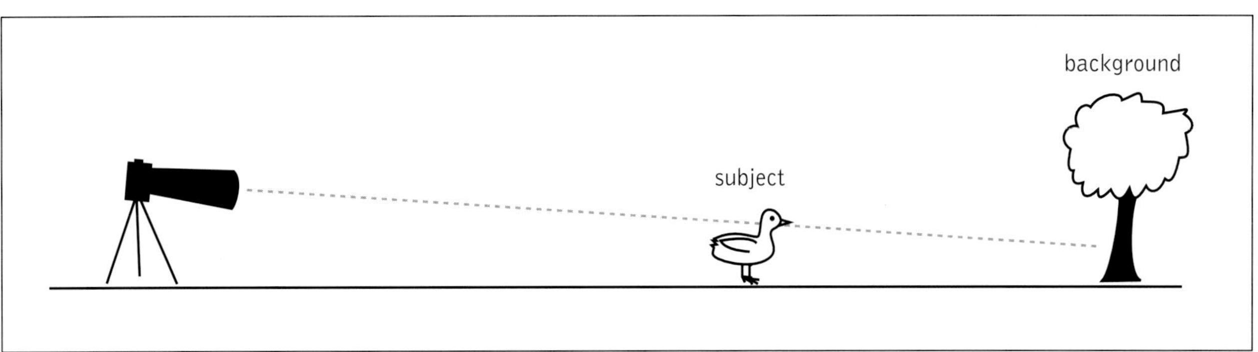

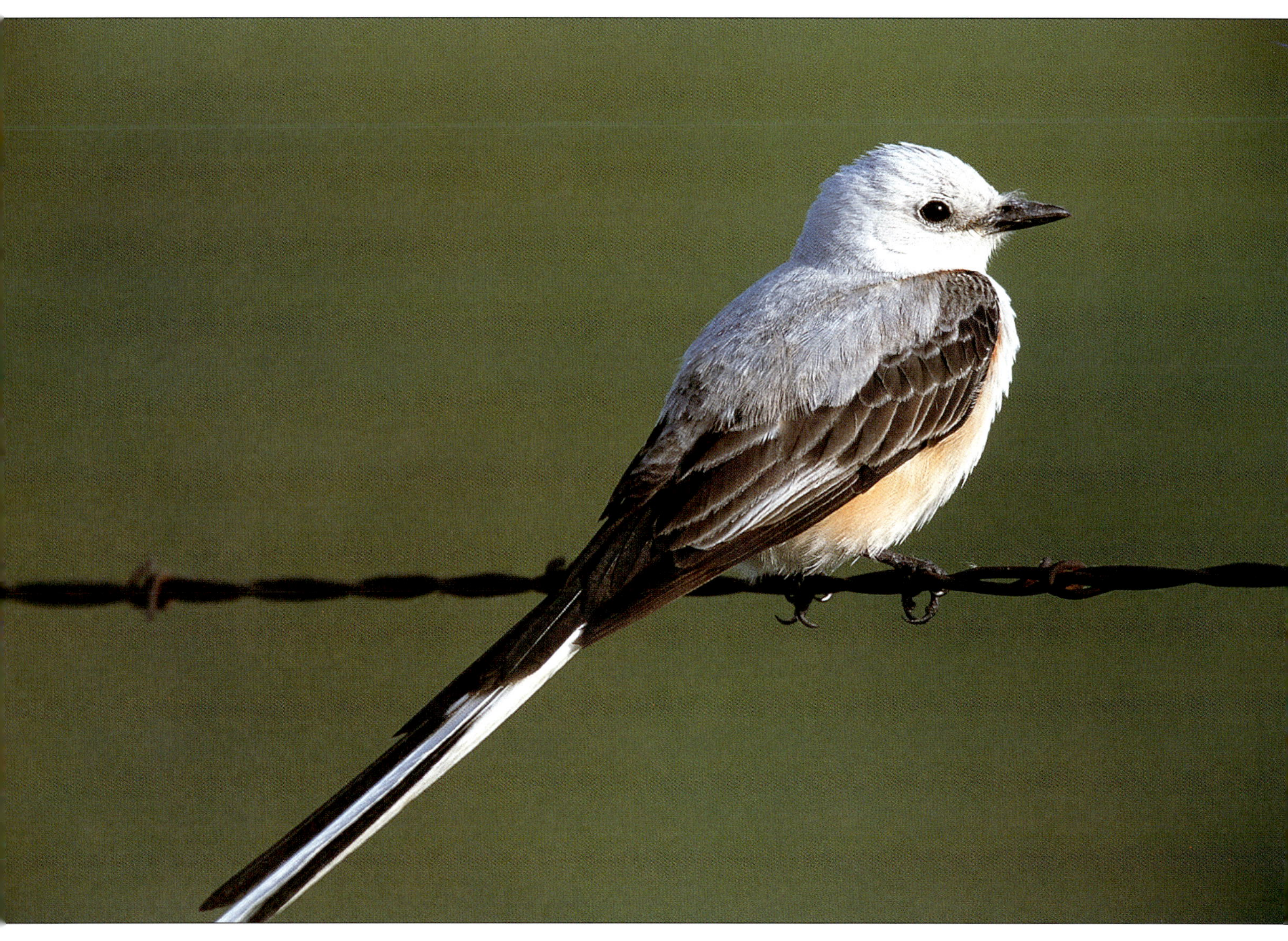

ground are in radically different geometric planes. If you're shooting down on your subject, the background is much closer to the plane the subject is in, and it becomes much more difficult to blur out distracting elements.

DON'T GET TOO COMFORTABLE

Occasionally, wildlife photographers have a chance to work with either a very large subject, like an elephant, or a smaller subject above them, perhaps a bird in a tree or a deer on a hillside. In such situations, it's possible to shoot from a relatively comfortable position and still obtain a strong perspective. Very few species, though, are as tall as most human beings. I haven't measured them and done the math, but regardless of where we travel, it seems like we rarely need to extend the legs on our tripods. We always seem to be shortening them in an attempt to get lower. Even animals that vastly outweigh us, like elephant seals and hip-

We photographed this scissor-tailed flycatcher from our truck, an ideal height from which to photograph birds perching on fences. It also illustrates how photographing the subject from its level makes it easier to blur out the background. Photographing the subject from its level usually puts the background further away from the subject than it would be if you were shooting down on the subject. Tallgrass Prairie Preserve, Oklahoma. 500mm lens with 2x teleconverter.

pos, are usually considerably closer to the ground than the position from which most people would prefer to operate a camera.

Some photographers say, "There's no way I'm getting down in the mud just to get a little better perspective." And I don't really blame them. It is messy, and you don't know who or what has crawled there before you. Also, some photographers' joints will no longer allow them to shoot from a low position unless they have a friend following with a block and tackle to help them stand up again. It won't be long before we join those ranks ourselves. Are these people forever doomed to images with a weak perspective? Of course not! We humans are very inventive.

There are all kinds of products on the market, many of them quite inexpensive, to help you get the perspective you want. Plastic tarps, groundcloths, or even an old sheet can protect you from the mud. Knee pads and the foam cushions that gardeners use can protect your knees while you kneel. And we know several photographers who bring a lightweight chair with them, not just to help obtain the strongest perspective, but to make waiting for those special images more comfortable.

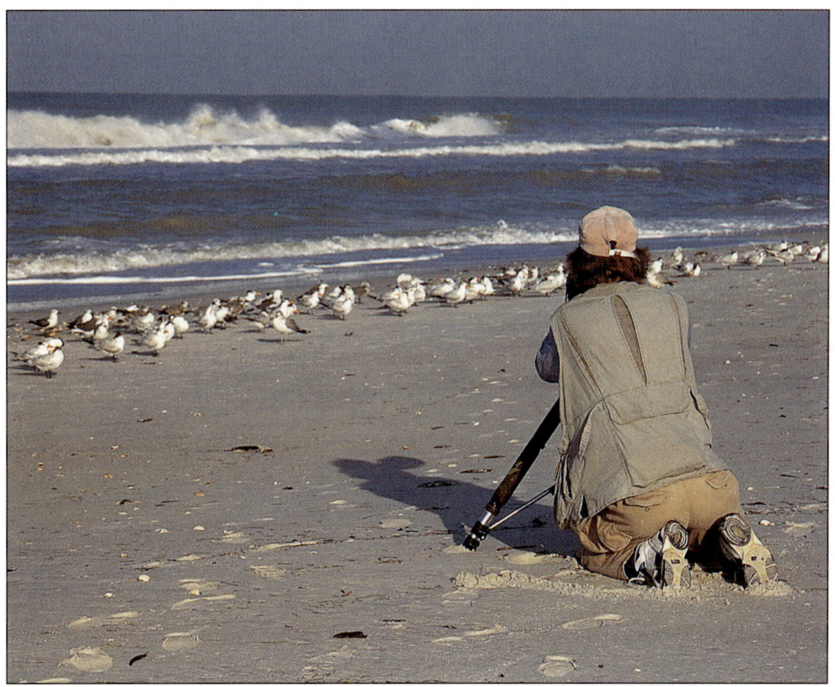

Beach sand made a relatively comfortable platform on which to kneel to photograph these royal terns. After an hour or two, though, even soft sand can become an instrument of torture. Photographers often have to earn images with a strong perspective. Sanibel Island, Florida. 28–80mm lens.

ABOVE AND BEYOND THE CALL OF DUTY

There are several photographers who deserve special recognition because they have been pioneers in the art of obtaining the lowest possible perspective on short subjects. Tim Fitzharris and Keith Szafranski did groundbreaking work on water birds, especially grebes. Using blinds and tripod heads mounted on float tubes, they were able to pho-

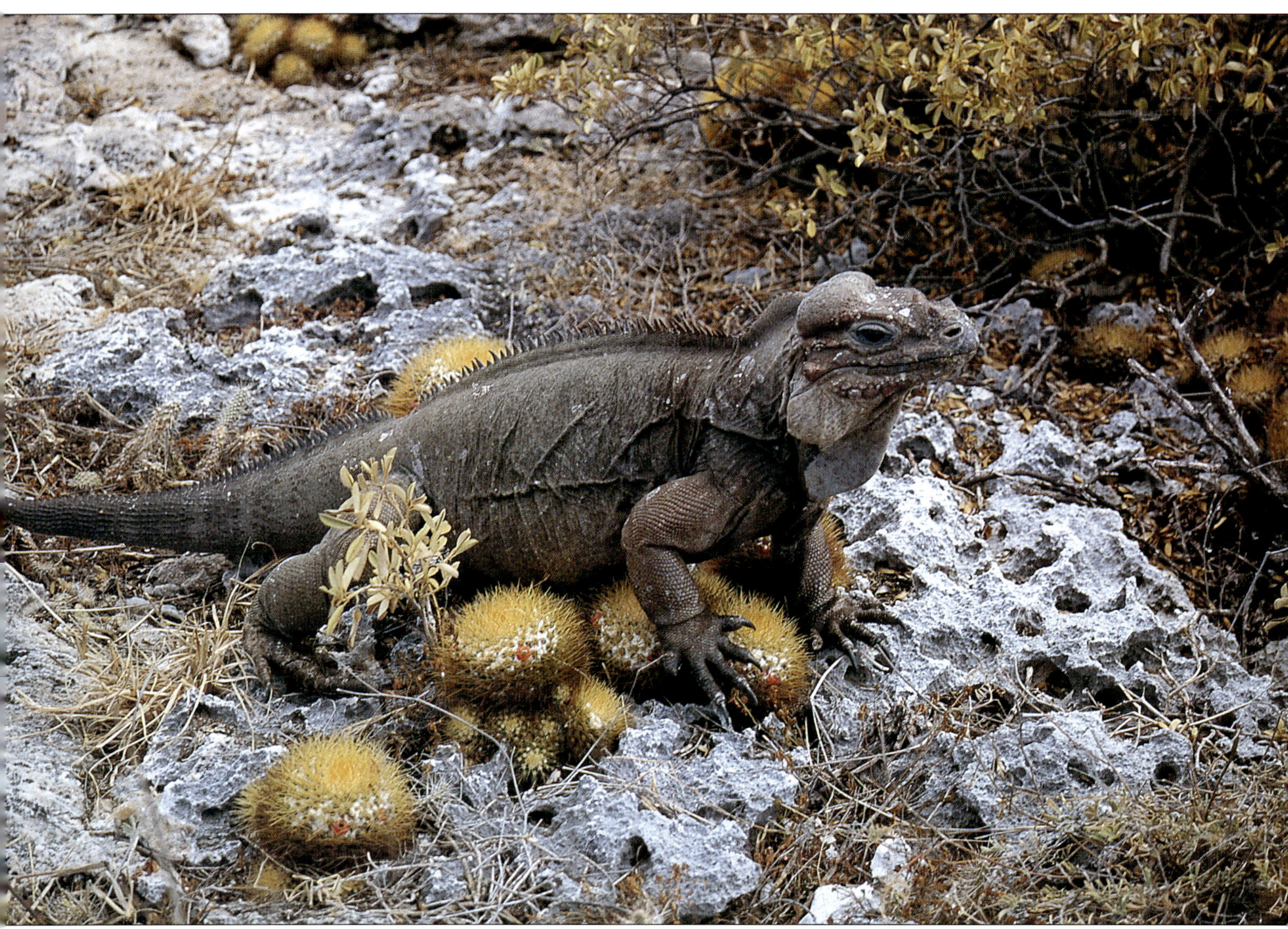

Not only was the ground sharp as razors, it was covered with cactus. There was no way we were getting down on this Mona ground iguana's level. Mona Island, Puerto Rico. 75–300mm lens.

tograph these aquatic birds from water level, a difficult perspective to achieve for photographers unwilling to get their feet wet.

Back on land, though not necessarily dry land, Arthur Morris has been pushing the perspective envelope. He has spent more time at the beach lying on his belly than most seals have. While trying to get the strongest possible images of shorebirds and seabirds, he decided that a tripod didn't allow him to get low enough for the best perspective, so he discarded it. At first, he simply balanced his long lens on its tripod foot. He has since helped develop a flat plate the lens attaches to, and using this plate he is able to shoot from much closer to the ground than is possible with the lens on a traditional tripod.

APPARENT PERSPECTIVE

There will often be times when you just can't get down to the animal's level. Either some regulation prevents you from joining your subject on the beach, it's unsafe to get down to the animal's level, the creature is crawling over ground littered with cactus, or you were up too late partying the night before (we wildlife photographers are notorious party animals) and the thought of lowering your head makes you cringe. Whatever the reason, there is a way around the perspective problem when you can't get down to your subject's level. It involves something called *apparent perspective*.

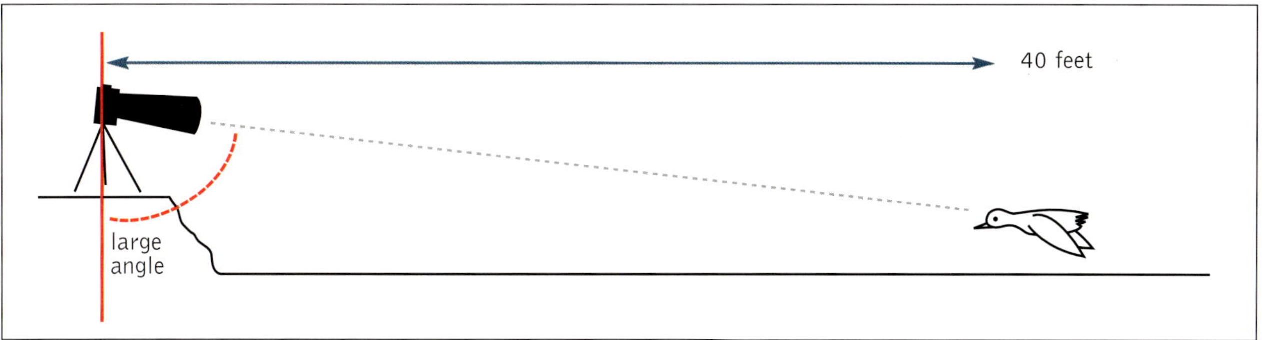

The closer to 90 degrees the angle is between your viewfinder and your subject, the closer to your level the subject will appear to be.

Imagine an elephant seal on a beach about five feet below the level of your camera. If that seal is only about ten feet away from where you're set up, the angle formed by drawing lines between your viewfinder and the ground, and your viewfinder and the seal, will be pretty small. If the seal is forty feet away, this angle will be much larger. The larger this angle is, the closer to your level the subject will appear to be. Even though both seals are five feet below your camera's level, the seal that is forty feet away will appear to be at almost the same height as your camera, while photos taken of the seal that is only ten feet away will obviously be looking down on the animal.

We spend so much time trying to get close to our subjects that sometimes we forget closer is not always better. If you find yourself in a situation like the one presented by the elephant seals, and it appears that you're looking down on your subject more than you would like, try backing away from the subject. Or if one's available, find another subject that is a bit farther away. By switching to a longer lens as you increase the angle between you and your subject, you can keep the subject the same size in the frame and still obtain a much stronger perspective. This situation doesn't occur very often in the field, but it does happen. And it's good to remember that you don't always have to accept the perspective that your subject presents to you.

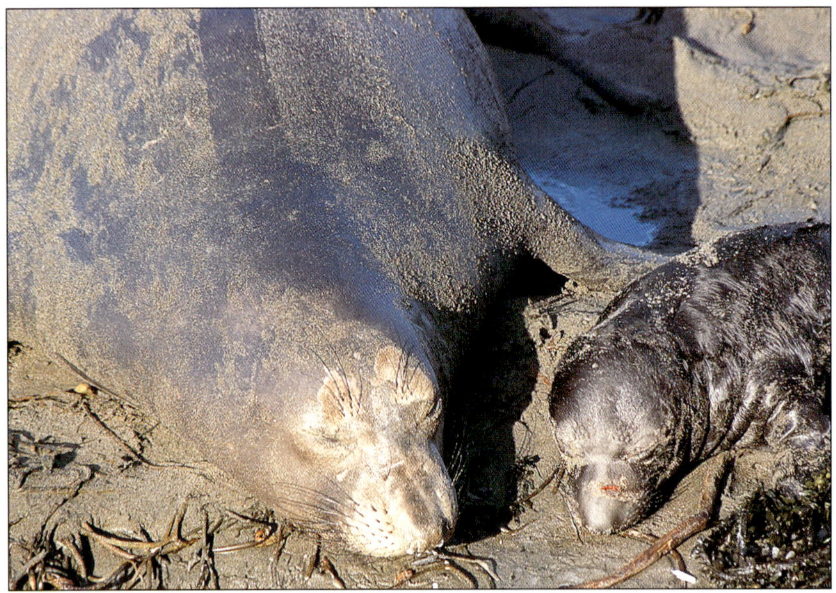

LEFT—These elephant seals were only about ten feet away, but they were at the base of a short cliff on a beach that was off limits to the public. There was no way to photograph them without shooting down on them, and it's obvious in the image. San Luis Obispo County, California. 100–400mm lens. BELOW—In this image, we let apparent perspective work for us. The seals were part of the same rookery as the seals in the previous photo, so they were also below us. However, they were also farther away, which made them appear at nearly the same height as the camera. San Luis Obispo County, California. 500mm lens with 2x teleconverter.

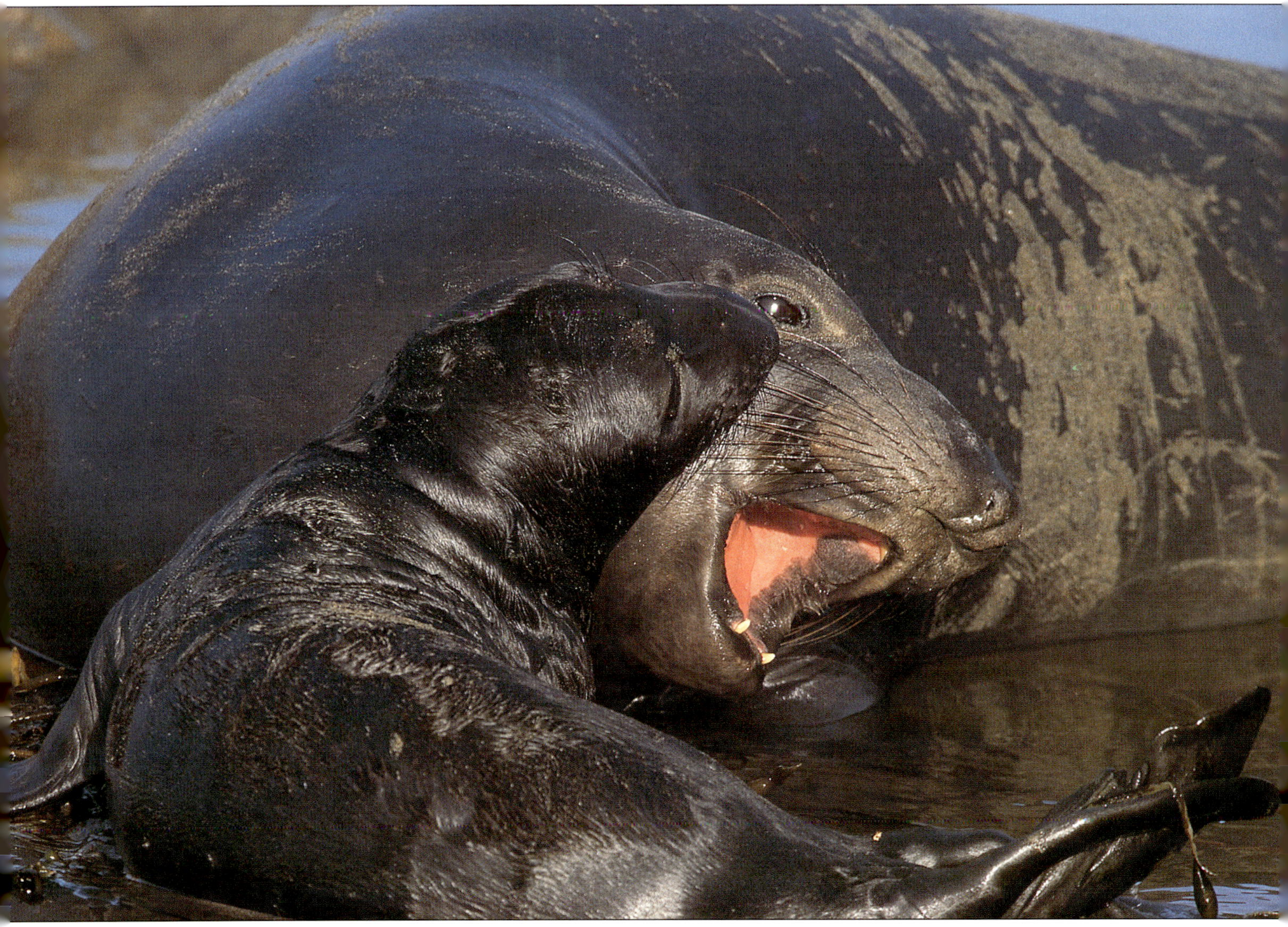

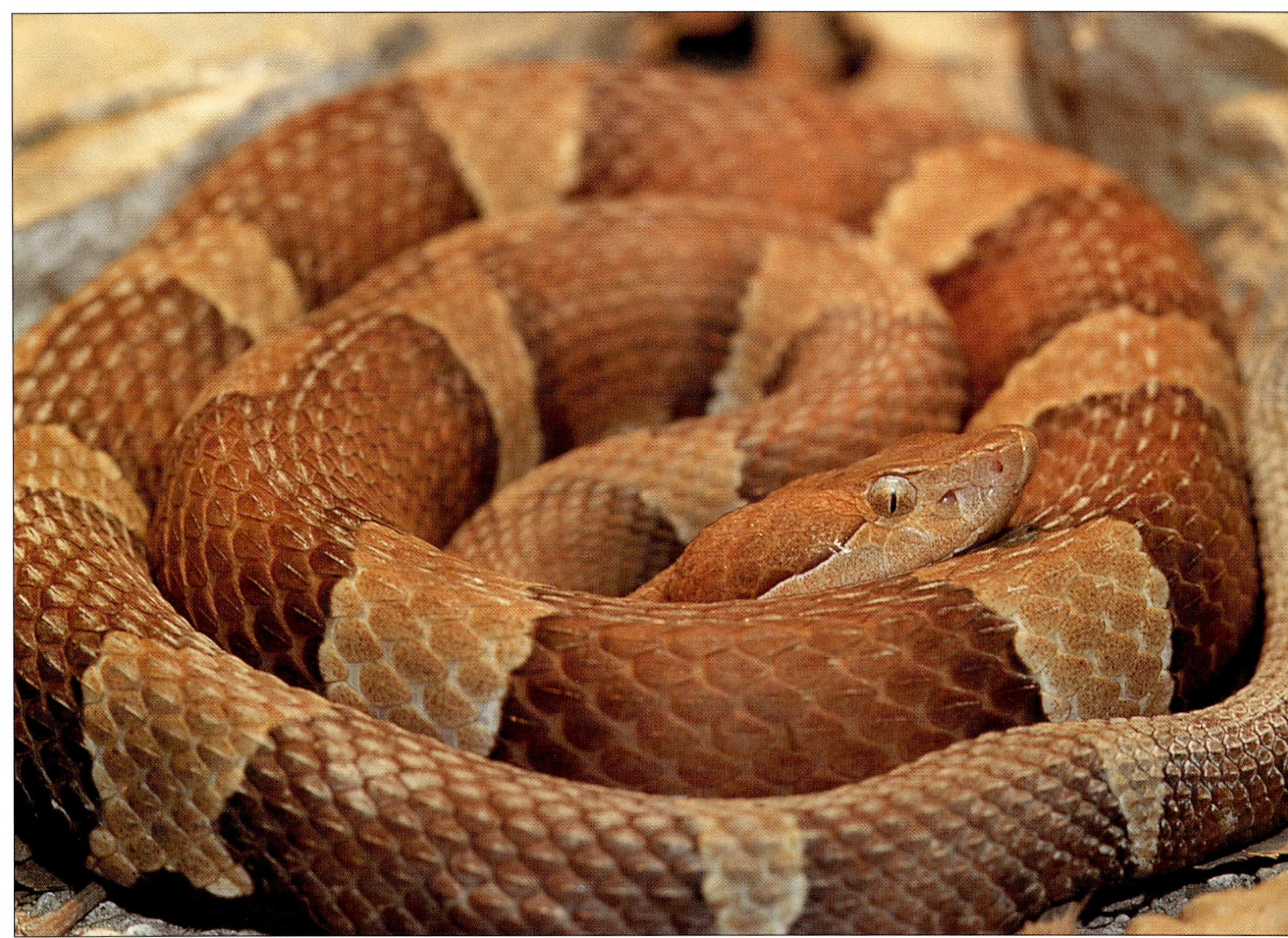

Obviously, when you want to capture the beauty of a design that is on top of your subject, like the pattern on the back of this copperhead, you need to shoot down on it. Captive. San Diego Zoo, California. 28–80mm lens with fill flash.

LOOKING DOWN ON YOUR SUBJECT

Just to make it confusing, there are situations in which it works to your advantage to shoot down on your subject. If you have a subject with a beautiful pattern on its back, like many snakes, obviously you need to be above the creature to capture the intricacies of its design. Groups of animals can also create some incredible patterns with their random wanderings. Being above them is often the only way to photograph these patterns.

Being above your subject can also make it easier when you include the creature as a small center of interest. In this kind of photo, you're trying to show your subject's relationship to the rest of its herd or rookery, or its relationship to its environment. If you photograph your subject from its level, it often will obscure or be obscured by other subjects or elements in the scene. If the landscape is rising in front of you, this isn't much of a problem. If the land is relatively level, shooting down on your subject will help prevent the different elements in your image

Often, photographing a group of animals, like this elephant seal rookery, works better if you can shoot from above your subjects. Because we were shooting down on these seals, they didn't obscure each other very much. Also, shooting down on them put more of them in the same plane as the film, making it easier for the depth of field to carry the entire group of animals. San Luis Obispo County, California. 75–300mm lens.

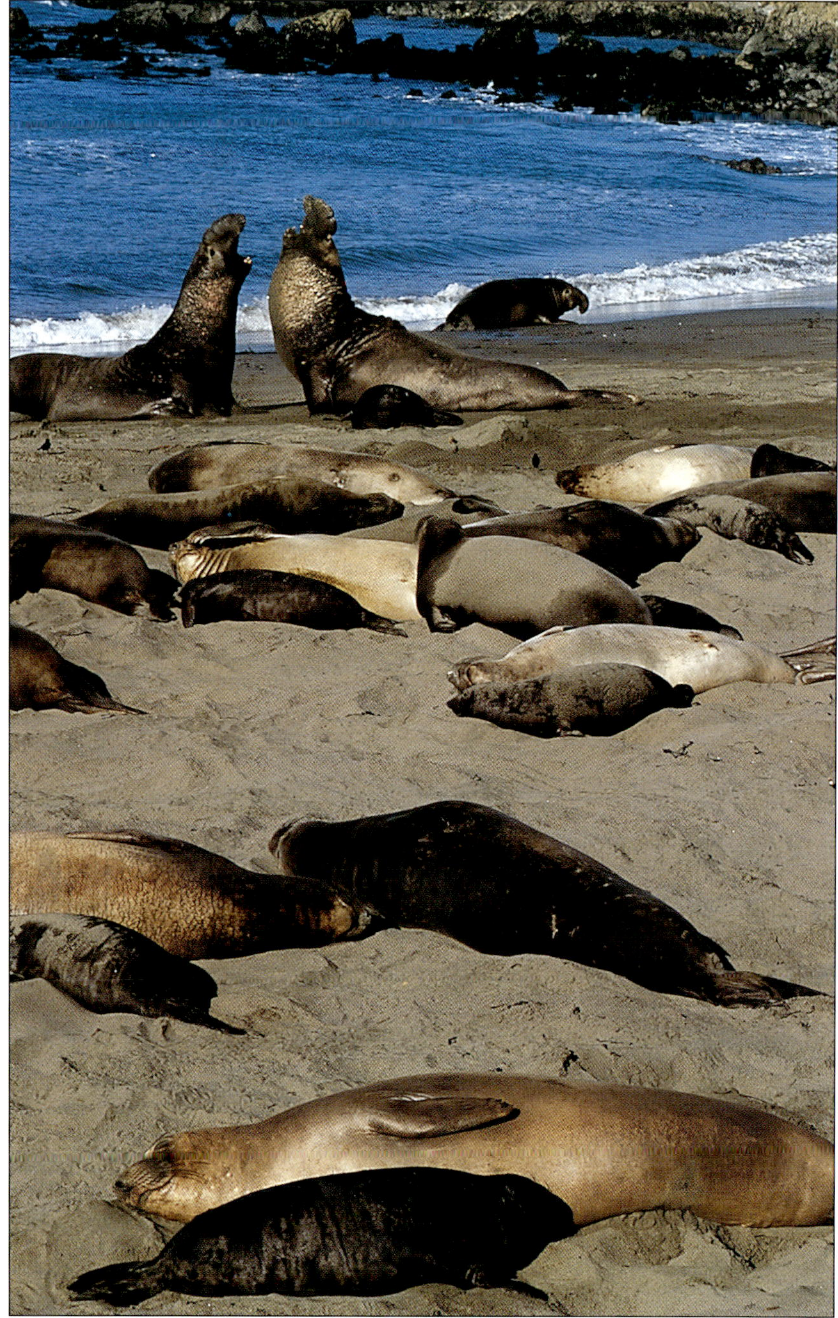

from hiding each other. Shooting down on the subject allows the viewer to see all the important elements in the scene.

It seems like such an unimportant thing, but how far you extend the legs of your tripod plays a big role in the strength of your wildlife photography. Your perspective of the subject implies not only a relationship between you and the animal, but also between the viewer and the animal. We want the viewer to see how important our subject is. Consequently, with the exception of situations where we're shooting patterns or showing environmental relationships, we want to shoot the subject from its level or lower. Going beyond documentation is much easier when you put your subject on a pedestal.

7. Capturing Animal Behavior

When you have seen one ant, one bird, one tree, you have not seen them all.

—E. O. Wilson

The avocets were part of a much larger aggregation of shorebirds and wading birds, and it was legitimately difficult to choose a subject. There were godwits and willets and egrets and dowitchers, as well as the avocets, all vying for our attention in a small corner of a tidal marsh at Tijuana Slough National Wildlife Refuge, south of San Diego. I had seen one of the avocets splashing in the water while its partner stood with its neck sticking out parallel to the water's surface, but it didn't mean anything to me. And besides, I was trying to capture a frame-filling image of a godwit and its reflection.

I glanced back at the avocets, and before I could react, they mated. And the show wasn't over yet. After mating, the birds crossed their long, saber-shaped bills just like cutlasses in a pirate movie, the male put his wing around the female, and they danced. The dance was both smooth and jerky, like a waltz seen under strobe lights, and it only lasted a few seconds, but it was one of the most enchanting sights I had ever seen.

Missing the opportunity to photograph their behavior was not the loss it would have been for many photographers. My equipment was not very good at the time, and my skills deserved no better, so I probably would not have obtained any outstanding images even if I had been ready (the godwit photos I did take were certainly nothing to write home about). This incident, though, taught me a very important lesson. And it taught me this lesson before I missed out on a situation I was equipped to photograph. Try to learn something about your subject before you pick up your camera.

Capturing animal behavior is perhaps the most obvious and often the easiest method of taking a photo beyond documentation. A portrait must be very striking, and an environmental shot must be very artistic before the viewer is going to give them a second glance. If you can show your subject engaged in some activity, however, then your viewer is going to at least spend enough time with the image to decipher just what the heck your subject is doing.

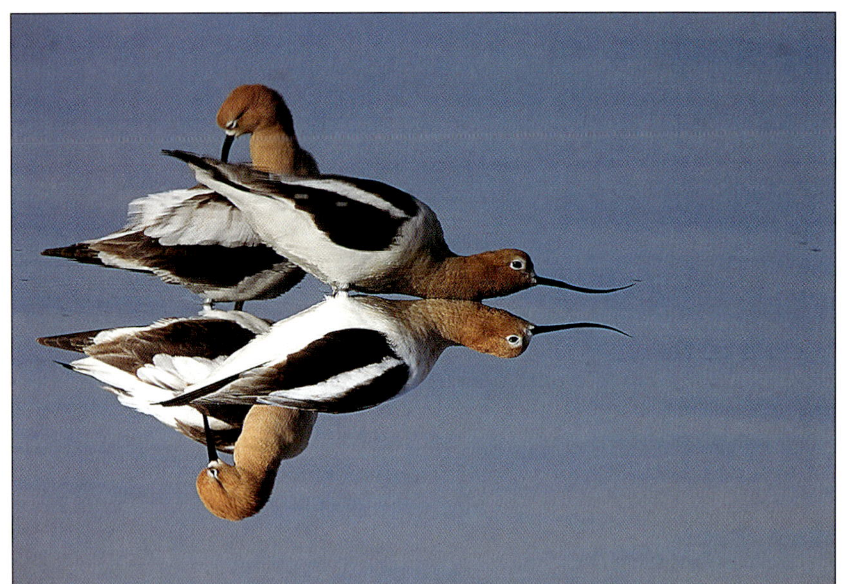

Not only is the pre-mating behavior of American avocets beautiful and interesting, it tells the knowledgeable photographer that the action in this scene is only just beginning. Jefferson County, Colorado. 500mm lens with 1.4x teleconverter.

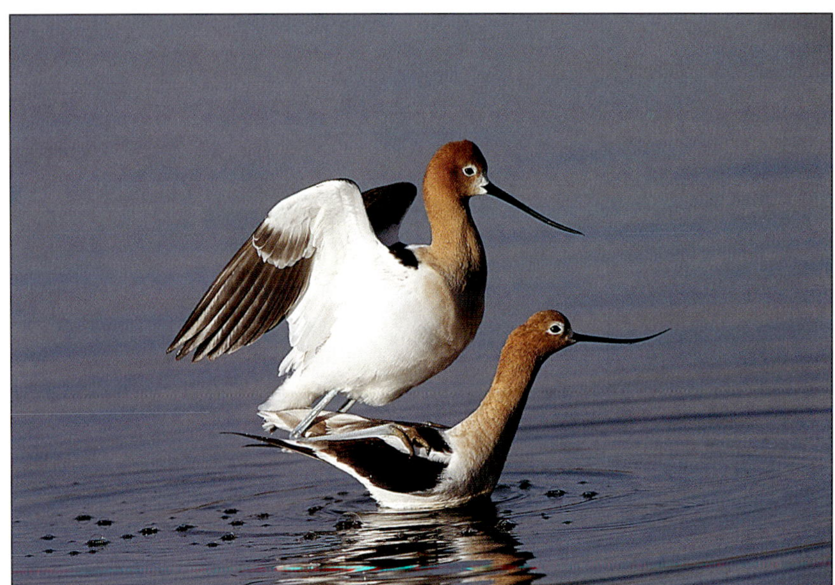

For most species, mating is a behavior that robs them of whatever grace they possess. For American avocets, on the other hand, it has all the elegance and beauty of an avian ballet. Jefferson County, Colorado. 500mm lens with 1.4xteleconverter.

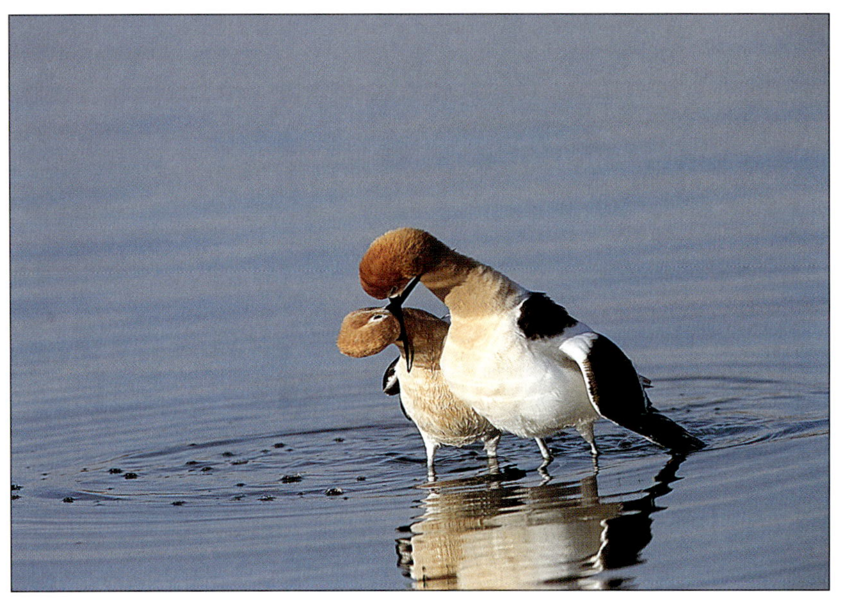

The post-mating dance that American avocets perform happens so quickly that it would be easy to miss the shot if you were unaware that it was coming. Jefferson County, Colorado. 500mm lens with 1.4x teleconverter.

WHAT DO WE MEAN BY "BEHAVIOR"?

Behavior can be almost anything. Actions that involve hardly any movement at all, like a nictitating membrane sliding across a raptor's eye, and the explosion of wings and water that accompany a flock of snow geese taking flight are both categorized as behavior. Behavior shots can feature a lone animal or groups of animals interacting. This subject is so wide open it boggles the mind. That's not to imply, though, that every behavior photo is an image that has gone beyond documentation. Simple behaviors, like walking or yawning, will probably not get a huge response unless the image has other things going for it as well. If nothing else, a photo of a nictitating membrane would have to be a very tight shot of the bird's head, just to show the membrane clearly.

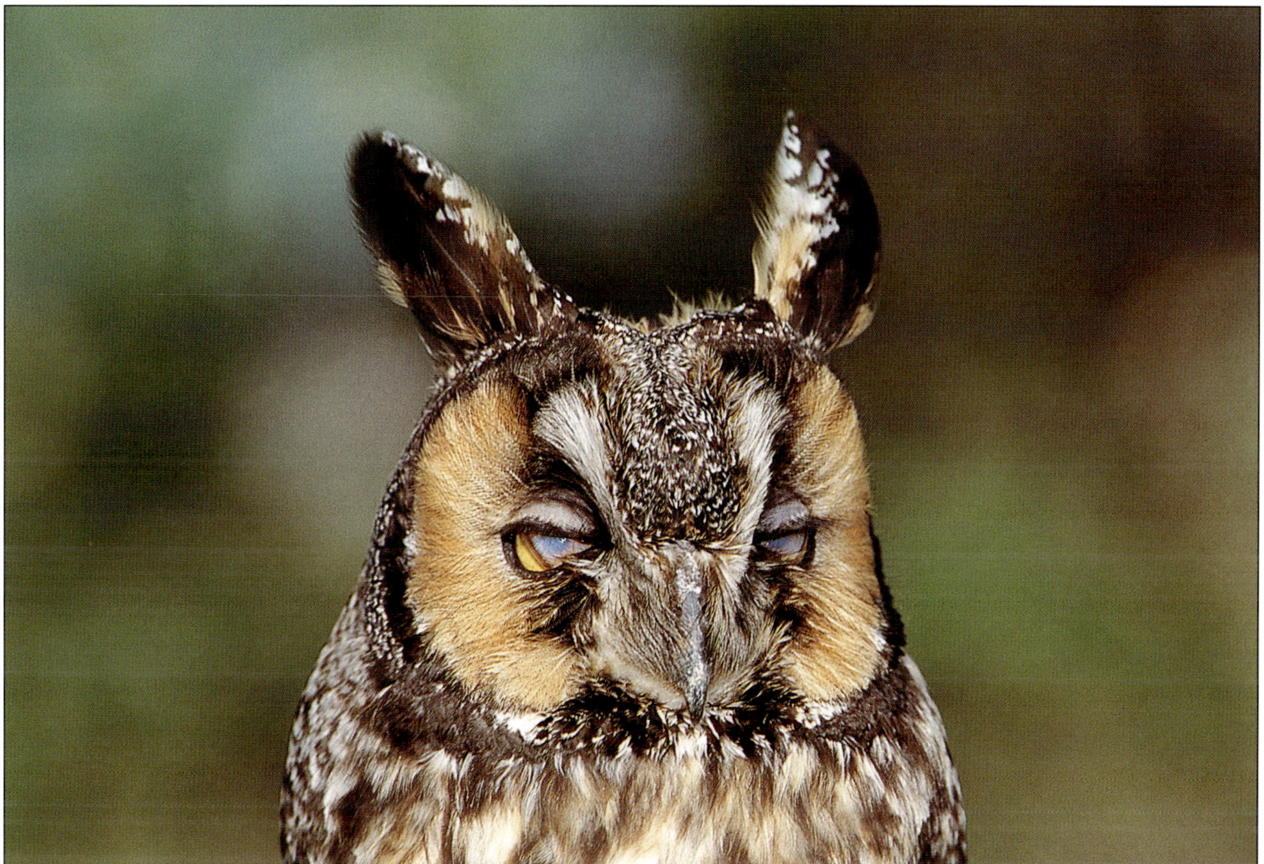

Photographing behavior can be as simple as showing the nictitating membrane lubricating a long-eared owl's eye. To show a behavior like this to the viewer, though, the photo needs to be tight. Captive. Larimer County, Colorado. 75–300mm lens with fill flash.

More complex behaviors, though, like pups playing or avocets dancing, are often interesting enough to capture your viewer's attention even if the composition is less than perfect. A subject whose size in the frame would put it in that no-man's-land of documentation if it were just standing there, can make an intriguing image if the animal is just doing something active. One of the reasons behavior affects photos so positively is that many behaviors are not even seen very often, let alone photographed. Great behavior images are an uncommon sight to most viewers for good reason. Even common behaviors can be maddeningly difficult to capture.

There are ways you can make it easier to capture various behaviors, and one of them is to know when to expect them. A couple of obvious examples of behavior-rich times are during courtship and when young animals are present. Most wildlife photographers dream of photographing subjects like fox pups or rutting elk just for the chance to bring home some exciting behavior images. And even though these are the stereotypical behaviors, who can resist photographing babies or the bizarre activities males engage in to attract females? Keep in mind, however, that these are only the tip of the behavior iceberg.

Social animals, like prairie dogs and chimpanzees, can be a gold mine of interesting activity as they go through their day-to-day lives. At the risk of sounding cliché, though, you have to stay focused on the activities going on around you if you want to capture images that go beyond documentation. And that's not always an easy thing to do. Fifty-nine minutes out of every hour they may ignore each other. Being aware of the behavioral possibilities, though, as well as being ready for them when they occur, plays a huge roll in bringing home those once-in-a-lifetime shots.

Social animals, like these black-tailed prairie dogs, make great subjects for capturing images of behavior. Here two siblings are taking a short rest after a wrestling match. Jefferson County, Colorado. 500mm lens with 1.4x teleconverter.

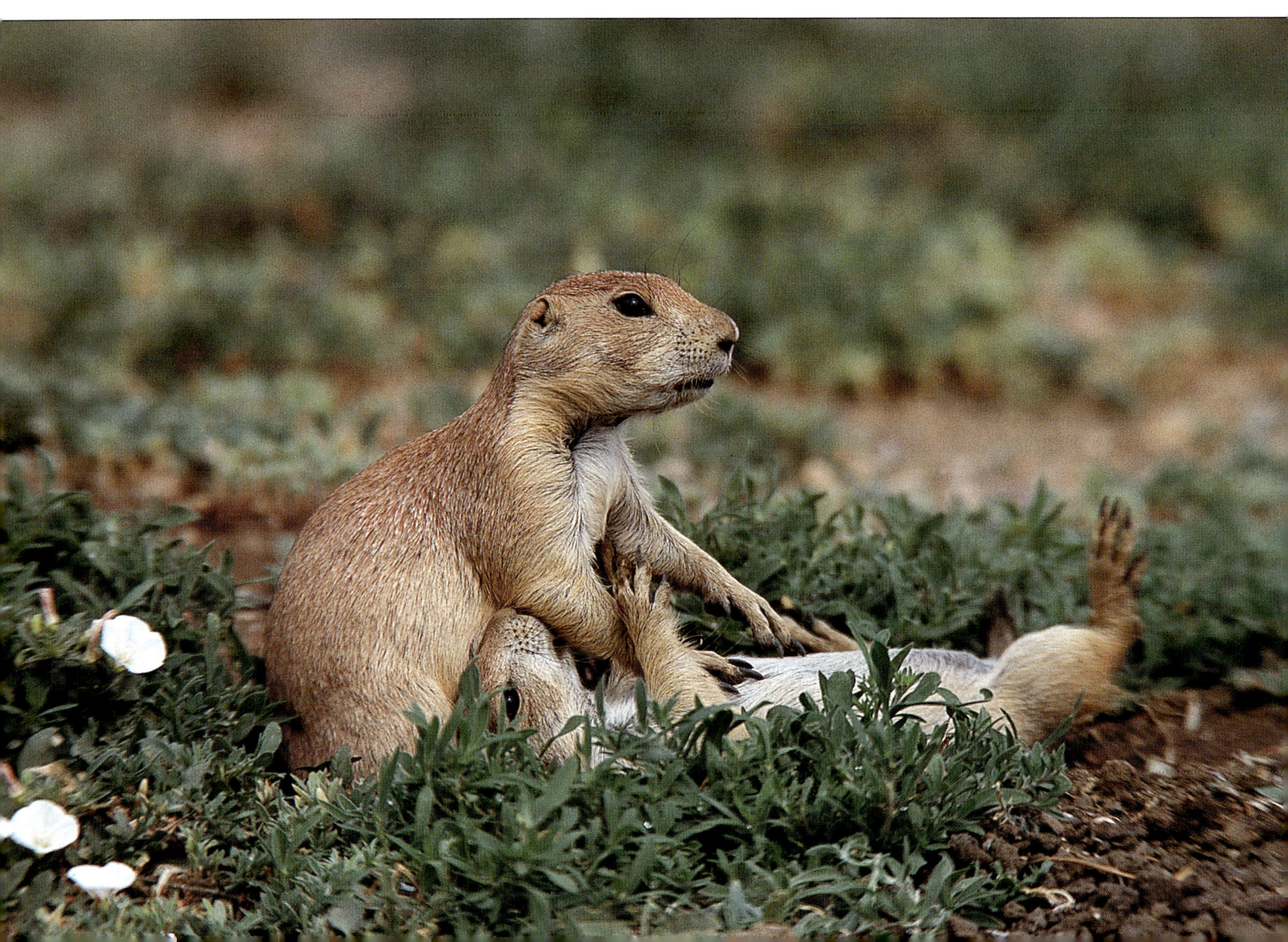

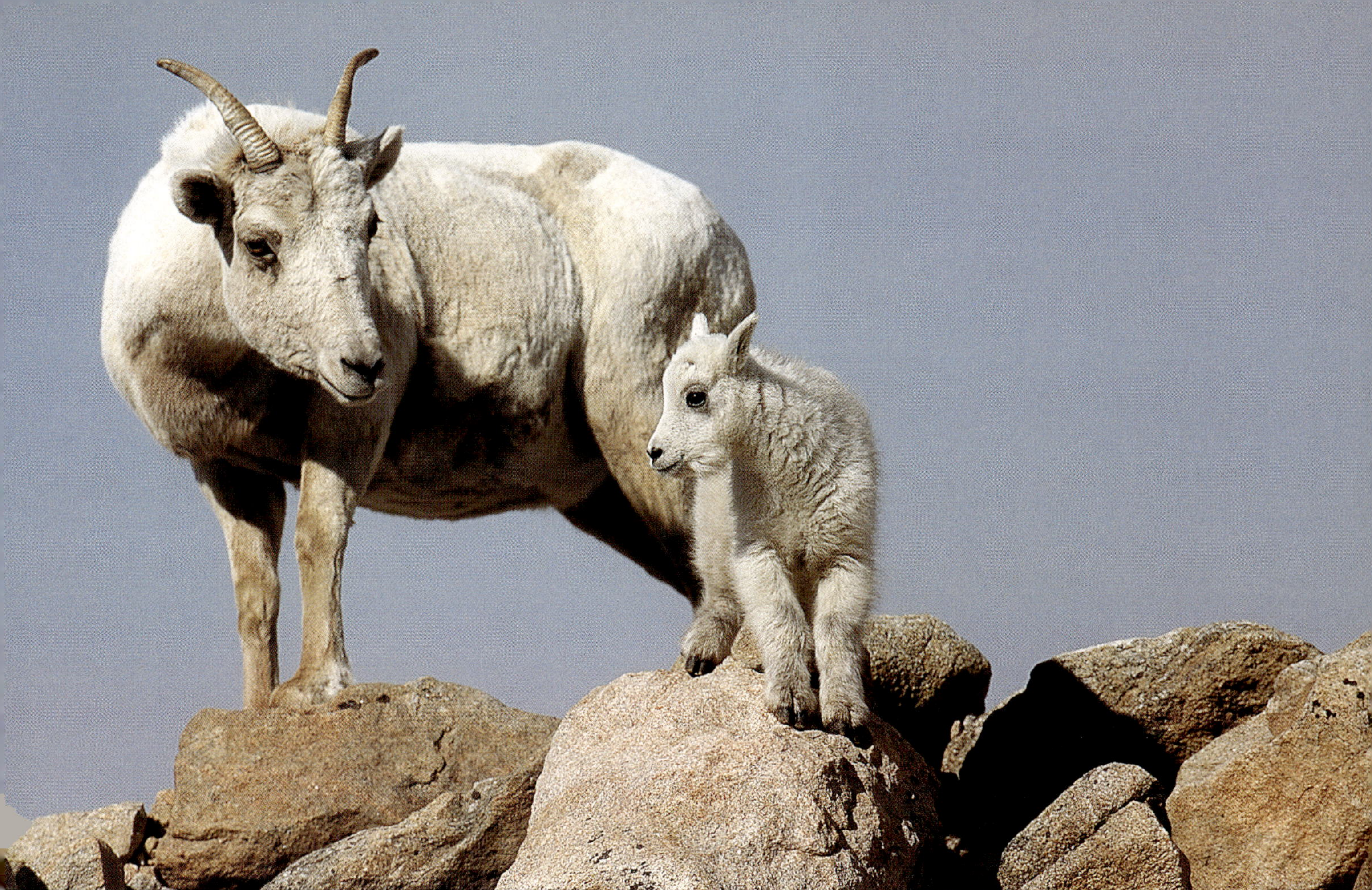

When a bighorn ewe approached this mountain goat kid, I was sure that either the kid would run away or the kid's mother would chase the bighorn ewe away. It was only because I was "on my toes" that I was able to capture a mother-to-be of one species checking out the baby of another species. Mt. Evans, Colorado. 500mm lens.

The same rule applies when two different species come together. Many times they will pay little attention to each other, like gulls and seals. Sometimes it depends on the time of year. Avocets will tolerate almost any species for most of the year. During nesting and chick rearing, though, they will attack almost everything, even species that are obviously no threat to their chicks. A general rule of thumb is this: When more than one potential subject is present in an area, you need to be on your toes.

LET ME SEE

The most important thing in capturing behavior is that the activity can be easily seen in the image. This doesn't mean that what is actually happening can be easily interpreted. Let's say we have a photo of a magpie poking around an elk's butt, of all the disgusting things to do. All we know from the photo is that there's a magpie showing a great deal of interest in the rear end of an elk. We don't know if the magpie is attacking the elk because the elk approached too close to the magpie's nest, if the magpie is looking for parasites, if the magpie is giving a proctological exam, or whatever. And it doesn't matter as long as the activity is clearly visible and it gives the viewer something to ponder.

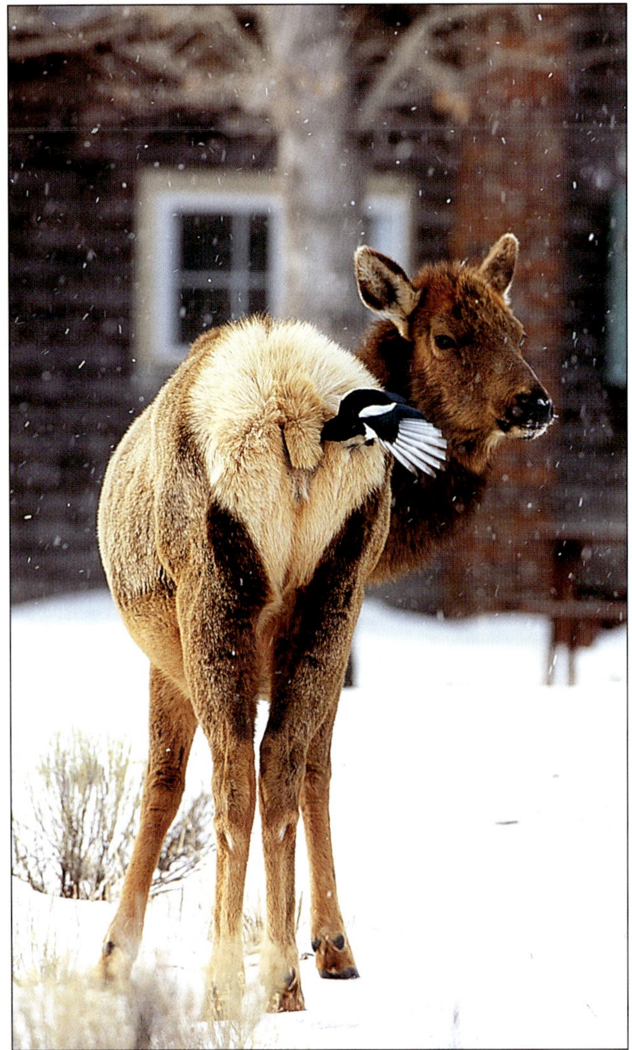

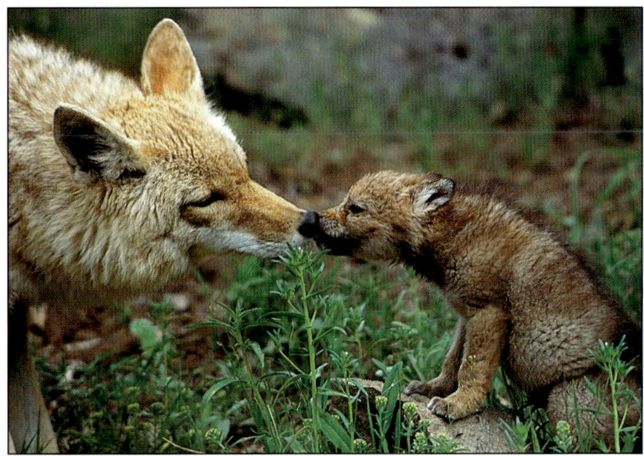

LEFT—This black-billed magpie is actually looking for parasites on a cow elk, but it's not particularly important that the viewers know that. The important thing is that there is something happening, and that it is easily visible. Give the viewers something to think about, and they may spend a good deal of time examining your image. Yellowstone National Park. 75–300mm lens. ABOVE—With behavior photos, the photographer can often get away with minor intrusive elements that might seriously weaken a portrait. The action of the mother coyote touching noses with the pup is so strong it takes a moment to even notice the plant covering part of her nose. Captive. Bridger Mountains, Montana. 500mm lens.

If you can capture some interesting behavior and make it easy to see, you can often get away with compositions that are less than perfect. Few people are going to pay attention to part of another animal or a distracting branch poking into the frame if your image shows a mother and baby touching noses. And this is a good thing because photographing behavior is usually hard enough—even without worrying about perfect composition.

Photographing behavior is usually hard enough—even without worrying about perfect composition.

When you're trying to focus on avocets dancing across the water, you're not thinking about shrubs that may adversely affect the composition. If people can see the birds with their crossed bills, though, it's usually enough to interest them in the image. Even if part of one bird is sticking out of the frame, it can still be an eye-catching photo because most people just don't see this behavior very often.

We're not saying you should pay absolutely no attention to composition and lighting when you're trying to photograph behavior. We are saying that a clear portrayal of that behavior should be the most important element in your image, especially if it's something a bit unusual or particularly dynamic. Besides, a "clear portrayal" usually means that excess clutter has been eliminated from the photo and that important elements are not hiding in the shadows. Behavior is such a strong element it can overshadow any minor problems with the photo, but the activity must be clearly visible.

MAXIMIZING OPPORTUNITIES

Okay. We've established that behavior is a great way to take your images beyond documentary. Just how do you go about doing this? What should you do to prepare for it? Well, it's time to crack the books. Did you think you were through with homework just because you're no longer in school? Many aspiring wildlife photographers imagine their choice of pastimes to be an outdoor life, a kaleidoscopic whirlwind of different habitats filled with the creatures they love. They didn't sign up for this just to spend hours in front of a computer screen or running down leads at the library. Sometimes, though, that's what it takes. Even the most vagabond of serious wildlife photographers spend a considerable amount of time researching the subjects they want to photograph.

Northern shovelers, like this drake jumping off the water, will often twitch their heads from side to side just before they take flight. A little research can help the photographer anticipate the duck jumping off the water. Jefferson County, Colorado. 500mm lens.

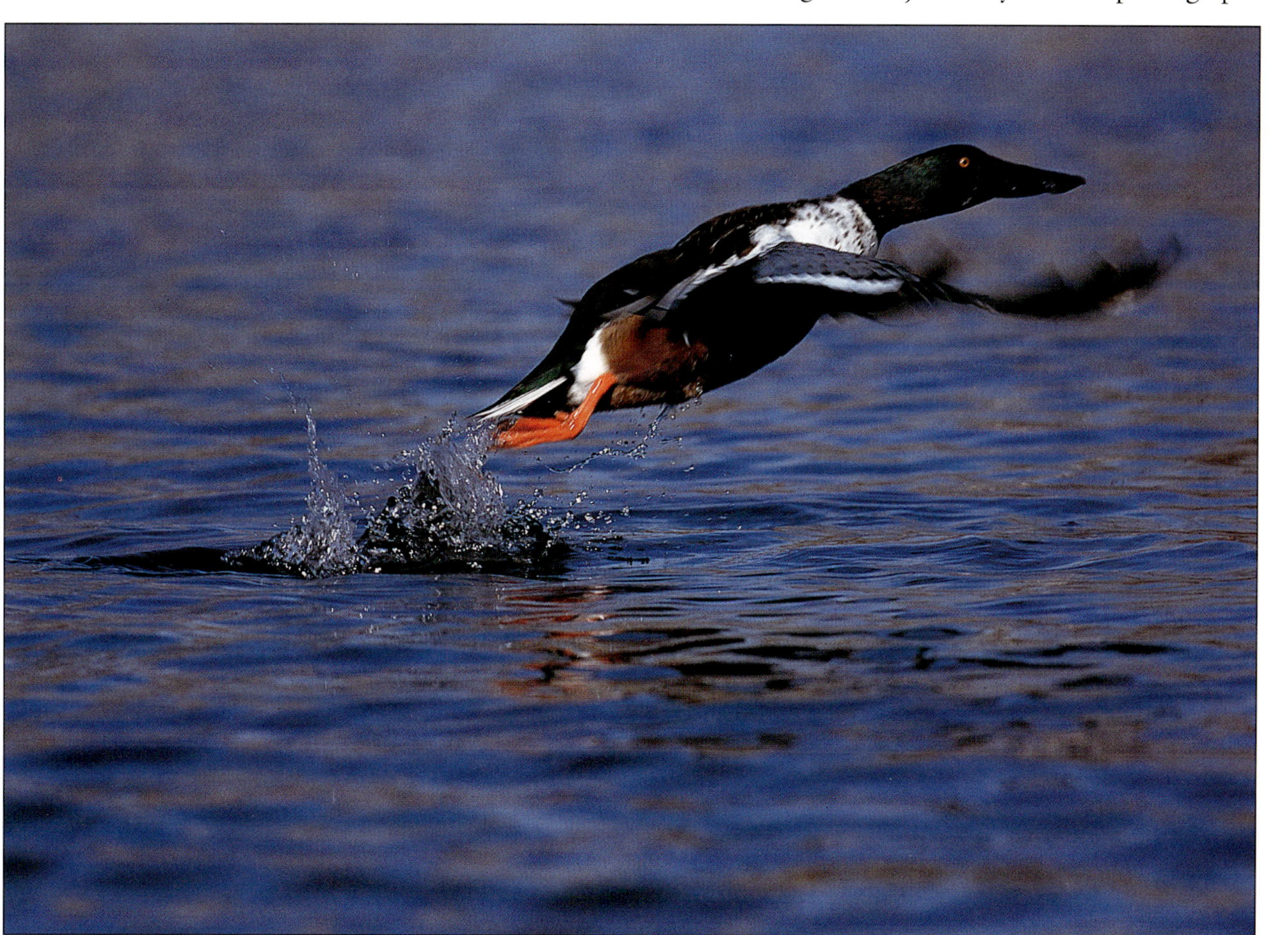

Research is important for several reasons. First, it lets you know what activities your subject engages in and what behaviors you might want to try to photograph. With a little research, you can determine the best places to find your subject at certain times of the year, when it engages in the behavior you're interested in, and how to anticipate that behavior. With a little research, I would not have missed my first chance to photograph dancing avocets.

Perhaps you're interested in photographing ducks, and you want to capture the drake jumping off the water—a difficult behavior to capture. Enter the field without doing any research and you would have no idea that some species often telegraph their intention to take flight. Mallards will usually twitch their heads up and down, like they're agreeing with you, before they fly. Shovelers do just the opposite. Before they fly, shovelers twitch their heads from side to side, like they think you're wrong.

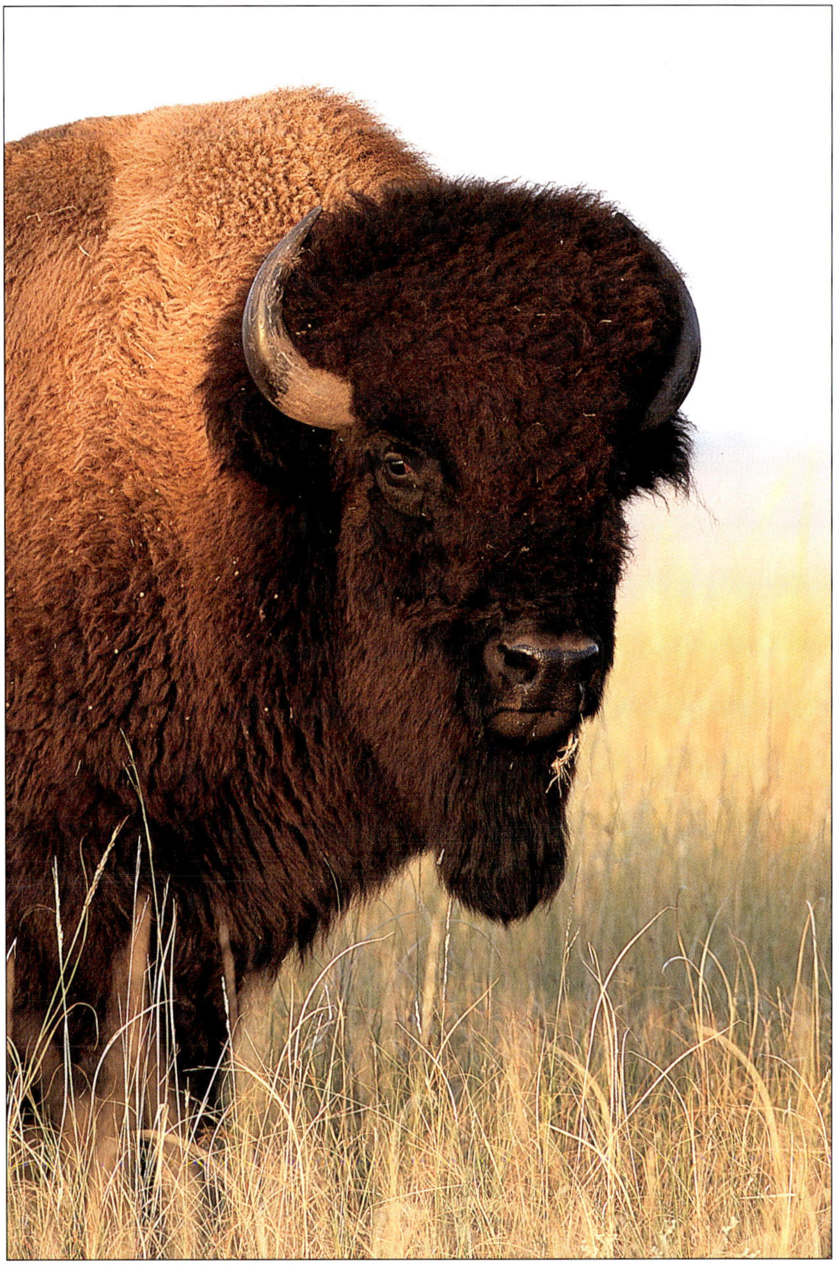

When a bison is staring at you and its tail sticks up in the air, you are in serious danger of being gored. A little research can keep you from getting into needlessly dangerous situations. Ft. Niobrara National Wildlife Refuge, Nebraska. 500mm lens.

Second, research is helpful in ensuring your safety. It can help alert you to dangers in your subject's habitat. For example, many photographers love to photograph the scenery and the wildlife of the Sonoran Desert in Southern Arizona, especially in springtime. Bees are very active at this time of year in the desert, pollinating the acacia and palo verde trees, and 99 percent of the bees in this region are now the Africanized "killer" bees. Forcing your way through the brush or swatting willy nilly at flying insects could be a very bad mistake.

Your subject itself could engage in behaviors that put your fragile body and more fragile gear at risk. If you are photographing bison, which are by far the most dangerous large animals in North America, a little research could save your life. You should know that if the animal's tail is sticking up and the beast is staring at you, you want to be somewhere else, soon.

Third, some research could help protect your subject from you. In chapter 5, we mentioned that there can be a fine line between trying to go beyond documentation with your wildlife photography and overstressing your subject, and that no photo is worth endangering your subject for. Well, we're repeating it now because it should be the basic tenet of wildlife photography. You should know your subject's body language, so you can tell when it's had enough of your presence. You should know how long the adults usually take between visits to their young, so you know if your presence is preventing the adults from returning. Wildlife photography is important to us not just because of our artistic natures, but because we love our subjects. Treat them with respect.

Research-wise, today's wildlife photographers have it much easier than their predecessors. Finding information on subjects has never been so easy. The amount of written material, on almost any species or habitat imaginable, boggles the mind. Between newspapers, magazines, books, research papers, the Internet, state game and fish publications, and national park publications, there is plenty of information available on just about every subject photographers are interested in. You can also contact wildlife biologists or even other photographers.

You should know your subject's body language, so you can tell when it's had enough of your presence.

Make your time with a camera pay off even if you don't get a chance to push the shutter button. Conduct your own research and make your own observations in the field. The differences between mallard and shoveler preflight behavior were observed during downtimes in various wetlands. And I have yet to see it mentioned in any publication. Do not discount the importance of research, though. It can often make the difference between a successful photography trip and a dud.

LADY LUCK

There is another factor that often plays a big role in the kind of behavior you are privy to, how close the activity is to you and whether or not you can get a clear shot of it. Photographers often speak of dedication and perseverance. They rarely speak of luck, and yet luck is often the only explainable reason for being able to witness some of the activities that have been captured on film. Do you think any amount of research would have helped the photographer whose coverage of orcas attacking a gray whale appeared in *National Geographic*? She could have read everything there was to read on orcas and gray whales, and it would

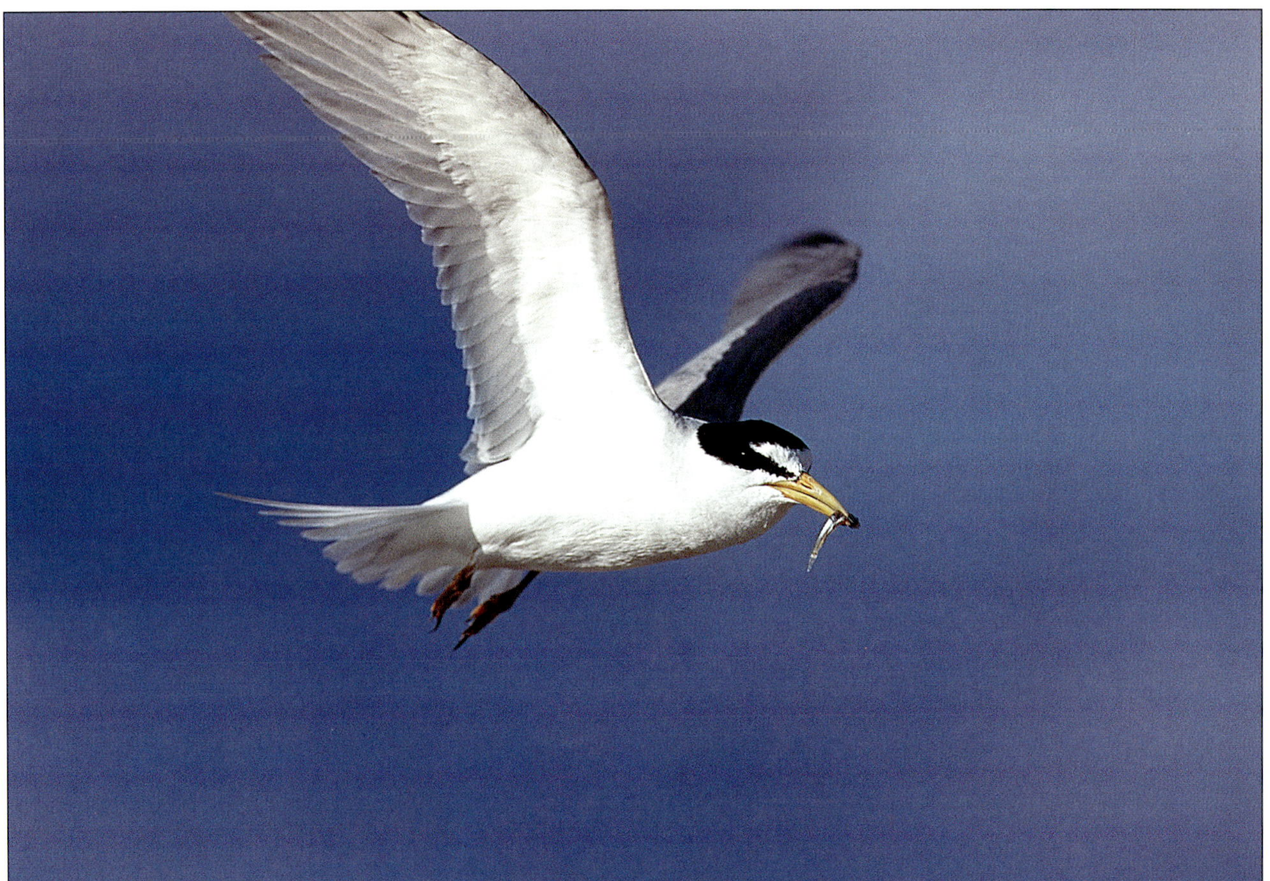

Photographing this least tern as it carried a fish back to its chicks was as much a matter of luck as anything else. Personally, however, we have nothing against being lucky. Lake McConaughy, Nebraska. 300mm lens.

have made absolutely no difference. For some reason that photographer was blessed that day, and she was in the right place at the right time with the right equipment.

Several years ago, Lake McConaughy in western Nebraska experienced unusually heavy spring runoff. The sandbars where the resident least terns nested disappeared, and the birds were forced to nest in a parking lot. The nesting area was cordoned off with red flagging, but it was easy to photograph the nesting birds from outside the flagging. We set up outside the nesting area, concentrating on an incubating adult about twenty-five feet away. No sooner had we set up, though, than another adult was hovering right in front of us, its screaming in no way diminished by the fish it was carrying in its beak. The bird was bringing food back to a camouflaged chick that was only a few feet in front of us, which we had not even seen. With a shorter lens we were able to get some great flight shots before backing up to see what invisible bird boundary we had crossed.

If we had set up on another nesting tern, and there were quite a few to choose from, we would never have gotten the great flight shots. Sure, we had studied the literature on least terns, but luck is what allowed us to get the flight shots we did. Don't overlook the role that luck plays in obtaining great photos, and keep in mind the only way to improve your luck and increase your chances is to spend more time in the field.

IT'S DOING *WHAT?*

Animals in unusual situations or places where you don't expect them to be can help an image go beyond documentation. Animals don't know they are not supposed to trespass on our property or mess with our toys and equipment. When they do cross this line, the results can be disastrous, like when deer get caught in fences. The results can also be interesting and humorous. Capturing these images is often more a matter of luck than research. Some years ago, we saw a shot of a cow moose resting in a child's wading pool in a backyard in Anchorage, Alaska. I definitely took a second look at that photo.

One of the campgrounds in Big Bend National Park now warns tent campers to knock their tents down if they leave camp. It seems the resident javelinas now associate standing tents with hidden food, and they will tear their way into any unguarded, standing tent. While camping there, we photographed a javelina standing on a collapsed tent, looking like he was wondering how to set it up. What the animal was really doing is unimportant. The important thing is creating an image that your viewers can weave a story around. Force the viewers to stay with your photo long enough to think up an interesting story or two to accompany it.

Make an effort to photograph any species you see in an unusual situation. This javelina was a member of a herd that roamed the campground in search of unguarded tents they could break into, looking for an easy meal. Standing on the flattened tent, the animal looks like it's wondering how to set it up. Big Bend National Park, Texas. 75–300mm lens.

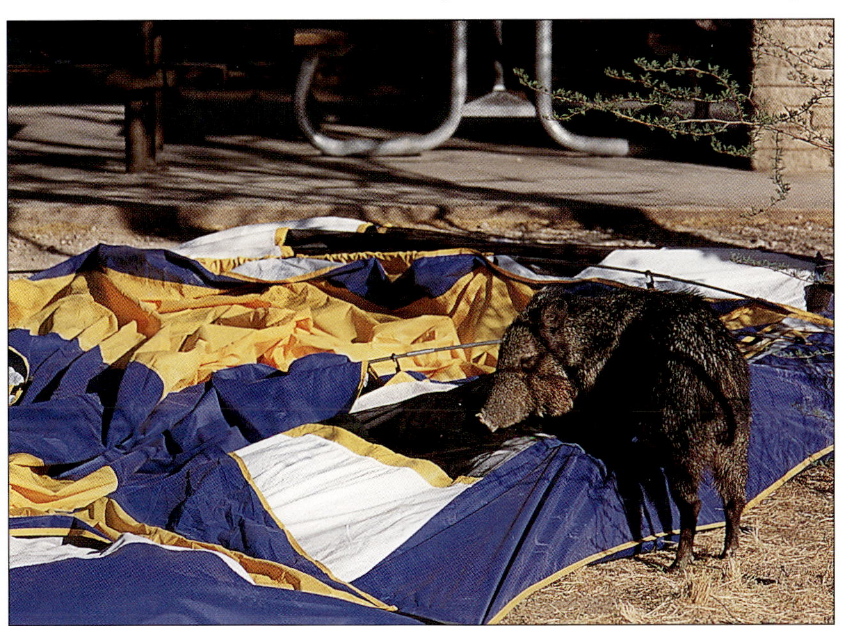

Capturing behavior is one of the best ways to take your photos beyond documentation, maybe because so many of our lives are now divorced from the lives of the animals around us. Most of our viewers have no idea what activities different animal species engage in, and they find these intimate glimpses into animal lives fascinating. Research plays a big role in helping the photographer capture animal behavior, but it can only go so far. So pray to God, bring out your good luck charms, get out in the field, and give luck a chance, too.

8. What's So Special About Your Subject?

In all things of nature there is something of the marvelous.
—Aristotle

In the last chapter we covered capturing your subject's behavioral traits. In this chapter we're going to be very superficial and judge God's creatures solely on the basis on their physical features. Doing so is only fair, because this is often what viewers will use to judge your images.

CASE IN POINT

The white-throated savanna monitor is a very impressive lizard, almost five feet long, with muscular legs and enormous claws, and we were trying to decide the best way to portray it, handicapped as we were. We were limited in what we could attempt because the lizard was in an enclosure at the San Diego Zoo, and a four-foot wall kept us from getting down on the lizard's level. On top of that, the enclosure was not very large, so we couldn't use apparent perspective to its full potential.

Then the lizard stuck out its tongue, fifteen inches long and ending in a black-tipped fork. That tongue overshadowed all of the creature's other attributes. It was the obvious feature to showcase. As is often the case, deciding what we wanted to photograph turned out to be the easy part. The lizard had to be in the right place with its tongue out. And these creatures are not constantly flicking their tongues in and out. They will do so constantly for twenty or thirty seconds, and then nothing for five or ten minutes.

We spent the next half-hour waiting for the lizard to wander over to the right spot and stick out its tongue. It finally did what it was supposed to, and we even had several chances to get the shot. Only one of those photos, however, showed what we wanted—the tongue extended at full length. The tongue is what makes the shot, though. Almost anything else we could have done with this subject, with the limitations we had there, would have shown a large lizard, slightly tighter or slightly wider, walking past rocks and dirt. It would have pretty much been documentary.

If your subject has some characteristic that makes it stand out from the menagerie, especially if it is known for that feature, try to make that

Many lizards, like this white-throated savanna monitor, have impressive tongues. Some species flick them so quickly an infrared beam and high-speed flash are needed to stop them. With monitors you just have to be ready to shoot when the tongue extends. Captive, San Diego Zoo, California. 75–300mm lens and fill flash.

trait stand out in your photo. The feature you're trying to accentuate could be almost anything—color, feathers, scales, hair, feet, teeth, nose, tongue, whatever. The trick is deciding how you need to photograph the feature to make it catch your viewer's eye. You need to decide what kind of light will work the best, what direction you want that light coming from, what environment will work best, what perspective you want, and how close you need to be. Even though it did not give us the strongest perspective, shooting down on the monitor lizard worked fine because its tongue stood out so well against the sand.

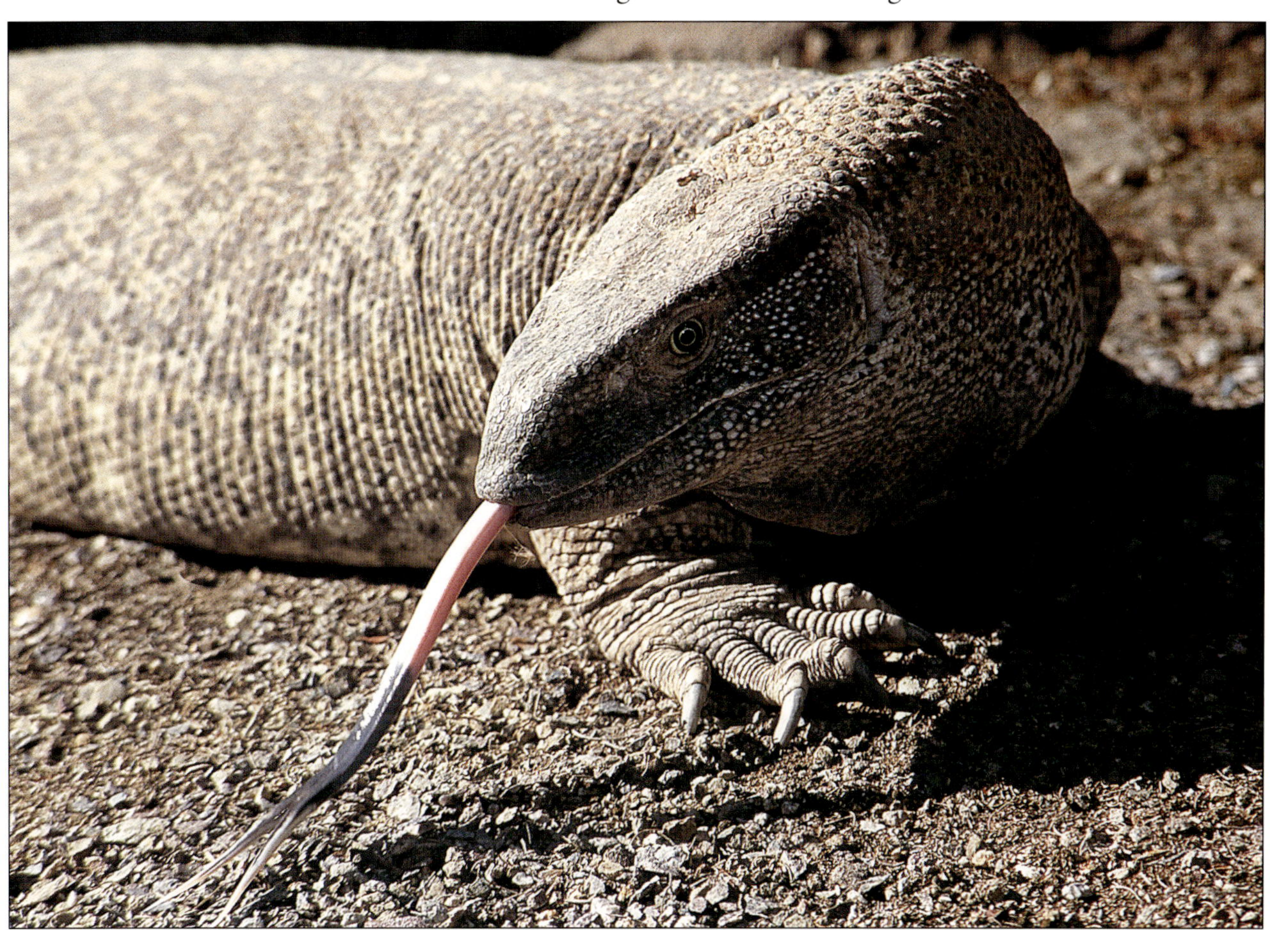

SHOW US WHAT YOU'VE GOT

Some animals have eye-catching features that are extremely large, like a whale's flukes. And some have features you can make stand out well enough in a fairly wide shot, like velvet deer antlers photographed in back light. For most subjects, though, you want to get in close. Unless it's an extremely rare animal, your viewer has probably seen many photos of your subject. You're trying to grab the viewers' attention by showing some part of the creature they may not have seen clearly, or at least not as often as they have seen photos of the entire animal. Showing these attributes clearly usually requires being quite close to your sub-

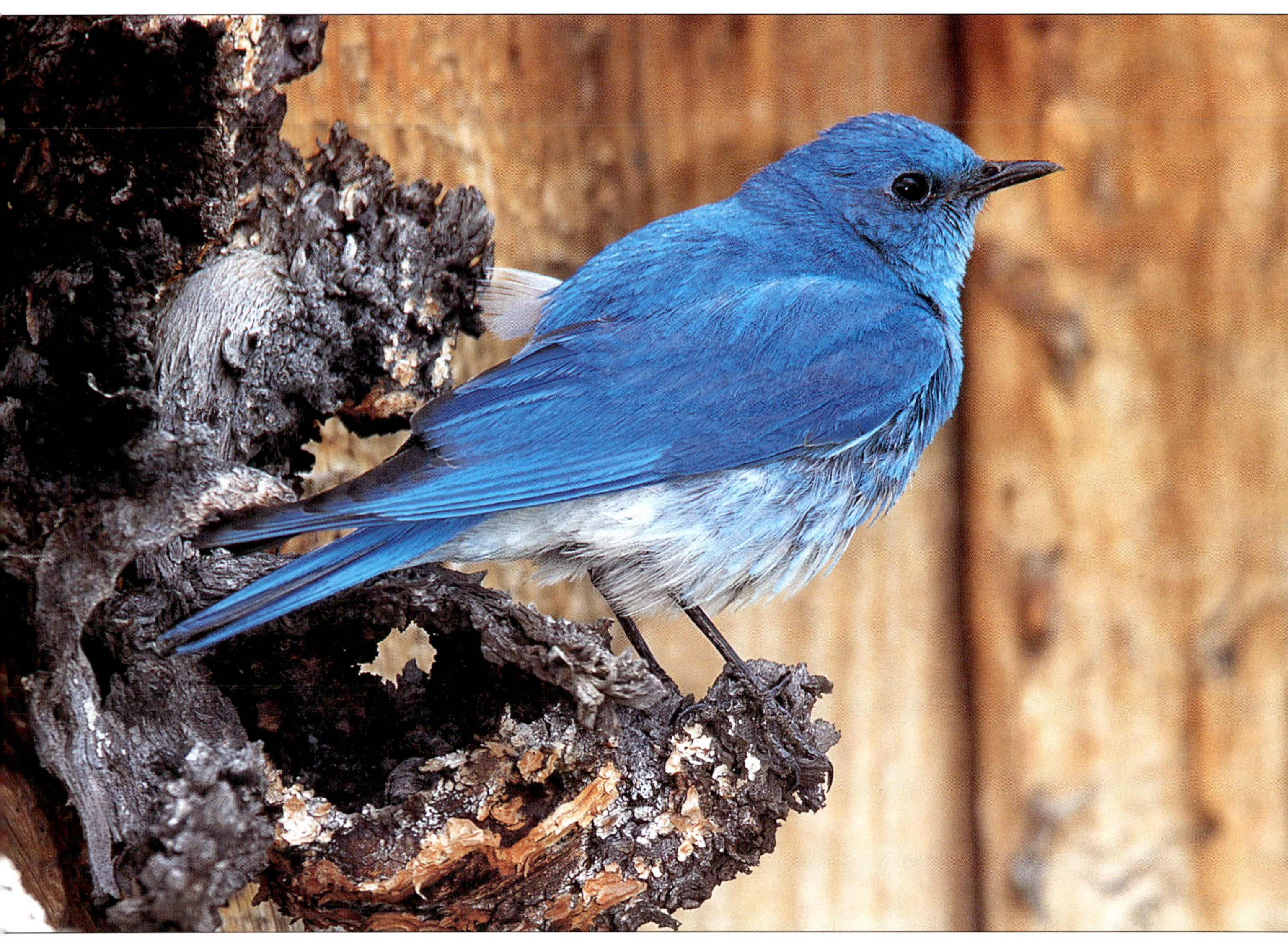

ject. Think about it for a moment. Individual features are usually quite small—even on large animals. The head of a grizzly bear is only about the size of a rabbit. If you want to show only the bear's head, you need to be pretty close.

You will probably need to shoot tight even if the feature you're trying to show is something found over the entire animal. Let's say you're trying to show the color of a mountain bluebird or the scales on a Gaboon viper. The characteristic needs to be seen in extraordinary detail because this is what you're using to attract your viewer's attention. The bluebird should be close to full frame, if not larger, because you're trying to blow your viewers away with the color of the bird. They should almost be overwhelmed by the amount of blue in the image. The bird should stand out well from its background, which means you probably don't want to photograph it against blue sky. Overcast conditions providing bright but low contrast light would be

We wanted to emphasize the mountain bluebird's color with this shot, and to do that with a relatively small subject, we needed to come in close. We also used a little fill flash to make the bird's color pop even more. Jackson County, Colorado. 500mm lens with 2x teleconverter and fill flash.

ideal, and you might want to consider using a little fill flash to bring out even more of the bird's color.

To show the scales clearly on the viper, again you want to come in close. If you show the entire snake, the details in the scales are not going to be visible. Pick a piece of the snake, and fill the frame with that. What piece you choose depends on both what you want to show and what the situation will allow. We picked the viper's head for two reasons. First, we also loved the crystal clarity of the snake's eye. And second, it was behind glass at a zoo, and its head was closest to us.

To show small details, like the scales or eyes of a Gaboon viper, the photographer must shoot very tight. If the entire animal can be seen in the frame, chances are the details you want to show will not be visible. Captive. San Diego Zoo, California. 28–80mm lens with fill flash.

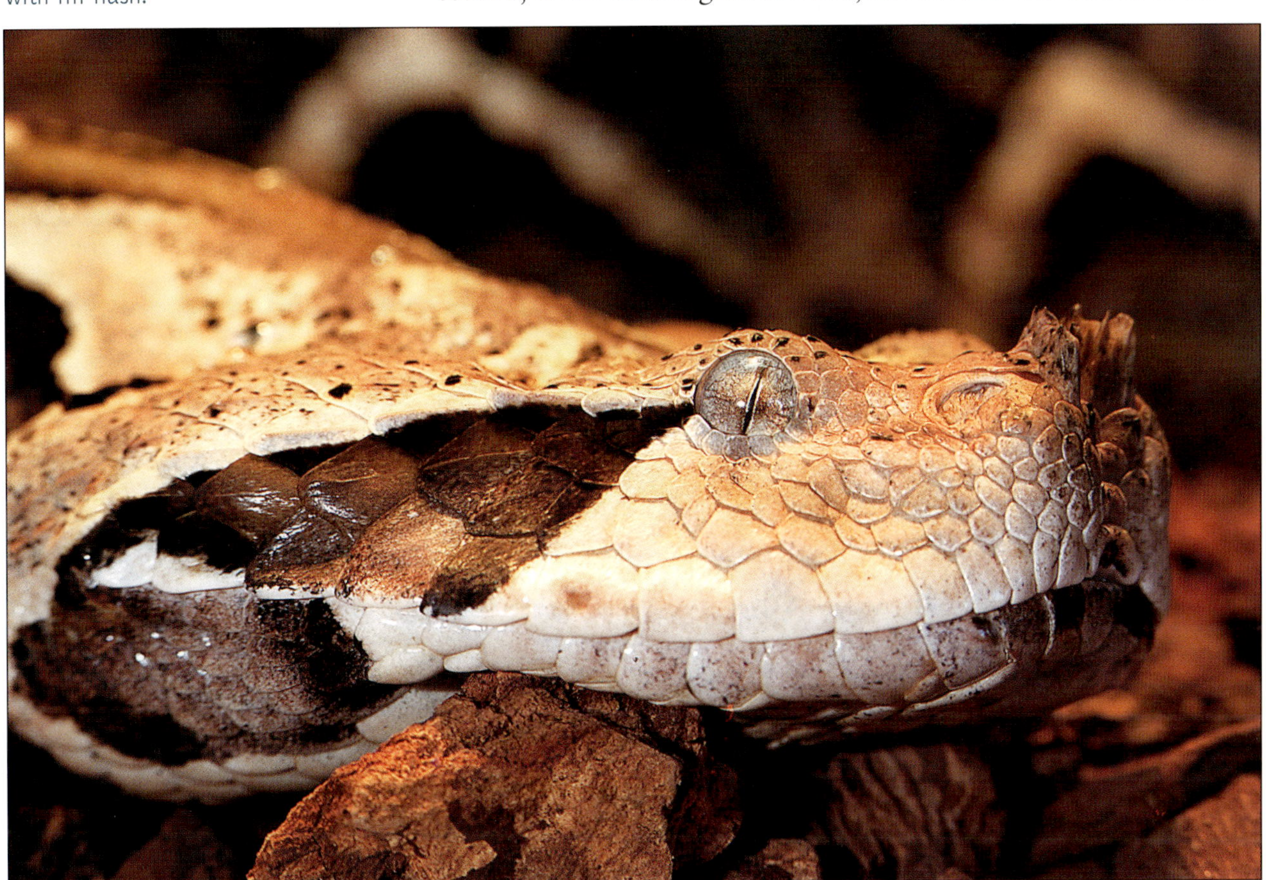

A LITTLE RESEARCH

Just as when attempting to photograph an animal's behavior, research can play a huge role in trying to photograph an animal's features. In fact, the feature you're interested in may only be visible during a behavior, such as a lizard sticking out its tongue. And if Cathy and I had done any research on monitor lizards before trying to photograph one, we would have known to watch for the tongue. Many creatures have interesting features that are not easily visible or are only visible for part of the animal's life cycle. A large number of bird species change their appearance just for breeding. The knobs on a white pelican's bill only appear during the breeding season. The beautiful plumes egrets are famous for, and that almost caused their extinction, are also seen only at this time of year.

A little research can actually alert you to traits you may not have even known about, traits that you may want to photograph once you do know about them. Again, lizard tongues would be a good example. Another would be a bison's black tongue, or the pit that a pit viper uses to detect infrared radiation, or the notch in a falcon's beak that it uses to break its prey's neck. The list is endless.

SURE, ANYTHING WOULD LOOK GOOD THERE

As you can see, in most instances you're going to be relatively close to your subject, trying to highlight something not easily seen. There will be times, however, when you want to employ just the opposite strategy. One of the most interesting things about a subject can be its relationship to its environment, and to show this we often need to back up and/or switch to a wider lens. Perhaps there's a marmot at the base of Mountain of the Holy Cross. One of the most visually exciting things about this creature is the view it has out its front door, and you want to capture that feeling.

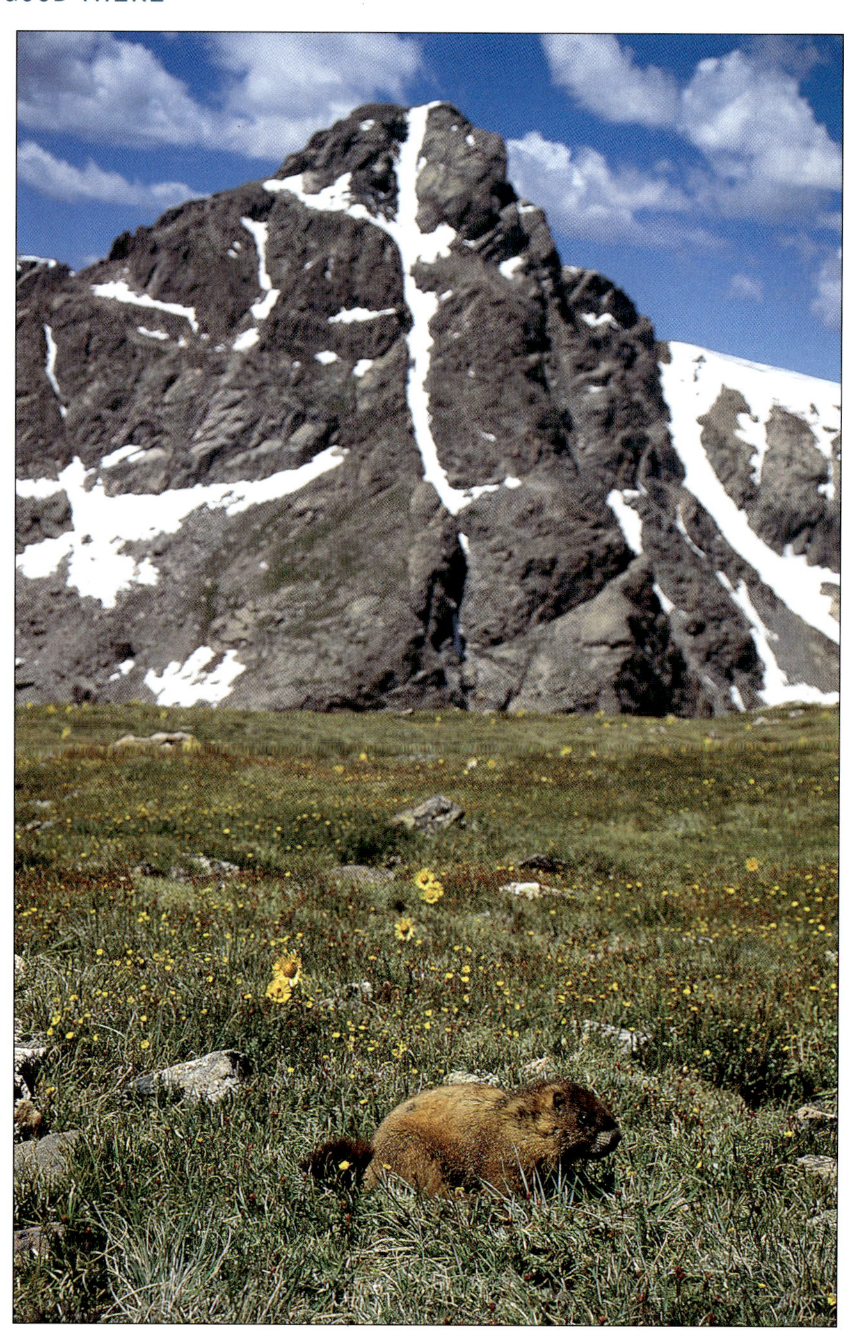

Mountain of the Holy Cross would probably be the most visually exciting thing about an image of any animal in this environment. Because of that we wanted to include the peak in this photo of a yellow-bellied marmot. For the shot to work, both the marmot and the peak must be easily visible, and competing elements should be eliminated. Holy Cross Wilderness, Colorado. 28–80mm lens.

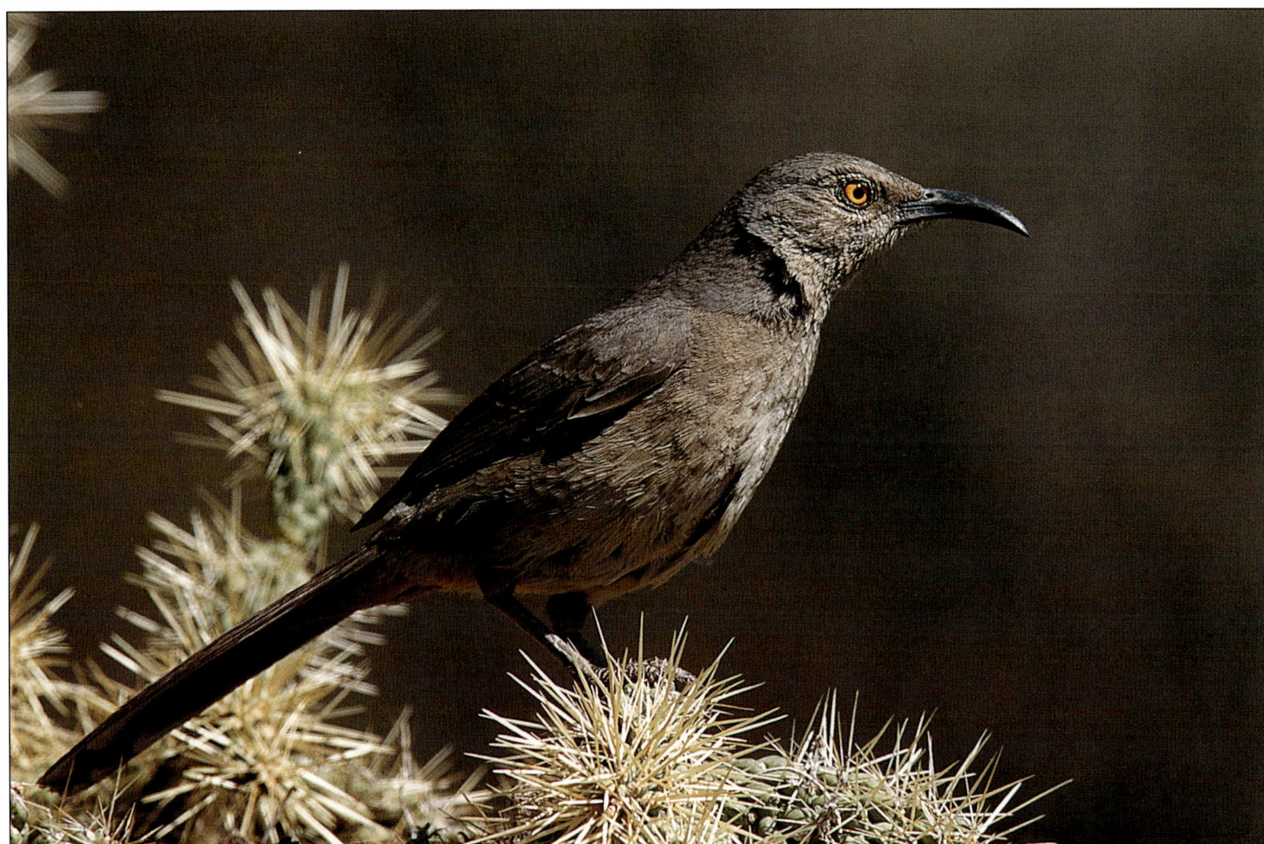

This photo of a curve-billed thrasher has a couple of things going for it. It's a simple shot with relatively few elements. It's tight enough to see details in the bird, including the color of its eyes. And showing the bird's ability to nonchalantly negotiate its way through the cactus spines adds interest. Pima County, Arizona. 500mm lens with 1.4x teleconverter.

In chapter 5 we talked about creating effective images that show the animal's relationship to its habitat, and that's what we're trying to do in this situation. Since our animal subject will be relatively small, it needs to be easily visible, and we want to keep competing elements to a minimum. Ideally, the marmot should stand out from a simple background, and there should be a clear line between the marmot and the cross of snow.

Incorporating only the subject's immediate surroundings into your photo can present similar problems. An animal's relationship to its immediate surroundings, though, is usually easier to include in an effective image than the creature's relationship to its entire habitat. It's easier simply because the image is tighter and there are fewer elements that have to work together. These relationships can be either merely interesting, like a thrasher walking among the thorns on a cholla cactus, or they can be the central theme in some incredibly beautiful wildlife photos.

These are some of our favorite shots. The most interesting thing about many subjects, especially when you're dealing with commonly-photographed animals, are the elements around them. Take a common creature, like a rock squirrel, put it in the middle of some colorful flowers, and the resulting image can be breathtaking.

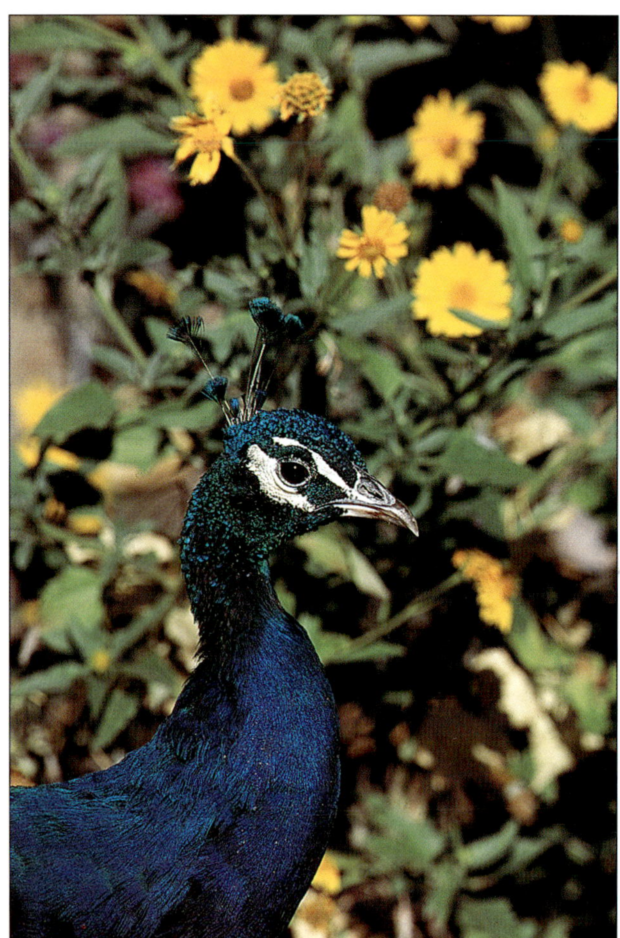

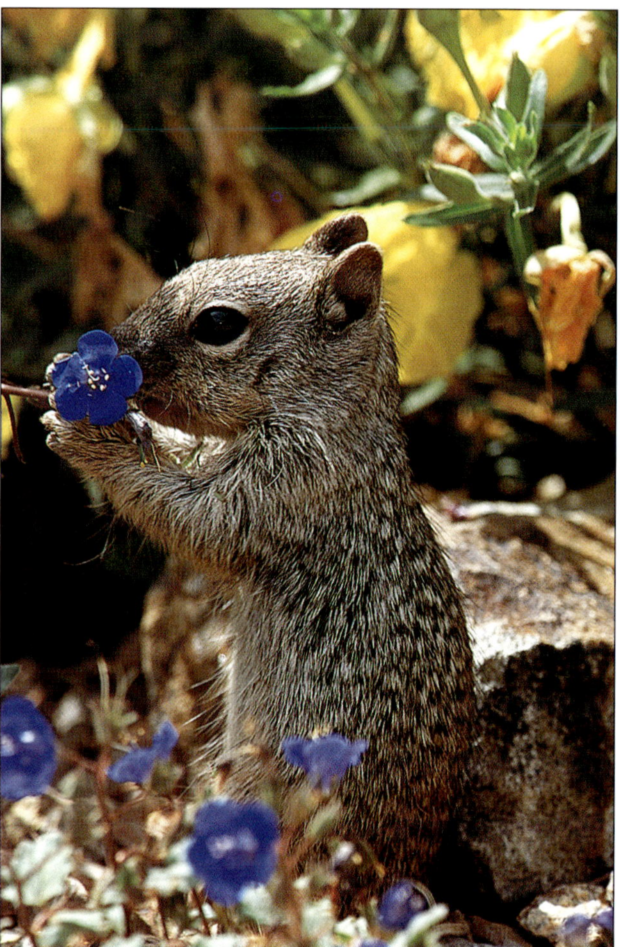

LEFT—Photographing your subject in flowers is a two-edged sword. The flowers can add considerable beauty to the image, but they can also compete with your subject. This is especially true when the flowers are a warm color and your subject is a cool color. This peacock is upstaged by the yellow flowers. Even though the flowers are out of focus, they are bright enough to compete with the subject. In fact, they are probably the first thing the viewer notices when looking at this image. Captive. Denver Zoo, Colorado. 500mm lens. RIGHT—This photo of a rock squirrel eating phacelia blossoms works because the squirrel is large enough to dominate the image, and the yellow evening primrose blossoms are shaded enough to dull their brilliance. Pima County, Arizona. 500mm lens with 2x teleconverter and fill flash.

How many blossoms should you include? Usually this is a rhetorical question because it's often decided for you by the size of your longest lens, how close you can approach the subject, and how many blossoms are available. It's also a bit subjective, and different viewers will react differently to the same image. Too many flowers, or blossoms that are too large or too showy, may compete with your primary subject—especially if the subject is a bit drab. In the rock squirrel image, the squirrel dominates the image despite the beauty of the flowers because the phacelia blossoms are a cool color and the yellow evening primrose blossoms are a bit out of focus as well as being slightly shaded.

AND ISN'T THAT A NICE REFLECTION ON YOU?

In lucky situations, the most striking thing about your subject can be its reflection. It's not often that still water, an uncluttered environment, and a cooperative subject work together for the photographer, and when it happens, the results can be simply poetic. Including a reflection gives your viewers another center of interest to study, and because of the properties of light, it often appears that there is eye contact between your subject and its reflection. This keeps the viewer's attention going back and forth between both centers of interest—your subject and its reflection. Who knows—the viewer may never walk away.

In lucky situations, the most striking thing about your subject can be its reflection.

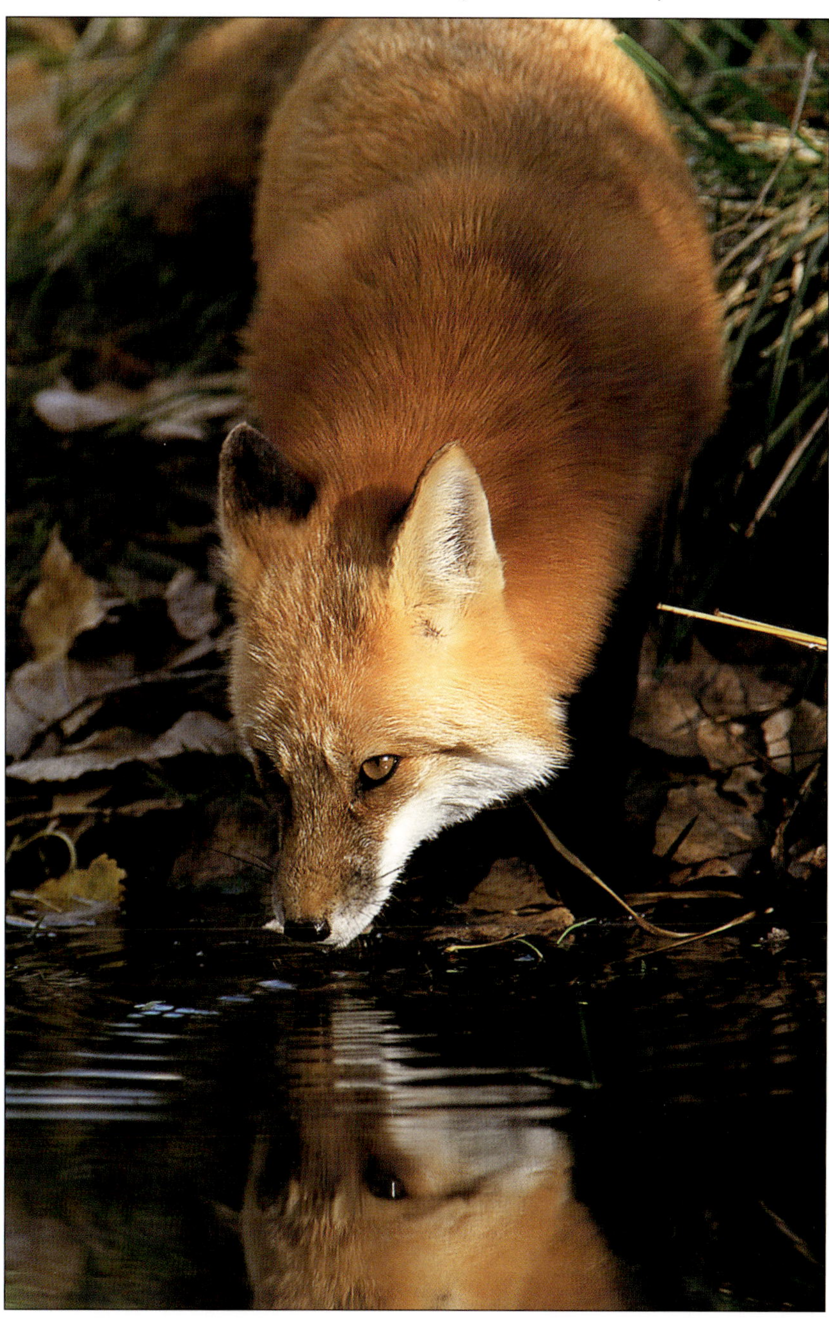

It's relatively easy to photograph red foxes. They are common in many urban areas, giving lots of photographers easy access to them. Photographing one with its reflection, though, is a different story, and it is the reflection that carries this image beyond documentation. Jefferson County, Colorado. 75–300mm lens.

THE TORTOISE AND THE HARE

What if the special attribute you want to emphasize is the subject's speed? Cathy and I were photographing a captive red fox one dismal autumn day, and the animal was continuously moving. The fallen leaves the fox was playing among offered incredible possibilities, but with the light levels what they were, it was almost impossible to get a sharp photo. Since opening the aperture up all the way still didn't give us enough shutter speed to stop the animal's motion, we experimented by doing the opposite.

We closed the aperture down and used a very slow shutter speed, between 1/10 and 1/20 of a second. The fox loved to run after its handler, so we had the handler run back and forth in front of us, and we photographed the running fox using a very slow shutter speed. Not only did we get a few interesting images of a running fox, but the animal's handler got some exercise. When using a slow shutter speed, the subject is not going to be perfectly sharp. As long as the viewers can see enough detail for the subject to be easily recognizable, though, and as long as the subject is sharper than the background, it can make a very strong picture. To me it seems counterintuitive that a slow shutter speed should make the animal look like it's moving faster, but that's

If the background is close to your running or flying subject, like this red fox, panning with the moving animal blurs the background, giving the impression of speed. It works especially well with a colorful background. Captive. Pine County, Minnesota. 75–300mm lens.

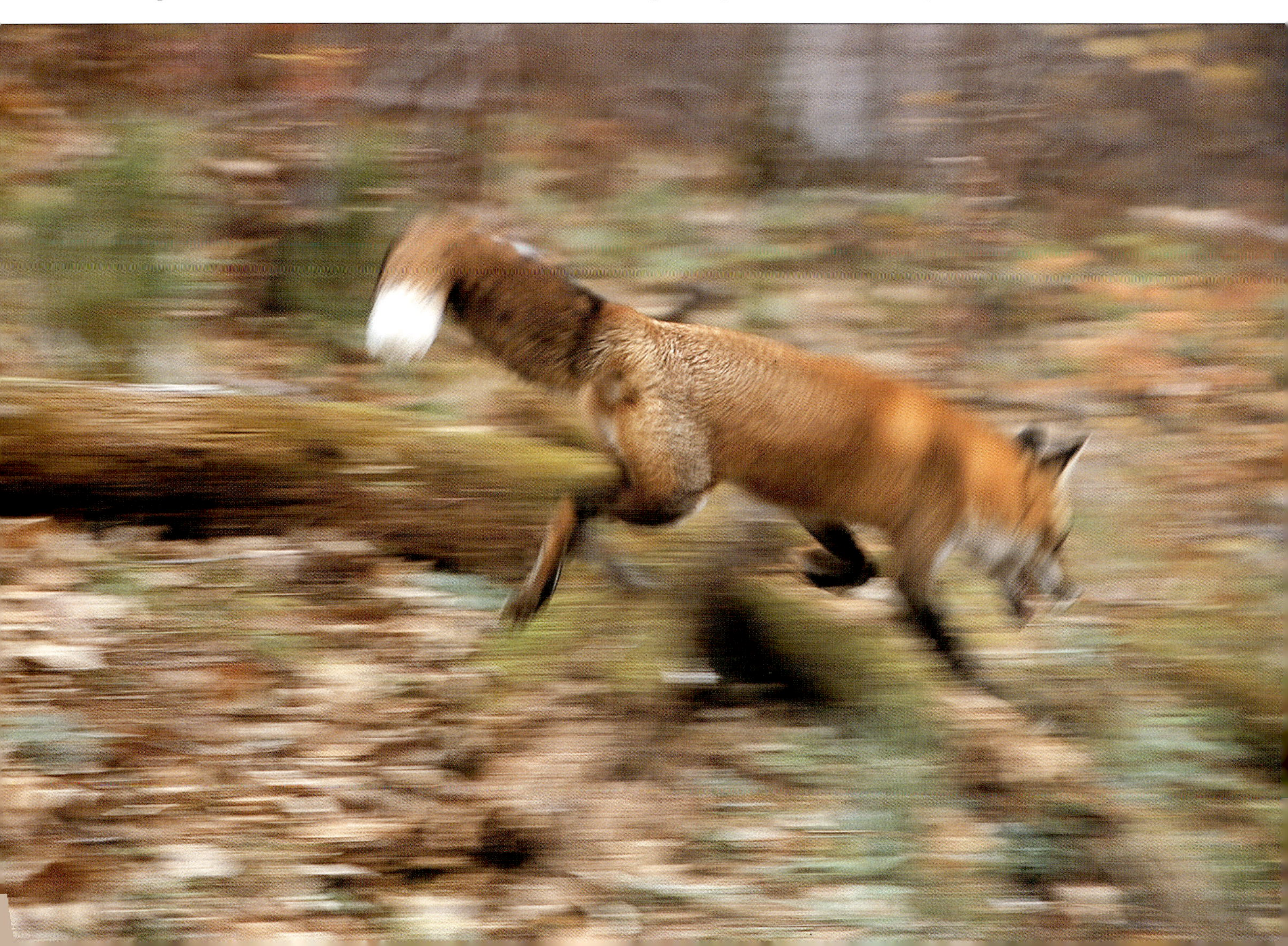

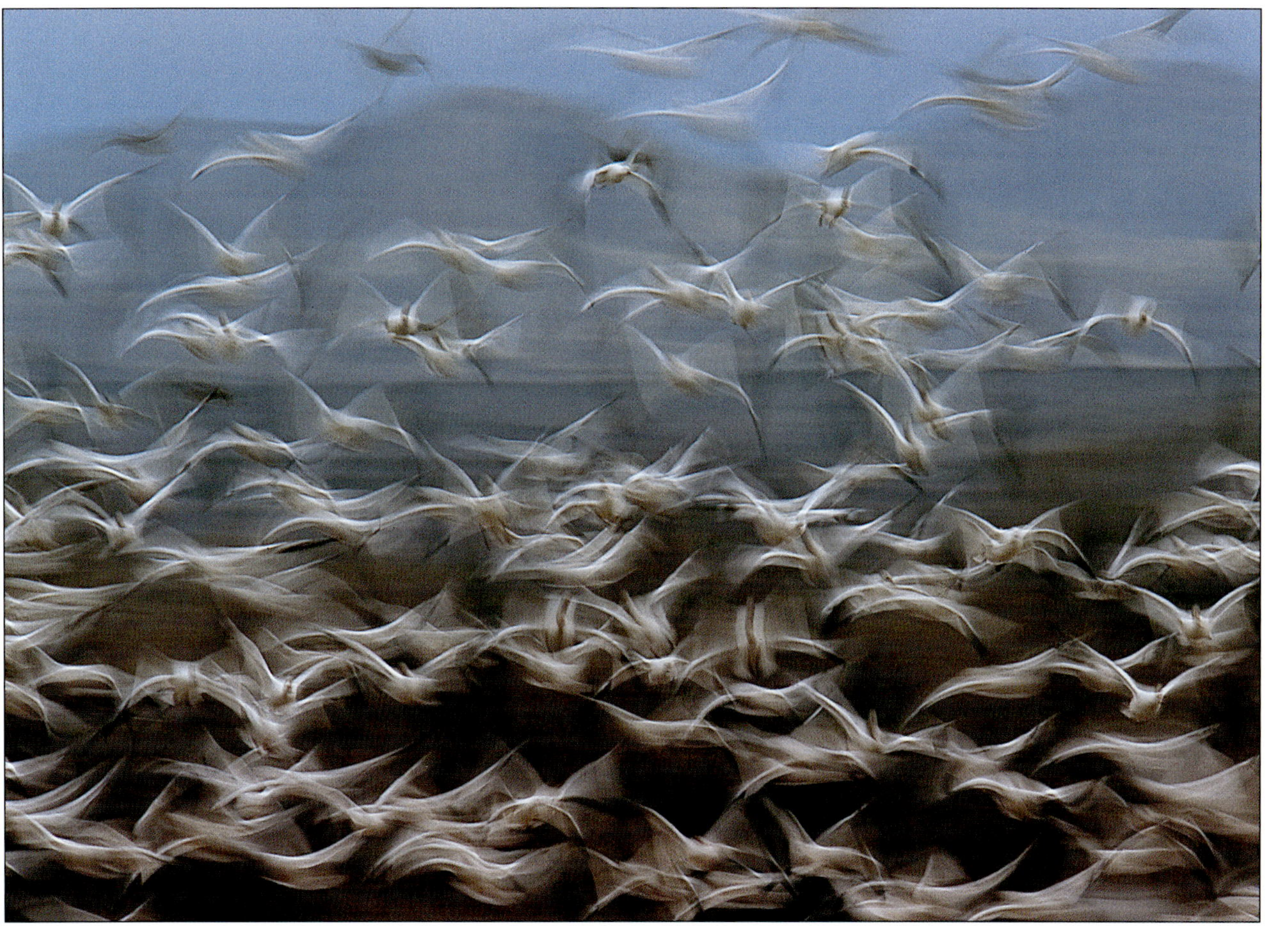

Using slow shutter speeds on a moving subject with a distant background will still give the impression of movement, but it won't necessarily be fast movement. These snow geese almost appear to flying in slow motion in this photo. Bosque del Apache National Wildlife Refuge, New Mexico. 500mm lens.

how it works. That red fox looked like it was flying over a red, yellow, and brown carpet.

Using a slow shutter speed is a great way to emphasize the speed of a fast subject, but it does have its limitations. We tried it with snow geese flying past distant mountains, and it didn't work the way we expected. Some of the images looked very artistic, but they didn't look like the geese were moving particularly fast. In fact, they looked like the geese were floating slowly, just the opposite of what we expected.

For this technique to work, the subject usually needs to be relatively close to its background. If the subject is close to its background (like the fox on the facing page), as you pan with the subject, the background will blur. The more the background blurs, the faster your subject appears to be moving. If the background is in the distance (like when we photographed the snow geese), it will not blur noticeably as you pan with your subject. If the background does not blur as you pan, then your subject appears to be moving, but not very quickly.

Showing how slow your subject moves is quite a challenge. Our method requires a wide angle lens, keeping the animal small in the frame, and showing it traversing an immense landscape. On an island off the coast of Puerto Rico, we photographed a terrestrial hermit crab dragging its shell through the dirt. By putting the track left by its shell in the foreground and having the crab in the middle of the frame, we captured the slow work of trudging over the landscape, carrying your house on your back.

Almost every animal you can think of has some interesting feature, and if you can draw attention to that feature in your photo, your viewer is going to spend a lot more time with your image. These features can be used to take your photos beyond documentation. It can work even if the interesting feature is part of the creature's habitat rather than part of the creature. Even the most common, humdrum species can look enchanting when they interact with the right elements in their environment.

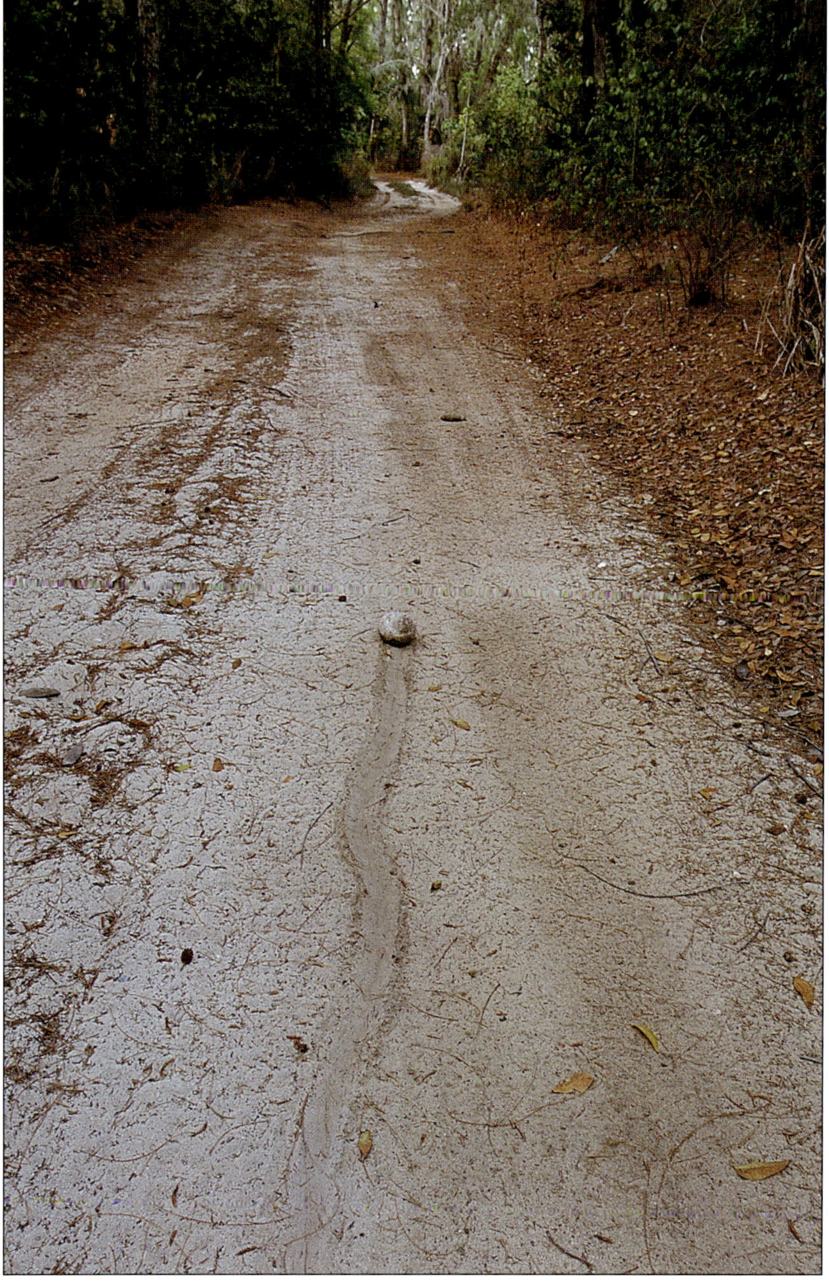

Emphasizing this hermit crab's trail, as well as the difference in size between the animal and the landscape it has to traverse, gives the impression of snail or crab speed and how long it takes to go anywhere. Mona Island, Puerto Rico. 28–80mm lens.

9. Celebrate the Seasons

Art or not, the most important criterion for good photography is whether people have an interest in viewing it.

—George Lepp

It wasn't the photo we had come to Rocky Mountain National Park to take. In fact, if we had known the weather was going to turn this nasty, we might have stayed home. It was late November, and most photographers, including us, visit the park at this time of year in pursuit of big game animals, specifically elk, mule deer, and bighorn sheep.

We went hoping to photograph these large mammals in calm, sunny weather, not because this weather makes for better pictures, but because it makes for more comfortable photographers. And the trip was looking like it would be a dud. Not only did we see hardly any of the

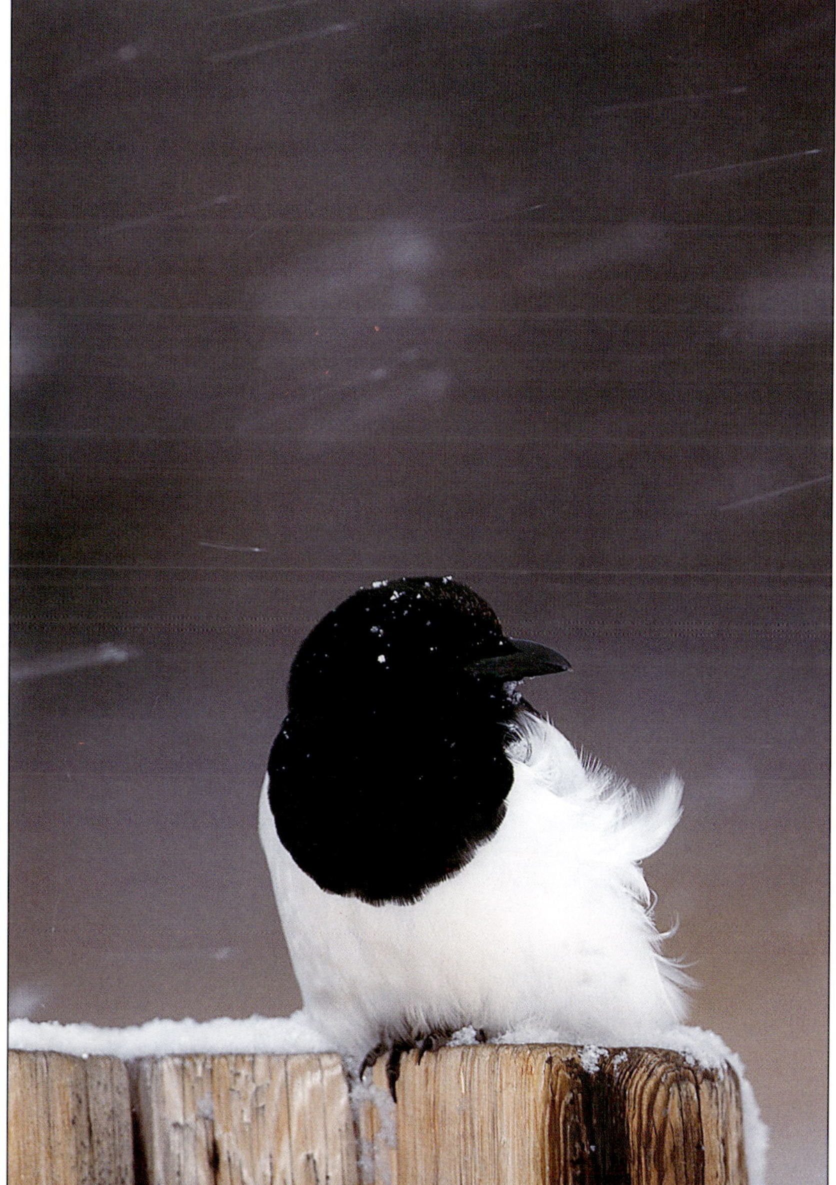

The blowing snow in this photo changes the central theme from just a black-billed magpie to the magpie's relationship with a harsh environment—a potentially much more interesting theme. Rocky Mountain National Park, Colorado. 500mm lens with 1.4x teleconverter and fill flash.

animals we were looking for, but the temperature dropped, it started snowing hard, and the wind picked up to gale force. Any lens pointed toward the northwest was almost instantly coated with snow.

A lone black-billed magpie perched on a stump in a parking lot seemed to be the only creature hardy enough or stupid enough (with the exception of two wildlife photographers) to brave the storm. We stopped to photograph it because there were no other animals around, and we knew there were film suppliers and processors back home who were depending on us for economic support. Also, we could photograph the bird from the relative comfort of the car, and we were beginning to see possibilities in the blowing snow.

Don't get me wrong: Magpies are neat birds, and very handsome in their black and white plumage. At that point in our photographic careers, though, we were enamored with large mammals, and we already had photos of magpies. However, we had never photographed one in a snowstorm before, and changing the weather totally changed the story in the photo. Without the snowstorm, we would have had a nice portrait of a magpie, a relatively easy photo to obtain. Because of the snowstorm, though, the subject of the photo was not an animal, but a concept—survival in a harsh environment.

Changing the weather totally changed the story in the photo.

Granted, you are making the viewers work harder when you force them to come up with a concept when they look at your pictures, but there is nothing wrong with that. Don't be afraid to make the viewer think a bit. Remember, the human brain actually enjoys working, far more than most of the owners believe. If you can give them a bit of a puzzle, even an easy puzzle with only two pieces, like a magpie and blowing snow, they will enjoy your image a great deal more.

WHAT'S THE WEATHER LIKE?

Even though most of us are relatively insulated from the worst the weather has to offer, we are still very interested in it. Look at the popularity of the Weather Channel. In spite of the way we try to hide from it, our lives still revolve around the weather. And the way wild creatures deal with it is fascinating to us.

If the weather turns the least little bit wet or cool, we hide inside. How do our wild subjects handle the cold, the heat, blizzards, floods, and droughts? If you can capture elements that indicate what season it is or what the weather is like in your wildlife photography, it will give your viewers more information to process. Make the viewers spend a little more time with your image by forcing them to analyze the relationships between two or more elements.

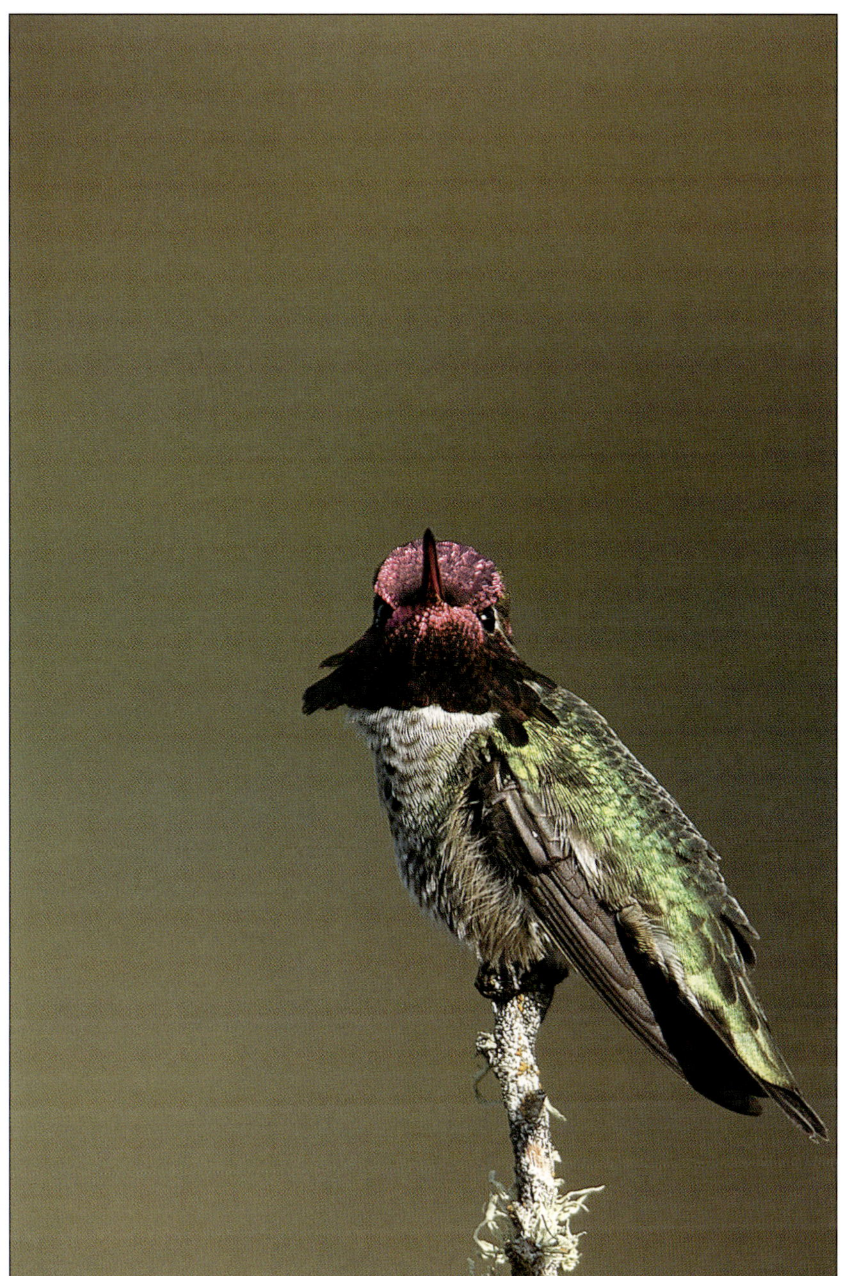

The inclusion of some species, like this male Anna's hummingbird flashing his iridescent feathers at trespassing males, can easily show the viewer what the climate is like regardless of what other elements are included in the image. San Luis Obispo County, California. 500mm lens with 2x teleconverter.

Some subjects are so representative of a particular climate that an image of the subject all by itself is enough to give viewers a good idea of the weather and the season. A tight shot of an emperor penguin is enough to know that it's cold outside. An Anna's hummingbird perched on a leafless twig still shows that the temperature is relatively mild and that flowers are in bloom.

With most animals you need to provide a few more clues to let the viewer know what's happening weather-wise around the subject. Flowers are always a good choice to indicate spring and summer in temperate climates. No one questions the season if a few autumn leaves can be seen around your subject. We are not suggesting that these shots are easy to get. In fact, just the opposite is true. Most creatures have an aversion to attractive flowers or colorful leaves, and capturing any kind of relationship between your subject and these elements is difficult at best. That's why images that do portray these relationships so often go beyond documentation.

It doesn't matter what season it was when you photographed your subject. What is important is that the image conveys an impression of a season, even the wrong season, to the viewers. Unless you're trying to show something of scientific interest, where seasonal accuracy is necessary, the important thing is just making the viewers recognize the relationship between the picture's elements. Many times that's all it takes to make them happy. If there's snow in the picture, they will

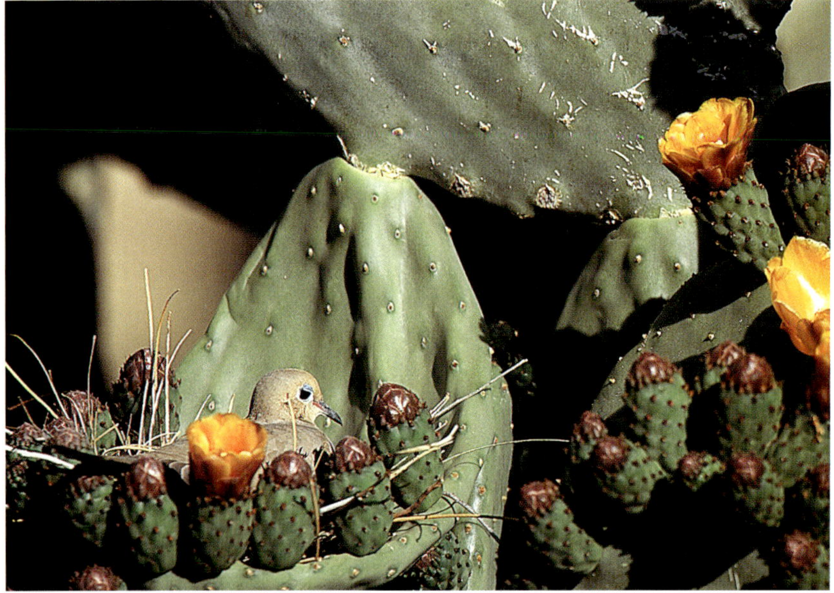

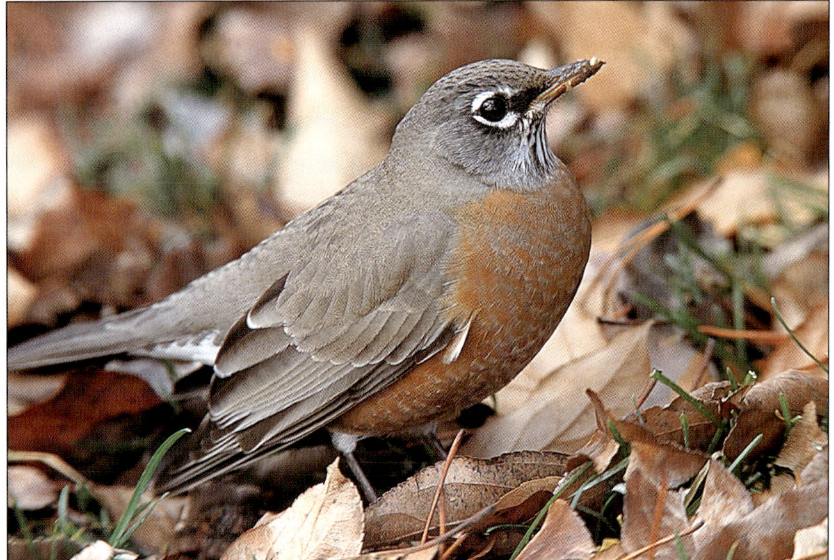

TOP—It's relatively easy to find and photograph nesting mourning doves, but finding one nesting in the middle of a bouquet of cactus blossoms is rather unusual. So even though the blossoms are almost bright enough to draw attention away from the dove, the image and its central theme are unusual enough to take this photo beyond documentation. Pima County, Arizona. 500mm lens with 2x teleconverter. BOTTOM—Without the fallen autumn leaves, this photo of an American robin would be nothing special. Including a seasonal element, though, is often all it takes to make a strong image out of a mediocre one. Jefferson County, Colorado. 500mm lens with 1.4x teleconverter.

deduce that it's winter. It doesn't matter that snow is relatively common in many locations while flowers are blooming. To make the viewer think even a bit more, try taking a species that represents one season and combine it with weather from another season. Examples that come to mind are bluebirds or robins—species that represent springtime—in a snowy environment.

HOW COLD WAS IT?

When the weather turns a bit inclement, try not to whine about having to protect your gear and the lack of light. This is your chance to make some ordinary species look extraordinary. Cathy and I look forward to snowy days just for the chance to make the local foxes and waterfowl look a little special. A common locale, like a nearby zoo, can turn into a wintry wilderness full of creatures new and wonderful when you sprinkle a little snow on it. Not only does the snow add an interesting element to your photos, it can help hide man-made objects, like fake rocks and culverts. Keep in mind that if you want falling snow to show up well in your image, you need a dark background behind it.

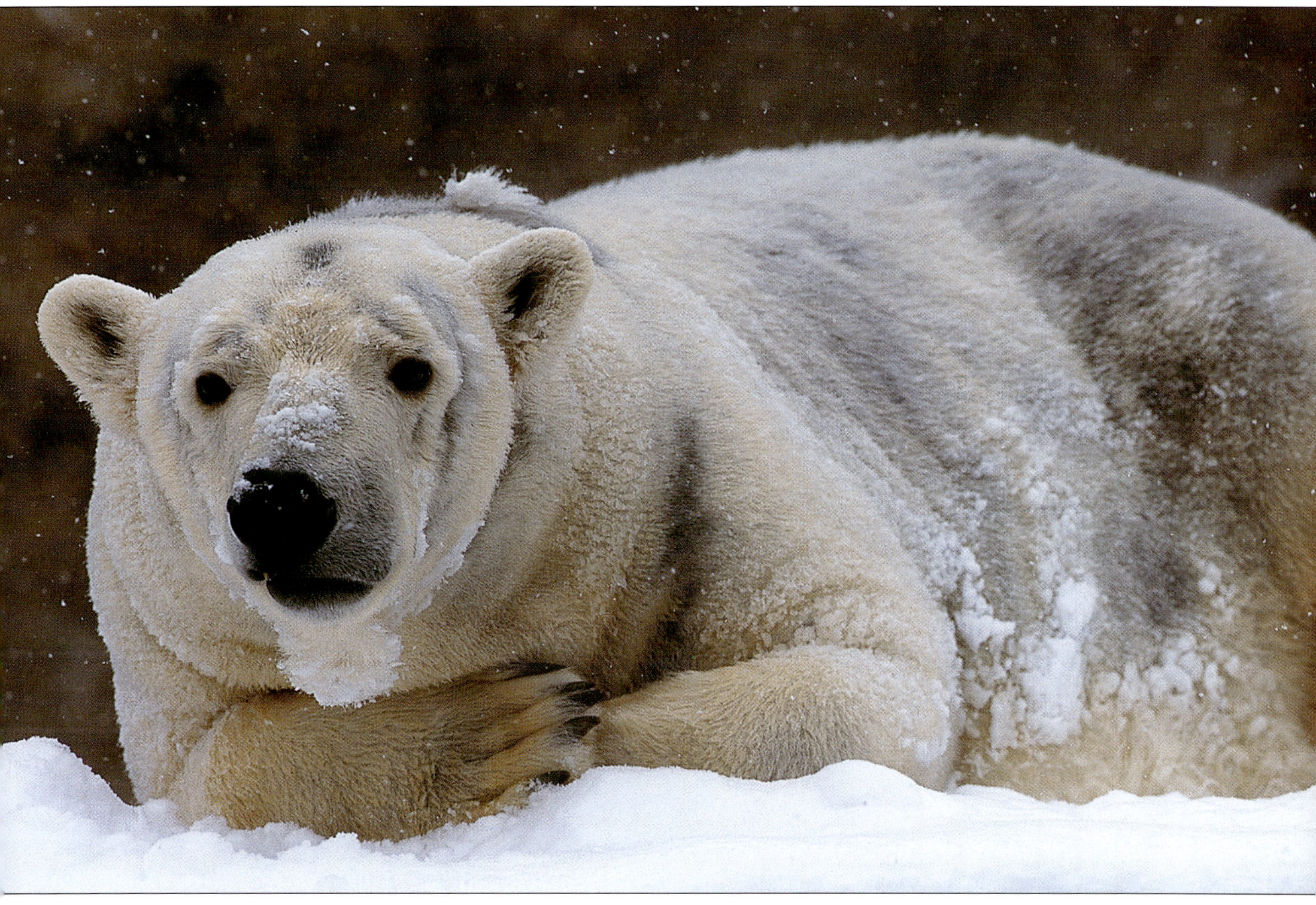

A little snow can add some magic to almost any wildlife experience. Even zoo animals, like this polar bear, can look special in a snowstorm. Highlighting the snow against a darker background helps it show up. Captive. Denver Zoo, Colorado. 500mm lens with 2x teleconverter.

Every so often, Denver experiences a good cold snap, making it easier to capture animals in circumstances that are at least a little unusual. During these times, the waterfowl all congregate in the few areas of open water. And when it's this cold, it's possible to photograph hooded mergansers swimming in what appears to be a frozen margarita. Your viewers almost can't help but imagine themselves in the animal's position when you present them an image like this. Because of your photos, people can experience the harshness of extreme weather from the climate-controlled comfort of their own homes. Whether or not this is a service to mankind is debatable, but it certainly helps take your images beyond documentary.

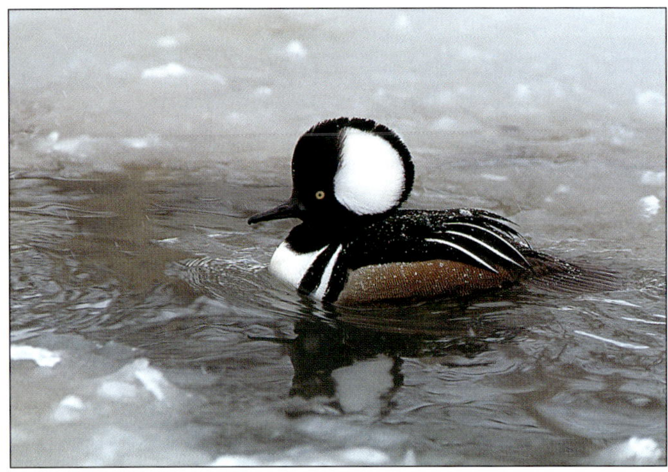

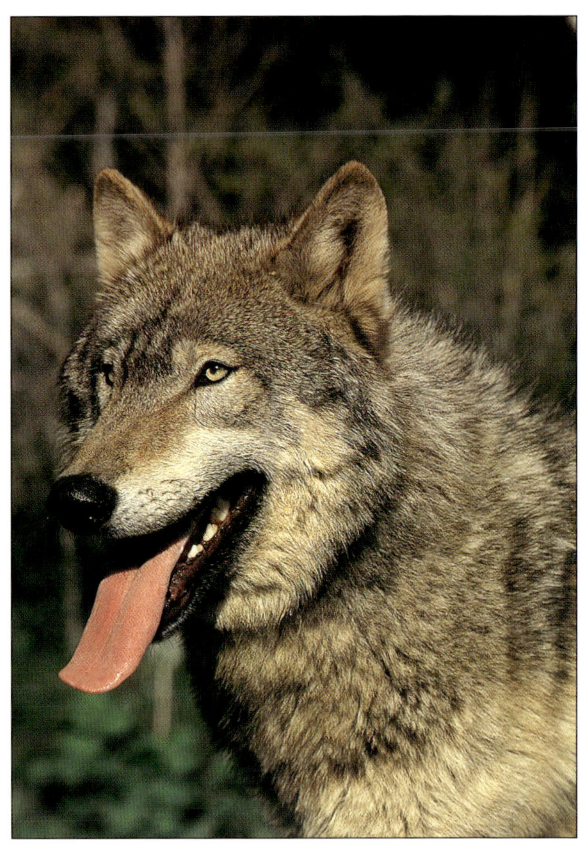

ABOVE—Make your viewers marvel at your subject's ability to handle the elements. I'm still baffled by a hooded merganser's ability to swim through icy slush without appearing to be cold. Captive. Denver Zoo, Colorado. 300mm lens with 1.4x teleconverter. RIGHT—Panting animals don't necessarily show that it's hot outside. This gray wolf was hot enough to pant on a mild day. Captive. Bridger Mountains, Colorado. 500mm lens.

It is easier to use cold or snow as a way to go beyond documentation than it is to use heat. That's because it's easier to show how cold it is in a photo than how hot it is. To portray *hot,* the common method is to show an arid landscape, maybe with a big, high sun, its rays spreading across the sky. Finding a wild animal to include in such a scene is usually difficult to say the least. And how do you show *hot* in an overgrown, tropical environment? I suppose you could always show the photographer drowning in his own sweat. However, when you try to incorporate a wilder subject in the image, it becomes a much more difficult situation. A panting animal can show that it's hot, but many animals begin panting when it's still relatively cool outside.

Part of the reason for this is most warm-blooded species can tolerate cold much easier than they can heat. And cold-blooded animals are deep in the shade when the temperature gets to be excessive. The animals that live in extremely hot locations tend to be nocturnal, or they have developed other strategies for dealing with the high temperature, strategies that usually make them hard to photograph. You only see these creatures in the relatively cool hours early or late in the day. Because it is so hard to capture the relationship between an animal and a hot environment, Cathy and I concentrate on showing winter's effects on the species we photograph.

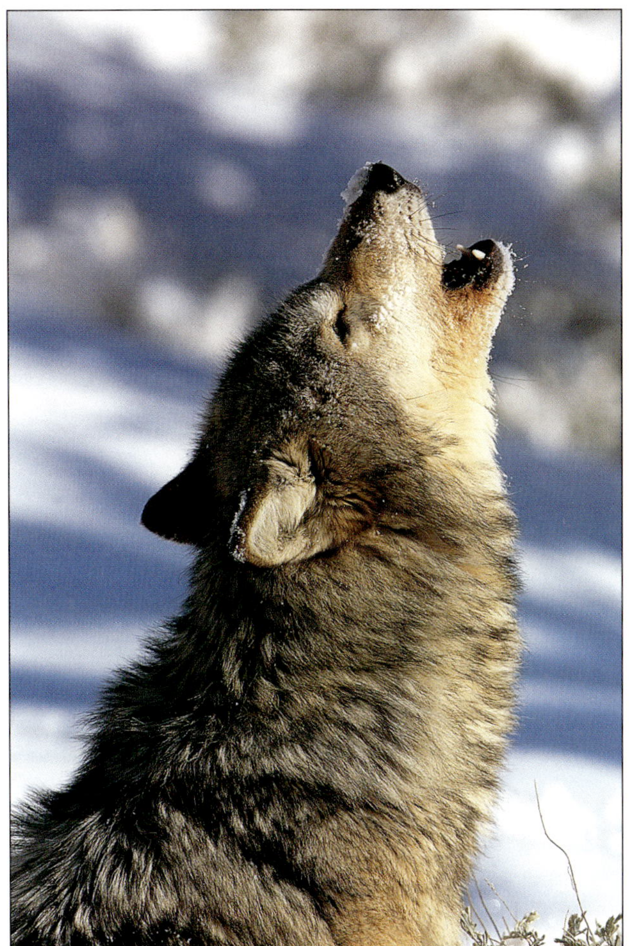

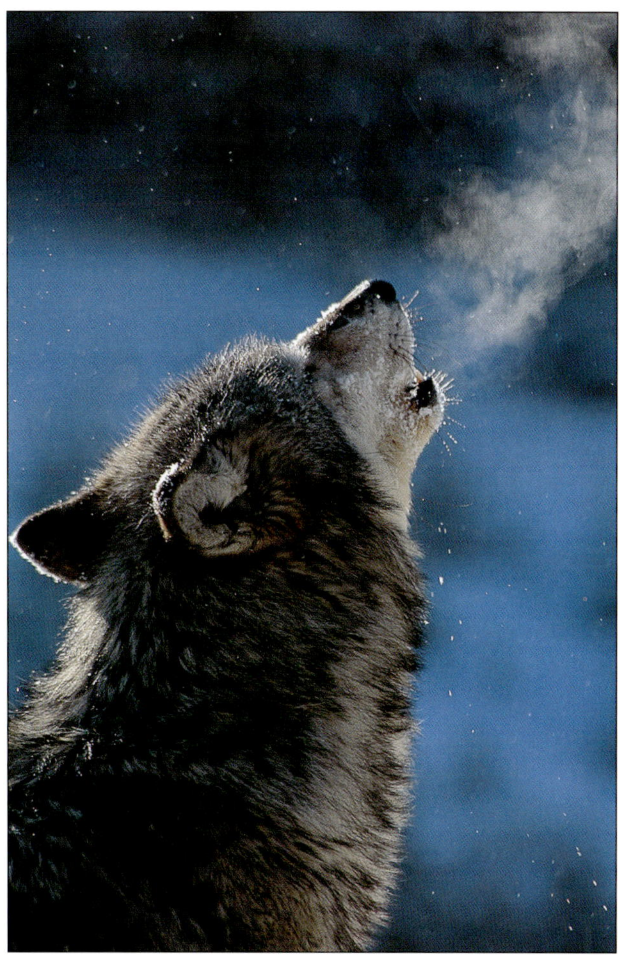

LEFT—This is a nice enough photo of a howling gray wolf, but there's nothing special about it. In spite of the behavior and the fresh snow, it's pretty much a documentary image if only because we've seen similar photos many times before. Captive. Bridger Mountains, Montana. 500mm lens. RIGHT—This photo, taken at the same time as the previous one, has several things going for it that the other one did not. It's tight enough to eliminate distracting elements, and back lighting gives the animal a nice rim light and highlights the rising steam. Captive. Bridger Mountains, Montana. 75–300mm lens.

SMOKIN'

What better way to add life to a static image than to show your subject's breath? As we mentioned in chapter 3, it adds another dimension to your picture, and it can only be done in cold weather. The trick to highlighting the steam the animal exhales is to photograph the subject with either back light or side light, and, just like with falling snow, a dark background is necessary behind the subject's head to make its breath stand out.

It was early March, and we were photographing captive wolves in Montana. The temperature stood at 0 degrees Fahrenheit, and we were trying to get in one more session before the sun disappeared behind the ridge to the west. The low, slanting rays of the sun gave everything a warm glow. The wolf we were imaging began to howl, and we were able to photograph it from two directions at the same time, one with front light and one with back light.

The traditional front-lit animal, the photos I took, looked fine. It was a good tight shot of a wolf howling, but it was a shot we've all seen before. And even though there was snow in the photo, it didn't look particularly cold. The late afternoon light even made it look quite comfortable. The shots Cathy took, the back-lit wolf, showed not only the steam rising as the creature howled, but tiny flecks of ice falling from the sky as the steam from the wolf's breath condensed and froze. You can almost see the wolf breathing and hear the music of its howl when you look at this photo. And because we can see the wolf's breath, it looks cold.

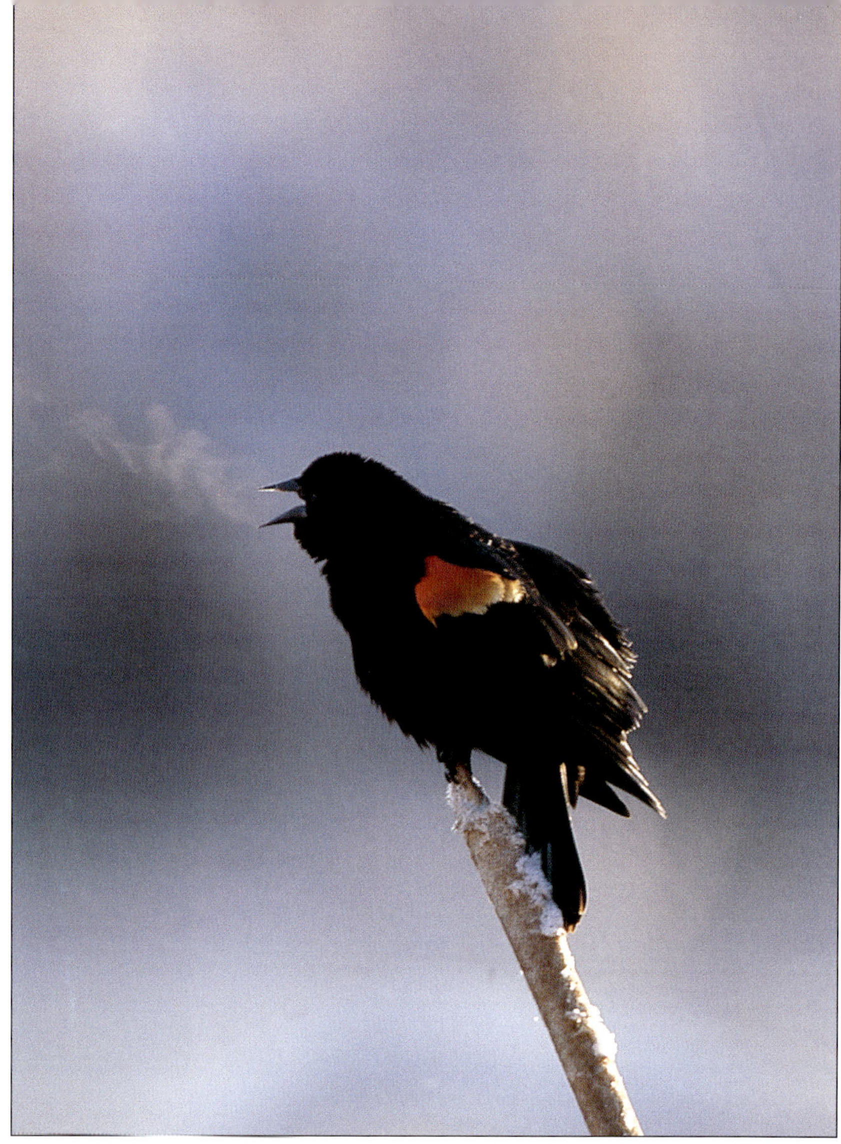

You don't need a large animal in order to capture the steam as it breathes. On cold mornings, even a red-winged blackbird's breath is visible as it sings. Jefferson County, Colorado. 500mm lens with 2x teleconverter.

This obviously won't work with cold-blooded animals, like reptiles and amphibians, but you don't necessarily need a large mammal either. All you need is a cold day to condense the moisture in your subject's breath and sunshine to illuminate it. The size of your subject and the humidity determines how cold the temperature must be before you can see condensing steam when your subject breathes. The larger the animal and the more humidity there is, the higher the temperature can be at which the animal's breath is visible. We've seen male elephant seals exhaling steam when the temperature was almost 50 degrees Fahrenheit.

Conversely, the smaller your subject and the drier the air, the colder it needs to be for your subject's breath to condense. Red-winged blackbirds migrate back to Colorado in mid to late March, and it can still get quite cold at that time of year. On cold mornings, you can see little wisps of steam trailing from their beaks as they make their territorial calls. You can almost trace the melody of their calls in those wisps of steam. And the fact that their breath is visible shows the viewers that red-winged blackbirds are busy establishing and defending their territories when it's still pretty darn cold.

JUST SHOOTIN' IN THE RAIN

Snow is much easier to work with than rain, and snow shows up a lot better in a photo. Cathy photographed bears for five days in a constant drizzle in Alaska, and except for the fact that everything looks wet, you can't tell it's raining in any of her photos. It has to be raining hard before it shows up in a photo. One of the few decent wildlife shots we've taken in which rain was actually a picture element was of an alligator. The gator's head is almost invisible floating in a shotgun blast pattern of raindrops, but it shows the reptile's relationship with rain very well. The photo was taken at a zoo, and we were able to get images from the protection of a ramada.

I'm sure that the expression "doesn't know enough to come in out of the rain" was coined by someone observing a wildlife photographer. And it's an expression Cathy and I try to live up to. Don't hesitate to follow your subjects through the seasons. Show your viewers how the creatures handle the vagaries of the weather. A picture element or two that shows the season or the weather and how your subject relates to it may be all you need to take that photo beyond documentation.

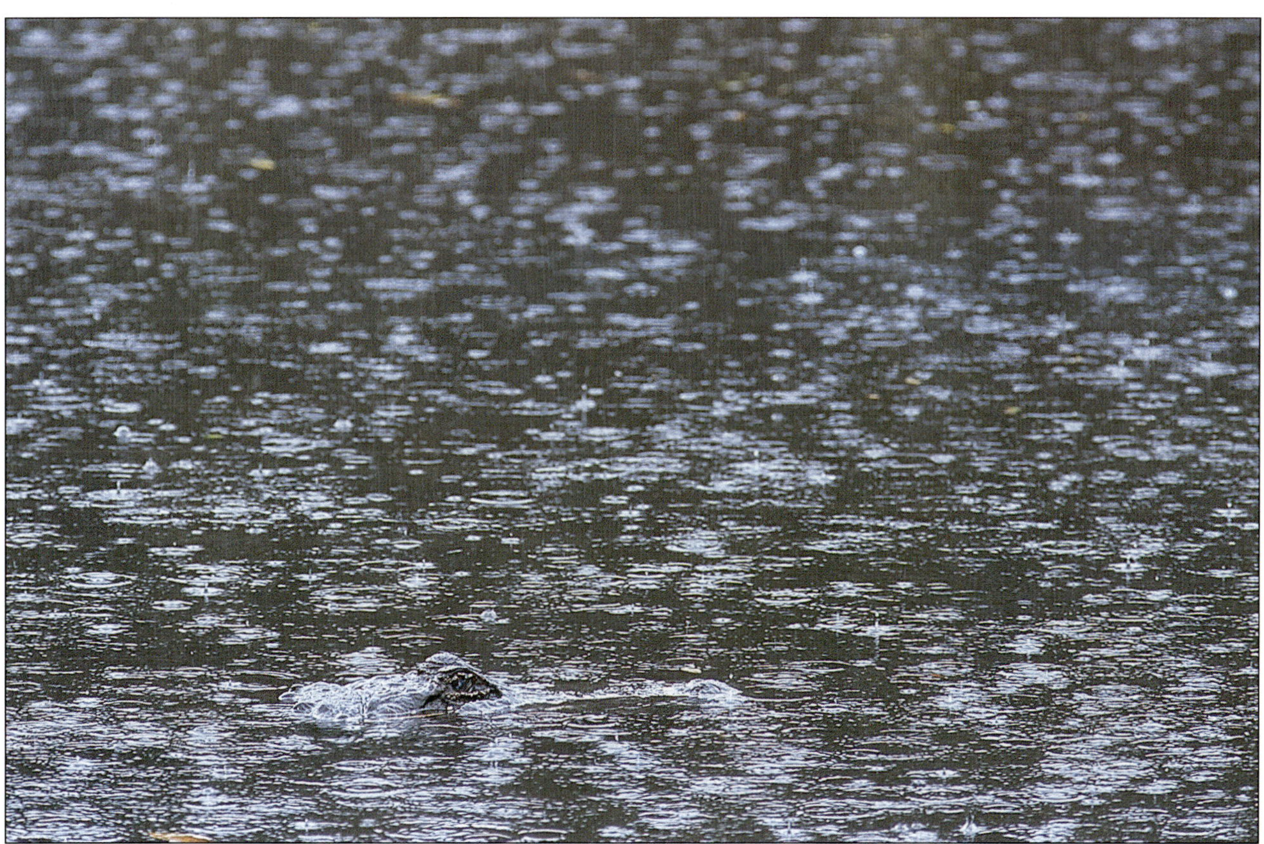

Rain is one of the hardest elements to work with and to portray. This photo of a nearly invisible alligator was taken in a downpour from the safety of a ramada. Captive. Alligator Farm, St. Augustine, Florida. 300mm lens with 1.4x teleconverter.

10. Capturing Your Subject's Moods

Our ability to perceive quality in nature begins, as in art, with the pretty. It expands through successive stages of the beautiful to values as yet uncaptured by language.

—Aldo Leopold

Photographing grizzly bears in the fog is a bit of a dicey proposition. For such large animals, grizzlies are able to disappear remarkably well even under clear conditions. When you can't see one standing in the open until you're within one hundred feet, well that can get the old adrenal glands working overtime. Or it would if the bears had been paying any attention at all to the photographers.

Cathy was in Lake Clark National Park on the west side of Alaska's Cook Inlet, and the bears—how many was impossible to tell in the fog—were intent on the grass they were eating. At rare intervals one of the beasts would lift up its head, and the cameras would begin clicking. When the bears lifted their heads and happened to be looking at the photographers, the resulting images had a feel of menace or impending danger, especially if the bear was taking a step forward. It didn't matter that the bear was only interested in grass, or that the photographers never felt the least bit threatened. To a viewer looking at a photo, a grizzly coming out of the fog and looking directly at you appears to be an aggressive bear.

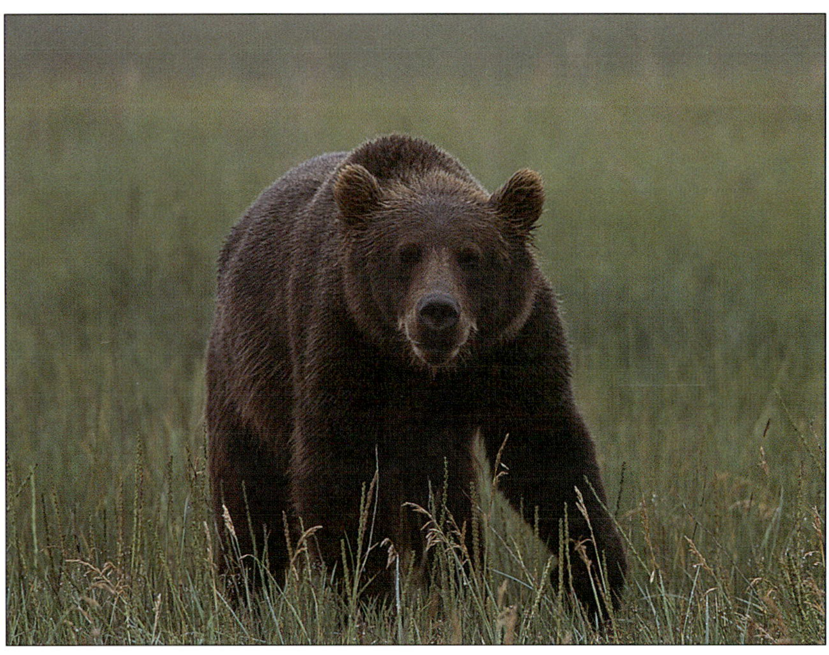

A grizzly bear staring at you, and approaching through the mist, appears to be an aggressive bear, even if the animal couldn't care less about the photographer. Lake Clark National Park, Alaska. 500mm lens.

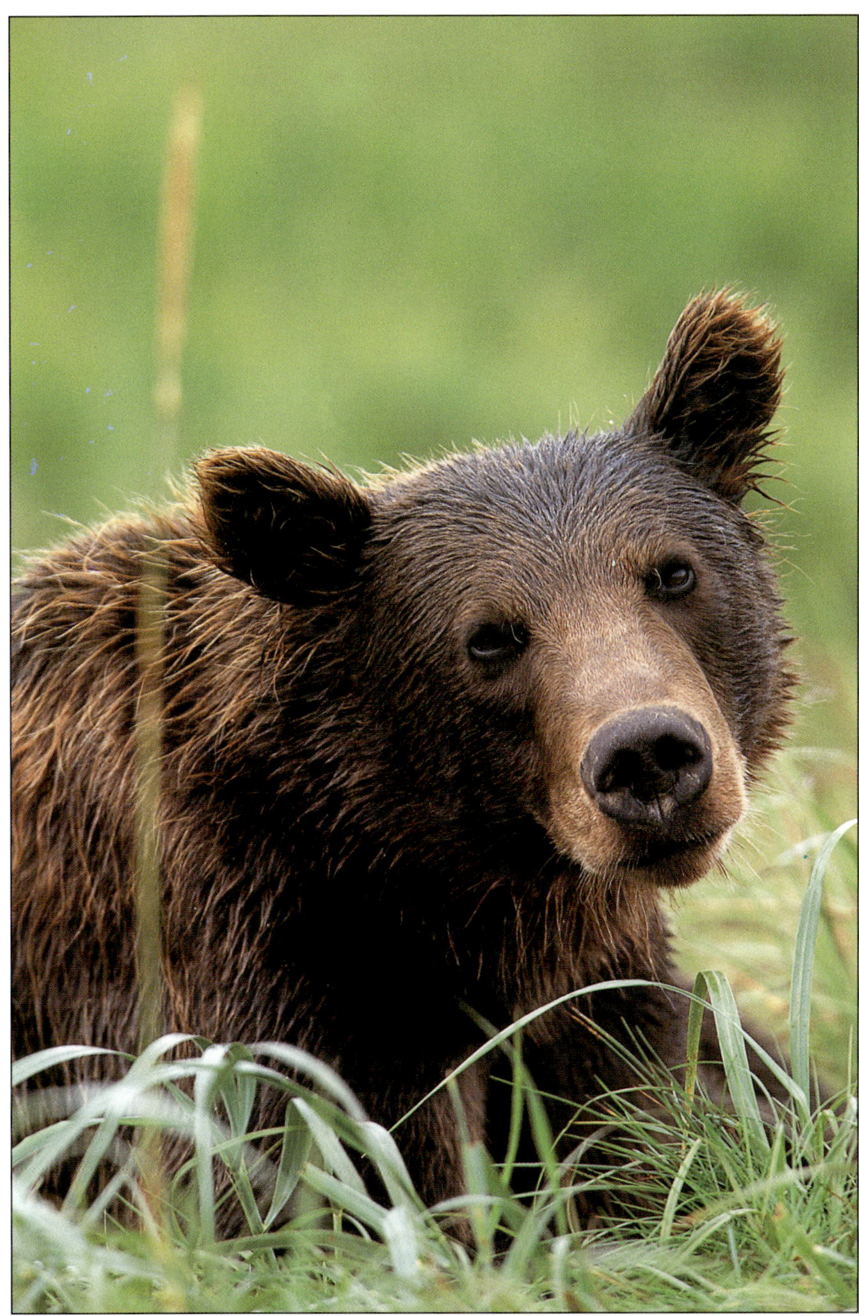

Take the same grizzly seen in the previous image, lay him down, and tilt his head to one side, and he looks like a curious puppy dog. Lake Clark National Park, Alaska. 500mm lens.

Later the fog cleared, and Cathy was able to photograph one of the same bears lounging against a fallen log. The bear looked at her, tilting its head to one side, much like a dog does when it's trying to understand just what in the world you're doing. The bear that had looked so aggressive in the foggy image now looked like you could scratch behind its ears with impunity—just a big, old teddy bear. Did the bear's mood change between one image and the next? Not very likely.

Humans, and nearly every other species of mammal and bird, can instinctively recognize a predator. A predator has its eyes set in the front of its head for binocular vision. A prey species has eyes on the sides of its head so it can watch for predators as it eats. Early in our evolutionary development, we learned that when a predator is looking directly at you, there is considerable cause for alarm. Having a grizzly bear looking at you and taking a step in your direction qualifies as a potentially dangerous situation. If the bear tilts its head, its gaze is no longer so intent, and the bear appears to be merely curious or playful rather than planning another course on its menu.

HOW DOES YOUR SUBJECT FEEL?

Capturing your subject's emotions or moods is an excellent way to go beyond documentation with your photography. Trying to photograph these feelings is often similar to photographing behavior. Many times it's necessary to either capture the subject engaged in some activity, or capture an interaction between the subject and other animals, if your

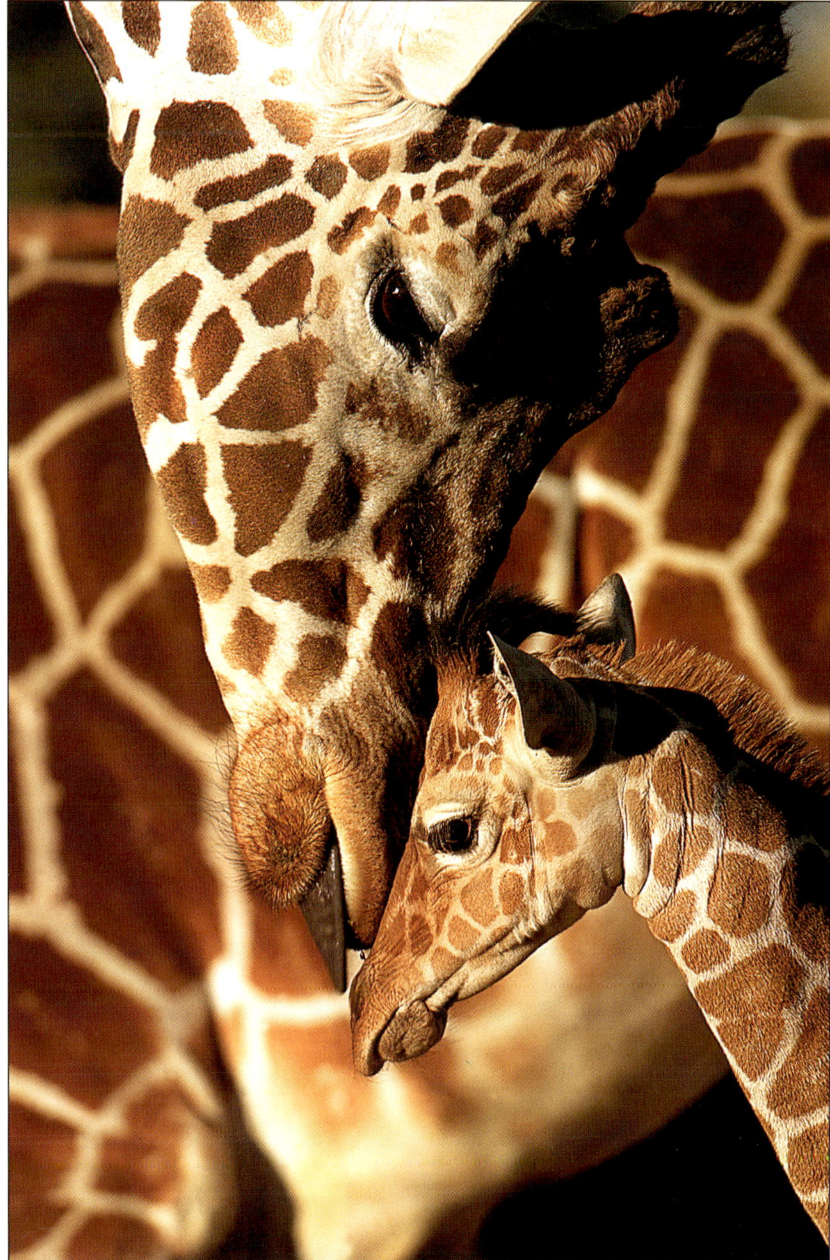

In this photo of a mother reticulated giraffe touching noses and licking its baby, the viewers will almost certainly see the scene as a depiction of motherly love. And it's not important if they are correct in their assumption. Just being able to attach a human emotion to a scene adds interest for your viewers. Captive. Denver Zoo, Colorado. 500mm lens.

image is to portray some emotion. And it doesn't matter if the feelings that seem apparent in your photos are the ones the animal actually experienced. All that matters is that the viewer reads them into the image.

The difficulty in capturing an animal's actual emotions varies considerably with the species. With some animals it's quite easy to show how they're feeling. Just try to take a wolf's food when it's eating. There's no question of how the animal feels in this situation. No ambiguity at all in what the animal is threatening to do to you. Animals with facial muscles—dogs, cats, and any species capable of snarling—are at least easy to read when they're warning or threatening.

When you're photographing animals without facial muscles, it can be very difficult to tell how they feel. Bottlenose dolphins have a perpetual grin. These animals could be terribly upset and they would still look happy as can be. Flamingos, on the other hand, always look unhappy because their beaks are curved in a permanent frown. Even if birds had facial muscles, they would find it hard to move their rigid beaks. Amphibians and reptiles also never change their expressions, and the mood you capture again has more to do with the set of their mouths than with the way they actually feel. Crocodiles are always grinning in a cheerful way. Horned lizards appear stern and humorless.

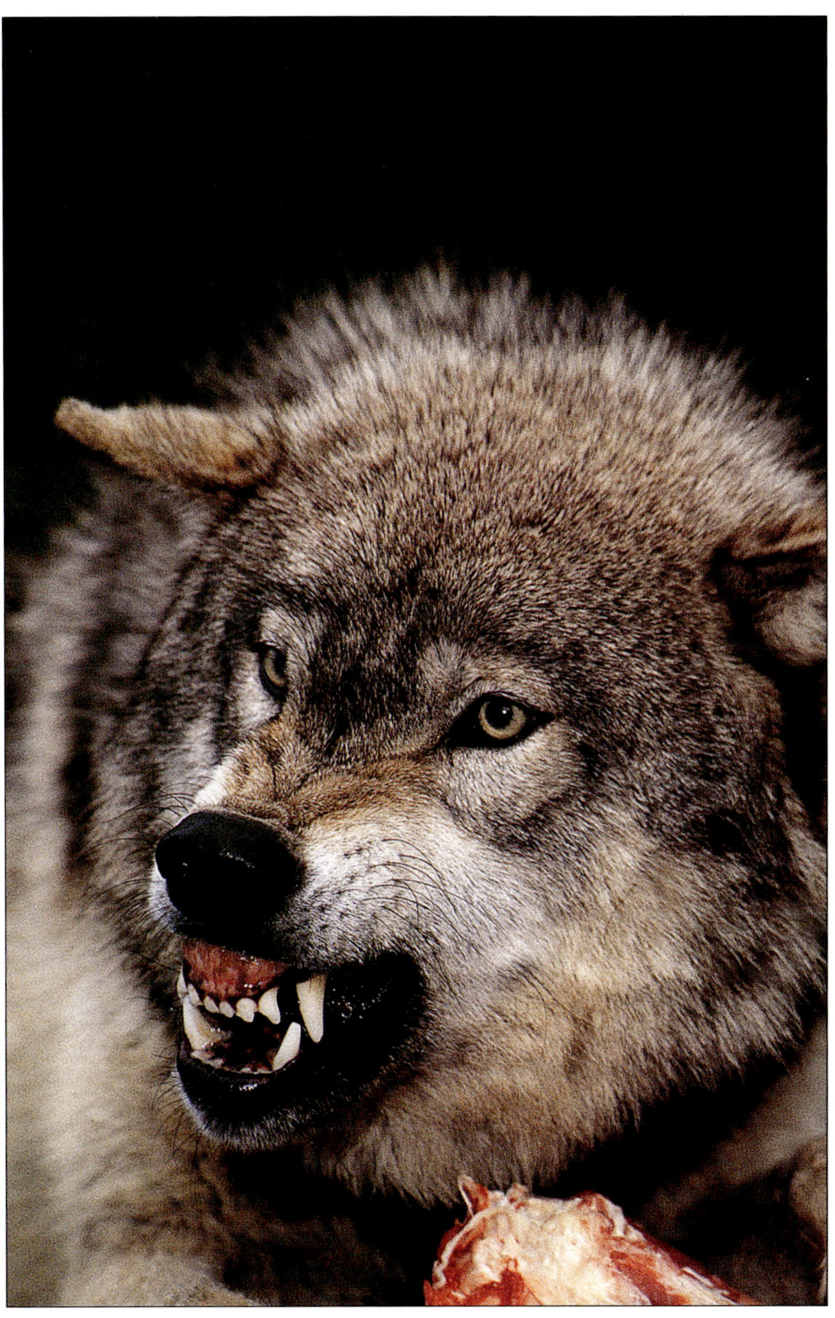

Any questions about how this gray wolf feels or what it's threatening to do? This is a warning in a language that anyone can understand. Captive. Bridger Mountains, Montana. 75–300mm lens with fill flash.

THE IMPORTANCE OF BODY LANGUAGE

To tell how these animals are feeling, you need to be able to read body language. While we were photographing a prairie rattlesnake that a friend of ours was releasing, we had no questions about how our subject felt. The snake made it very clear that it was tired of being carried in a sack. Many times, though, being able to read an animal's emotions means hitting the books again. Once again, research can play an important role in wildlife photography. The key to understanding a dolphin's moods is noticing how it holds its fins and the arch of its back, and being able to decipher what you've seen.

Being able to read your subject's body language is also important in terms of both the animal's and your own safety. If you're photographing grizzly bears in the fog, it's a darn good idea to be able to recognize when the beasts are tired of putting up with the paparazzi. It's also nice if you can tell when your continued presence is bothering some creature that's unable to flee and is too small to eat you.

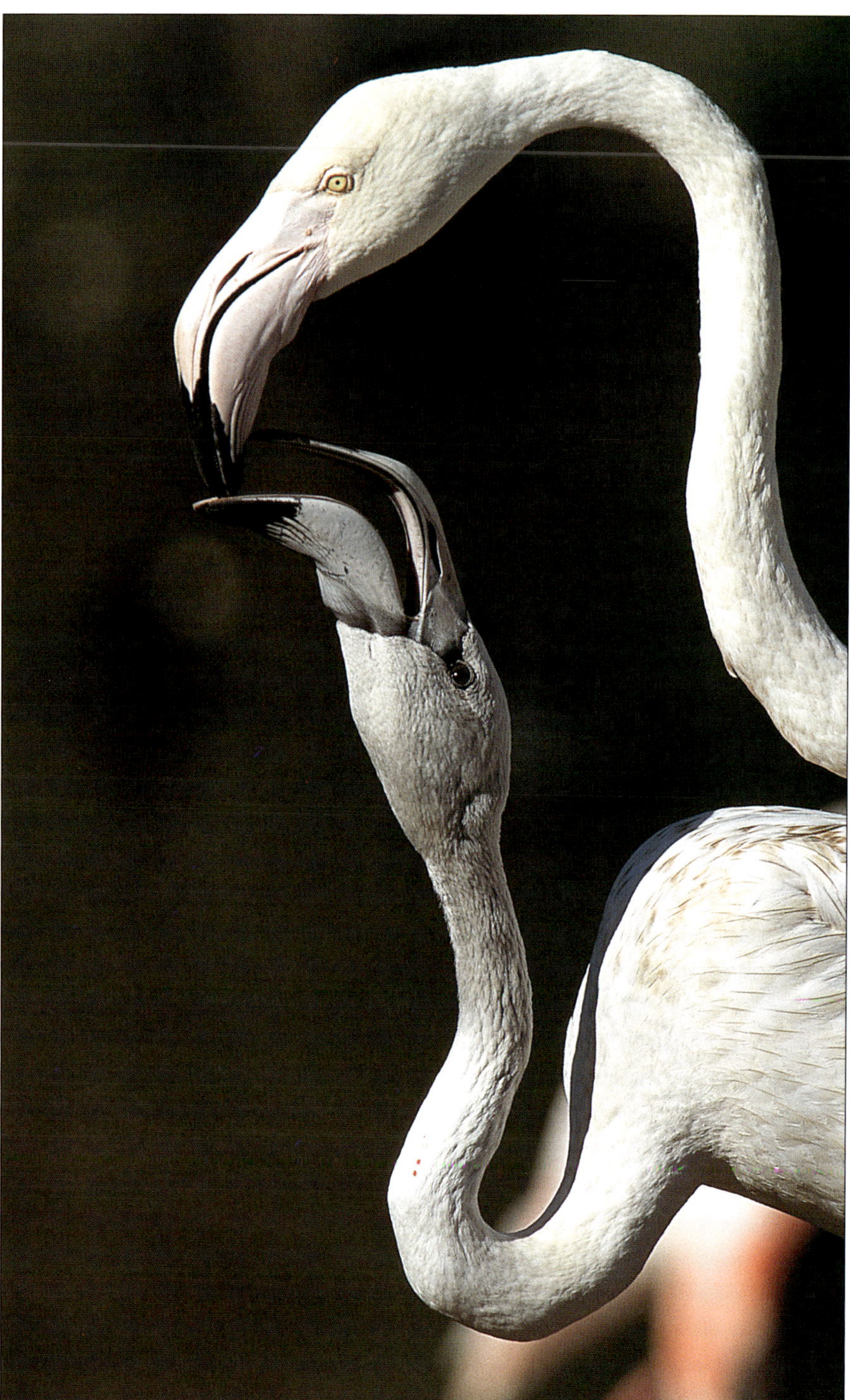

Flamingos are destined to always appear unhappy and humorless just because of the way their beaks are curved in a perpetual frown. Here a greater flamingo juvenile is begging food from an adult. Captive. Denver Zoo, Colorado. 500mm lens.

It's important to realize, though, that with most species you photograph, few of your viewers are going to understand the body language they see in the image. Your viewers will probably not react to the actual mood or emotions of the subject. They will react to how the animal appears to be feeling. However, unless you're documenting the animal's body language for study or some other scientific reason, it doesn't matter. Creating an image in which the subject appears to have some human emotion will give another element of interest to your picture. It probably won't matter to your viewers that the animal didn't feel that way at all. Most viewers just want to see an interesting photo.

A LITTLE HUMOR

One sure way to draw your viewers into an image is to inject a bit of humor into it. There are almost as many ways to add a few laughs to a photo as there are subjects to photograph. Courtship can offer some outstanding opportunities for humorous images. Males, especially, will engage in the most outrageous conduct in an attempt to attract a mate. For example, common goldeneye drakes look like they are trying to break their own backs as they show off for the hens.

Sometimes there is little action involved in a funny situation. Pay attention to the look on the subject's face. Some animals have expressions that are downright funny all by themselves. Be forewarned that capturing expressions will probably require both a long lens and a tol-

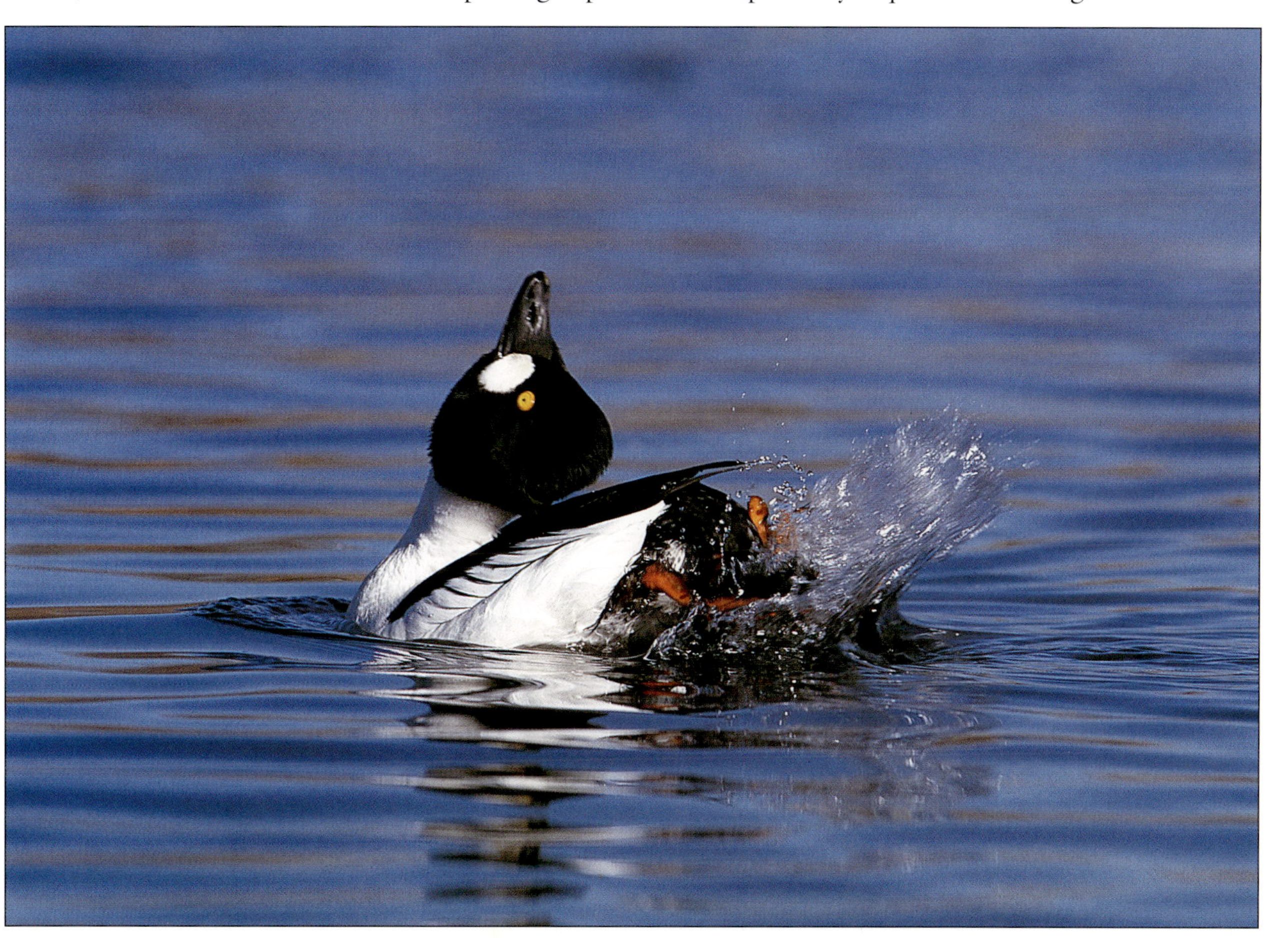

Many duck species appear to do little but swim and nap. Spend a little time with them, though, and you never know what behaviors you may capture. Many of them perform interesting courtship rituals. Common goldeneye drakes appear to break their backs just to impress the hens. Jefferson County, Colorado. 500mm lens.

erant subject. You need to shoot tight if you want to give the viewers a detailed look at the animal's expression. Orangutans seem to be especially good subjects if you want to capture comical expressions.

Despite the fact that there are many ways to capture humor, it's not an easy thing to do. Most of the moments you're trying to photograph are fleeting. If you're not paying attention constantly, or if the subject isn't in exactly the right spot, the moment goes unrecorded. Don't get discouraged if your files have a dearth of comical images. Keep an animal or two in your viewfinder as often as possible, and try to be ready when those fleeting moments occur.

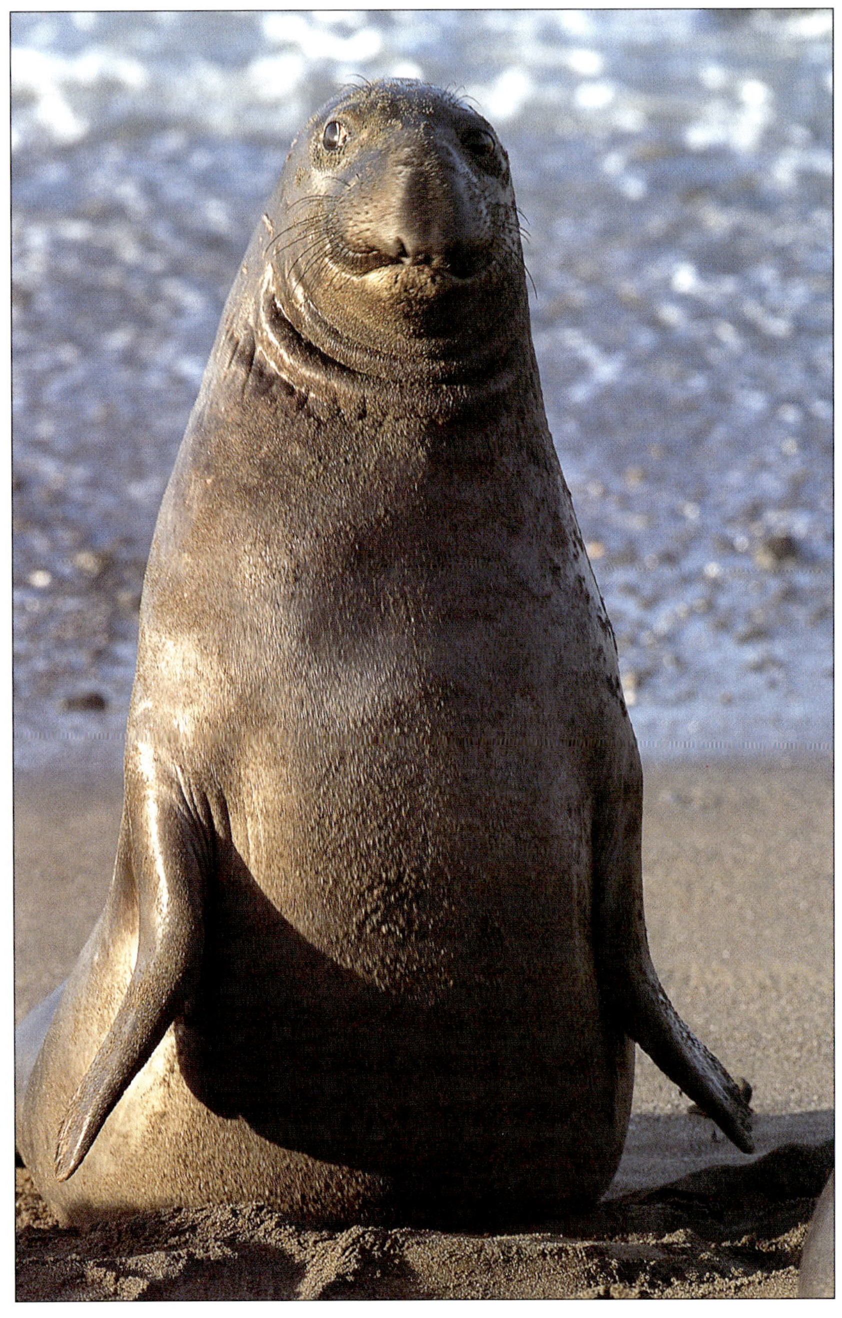

Sometimes there is little direct action involved in a humorous situation. This young bull elephant seal adopted this comical expression just after coming out of the water. Who knows why? San Luis Obispo County, California. 100–400mm lens.

Although it shows only a minimum of behavior, this image of an ocelot clearly lends credence to the clichés regarding a cat's natural curiosity. Captive. Arizona–Sonora Desert Museum, Arizona. 500mm lens.

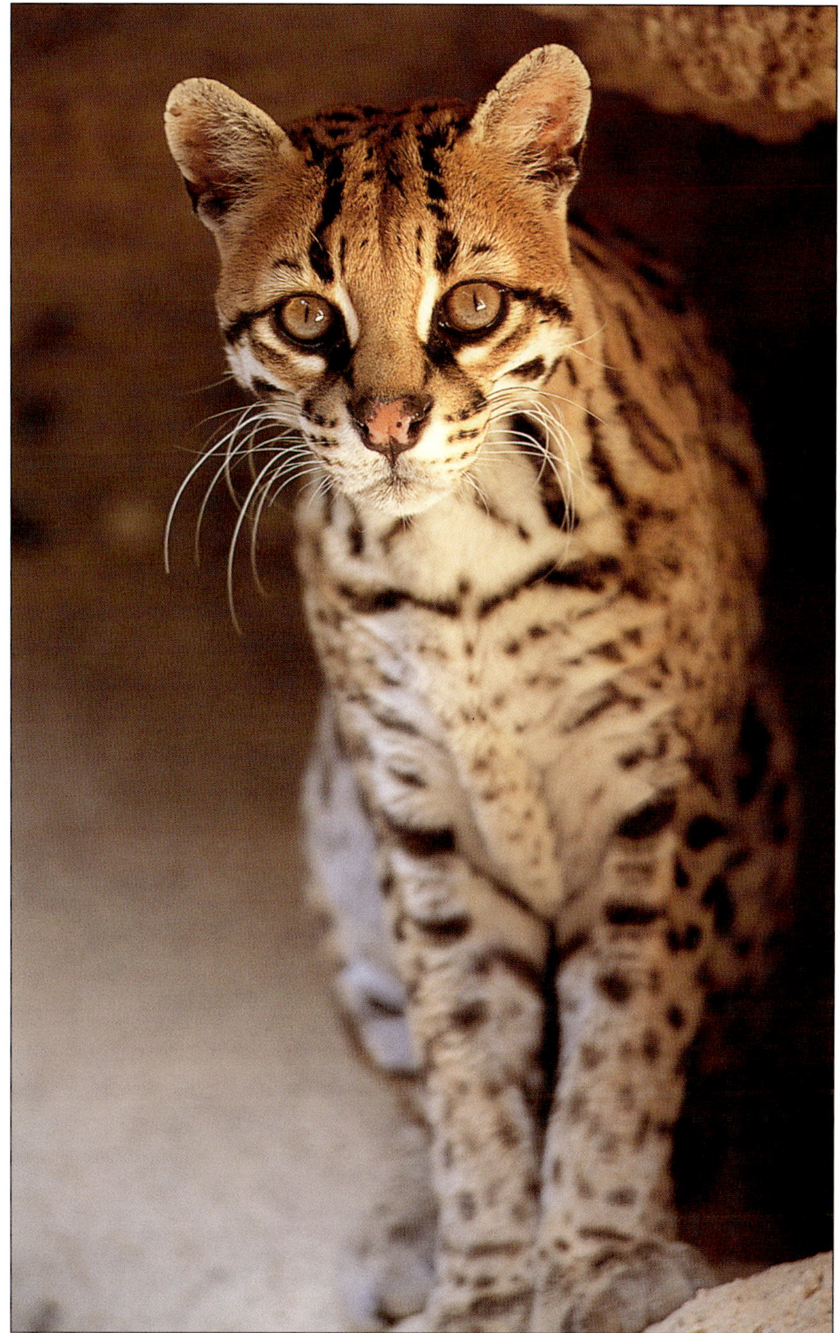

For the photographer, shooting the moods and emotions of animals can mean trying to capture fast moving action, moments of quiet tenderness, and your subject's expressions in exquisite detail. This is anything but slam-dunk easy. If you can do it, however, animal emotions can go a long way toward lifting your images above the ordinary. It's not important if you capture the way the animal actually feels, as long as you capture a look that says happy, sad, upset, bored, or curious to your viewers. A clearly portrayed emotion that your viewers can identify with will often take an image beyond documentation.

Conclusion

Today's wildlife photographers have it both easier and harder than those of a couple generations ago. We have much greater access to subjects all over the world. Granted, some of those species may not be with us too much longer, but we still have access even to many highly endangered species. And the equipment at our disposal is absolutely mind boggling in its capabilities. Our major difficulty is in trying to impress an audience that has seen many, many wildlife photos. Several decades ago, photographers could impress their viewers with photos that often would be weak by today's standards. With few exceptions, the wildlife images of that era would be called documentary by today's photographers.

The simplicity of this shot of a common goldeneye floating in a colorful reflection is part of what takes this image beyond documentation. Jefferson County, Colorado. 500mm lens with 2x teleconverter.

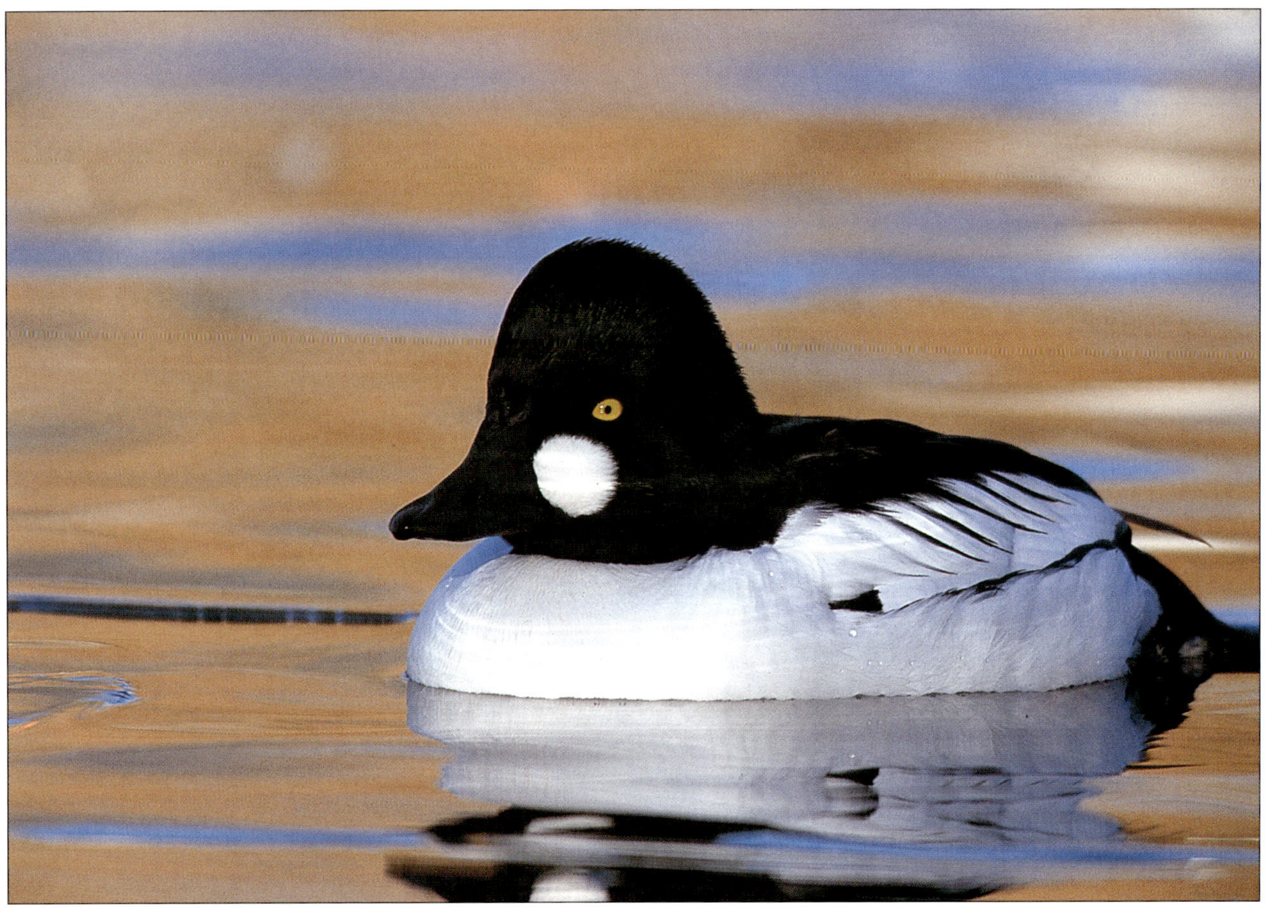

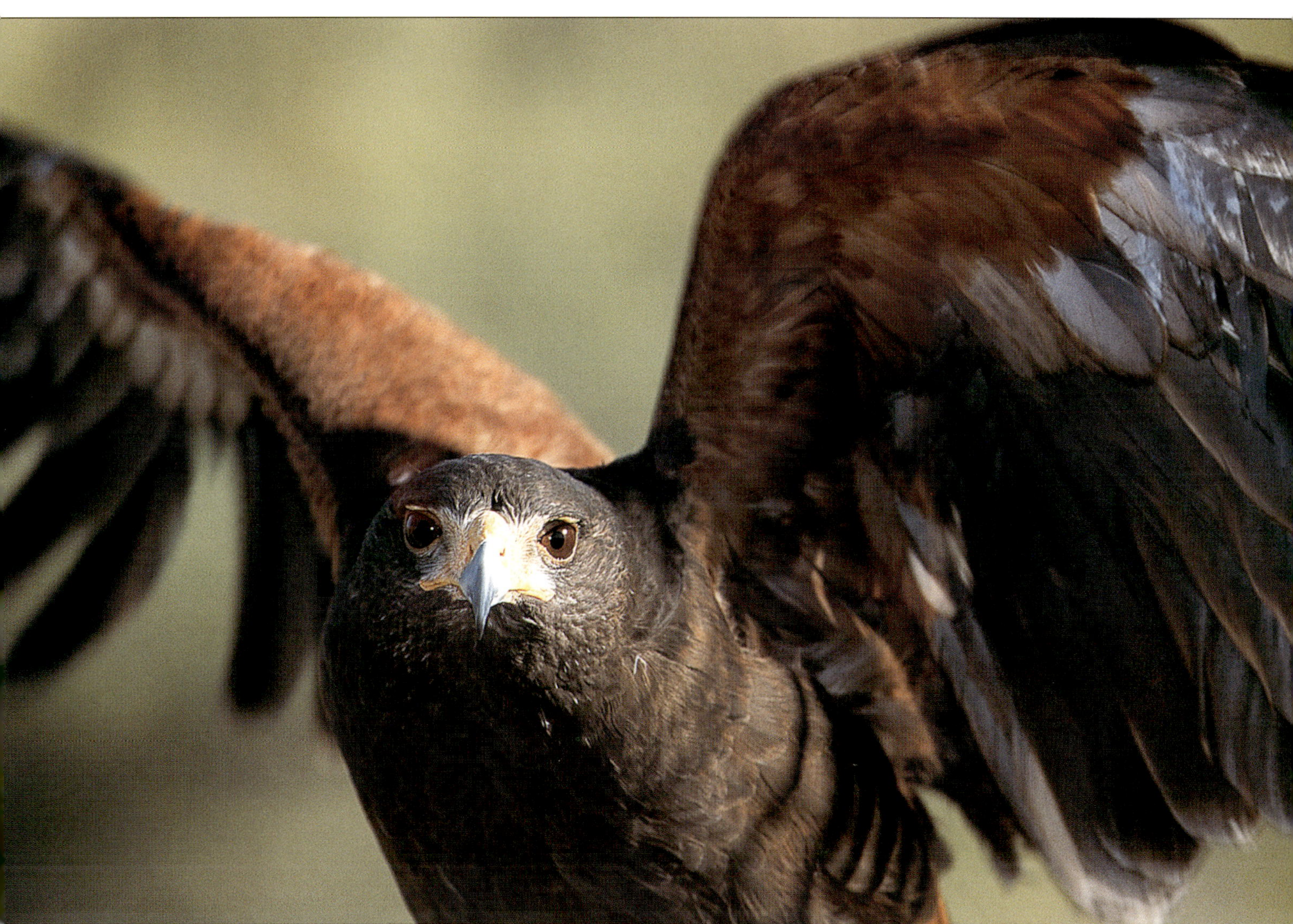

This Harris' hawk spreading its wings shows the importance of capturing behavior. Without the spread wings we would have had a nice but ordinary portrait. The spread wings add drama and action to the image. Captive. Arizona–Sonora Desert Museum. 500mm lens.

The current generation of wildlife photographers may have to go beyond documentary to make their viewers take notice, but they also have the tools to do so. Today's camera gear can do some amazing things in the right hands. If you want to expand your horizons, there's no reason to settle for documentary. Just be sure of your reasons for doing so. Viewers may call your work interesting, but going beyond documentation may not win you any more awards in photography competitions. It may not have a positive effect on the number of sales you make. If you choose to go beyond documentation, do so because you're not satisfied with your work until it stands out from the crowd.

Taking wildlife photos that go beyond documentation is not an easy thing to do. Don't get too frustrated if your rate of return is relatively small. Most of the images that Cathy and I return home with are documentary, and the same is true for every other wildlife photographer out there. I hope it will always be that way. It's the difficulty of going beyond documentation that makes the photos that do accomplish it so special.

This is a time-intensive endeavor, so concentrate on subjects you enjoy photographing. Photographers have been everywhere anyway, photographing anything they considered exciting, beautiful, or even interesting. There are very few animal subjects left that haven't been covered, so don't worry about what you photograph. Worry about your treatment of that subject.

Sure, nearly every subject has been photographed, but there are always new things to show about every creature and new ways to portray the animal. Experiment with the light, play with the composition, shoot the subject tight, shoot it wide, highlight an interesting feature, capture its emotions. No animal has been covered so extensively that we have seen photos of all of its behaviors. The main thing is to spend lots of time with the subject, and try to share what the creature is willing to show you. That is the reason we became wildlife photographers in the first place, so we could spend more time with wildlife. And in the end, whether we get the shot or not, having a wild animal share its life with us is its own reward.

Whether we get the shot or not, having a wild animal share its life with us is its own reward.

Appendix

RESOURCES

Morris, Arthur. *The Art of Bird Photography: The Complete Guide to Professional Techniques.* Watson-Guptill Publishers, 1998.

Burian, Peter and Robert Caputo. *National Geographic Photography Field Guide: Secrets to Making Great Pictures.* National Geographic Society, 1999.

Campbell, Laurie. *The Royal Society for the Protection of Birds: Guide to Bird & Nature Photography.* David & Charles, 1990.

Fitzharris, Tim. *Nature Photography: National Audubon Society Guide.* Firefly Books, 1996.

———. *Wild Bird Photography: National Audubon Society Guide.* Firefly Books, 1996.

Lepp, George. *Beyond the Basics, II.* Lepp & Associates, 1997.

McDonald, Joe. *Designing Wildlife Photographs: Professional Field Techniques for Composing Great Pictures.* Amphoto, 1994.

Norton, Boyd. *The Art of Outdoor Photography: Techniques for the Advanced Amateur and Professional.* Voyageur Press, 1993.

Shaw, John. *The Nature Photographer's Complete Guide to Professional Field Techniques.* Amphoto, 1984.

Wolf, Art and Martha Hill. *The Art of Photographing Nature.* Crown Trade Paperbacks, 1993.

FURTHER READING

Jim Brandenburg, *Chased by the Light* (Creative Publishing, International: 1998).

Frans Lanting, *Eye to Eye: Intimate Encounters with the Animal World,* ed. Christine Eckstrom (Taschen Verlag: 1997).

Art Wolf, *The Living Wild* (Wildlands Press: 2000).

Jim Brandenburg, *Looking for the Summer* (NorthWord Press, 2003).

Index

OTHER BOOKS FROM

Amherst Media®

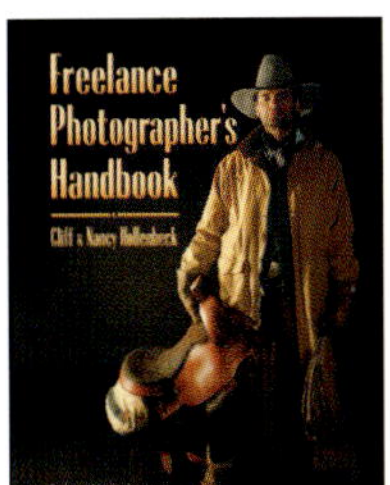

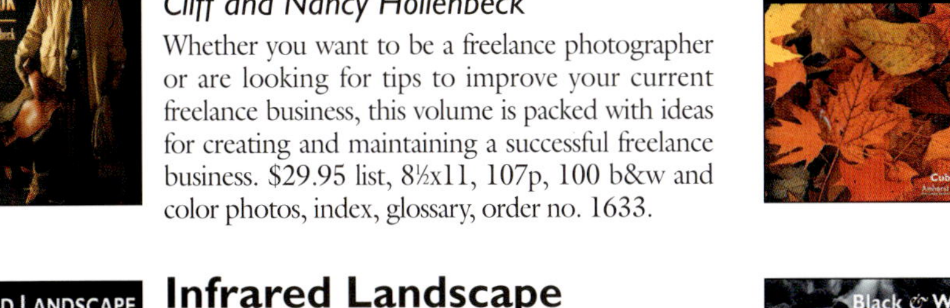

Freelance Photographer's Handbook

Cliff and Nancy Hollenbeck

Whether you want to be a freelance photographer or are looking for tips to improve your current freelance business, this volume is packed with ideas for creating and maintaining a successful freelance business. $29.95 list, 8½x11, 107p, 100 b&w and color photos, index, glossary, order no. 1633.

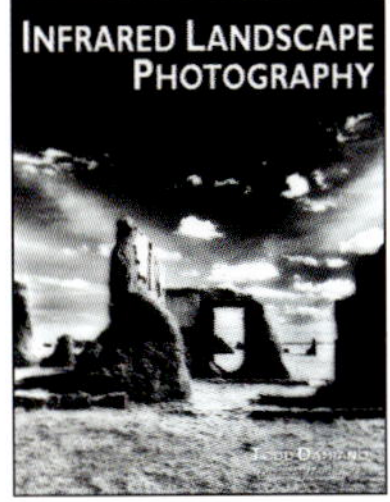

Infrared Landscape Photography

Todd Damiano

Landscapes shot with infrared can become breathtaking and ghostly images. The author analyzes over fifty of his compelling photographs to teach you the techniques you need to capture landscapes with infrared. $29.95 list, 8½x11, 120p, 60 b&w photos, index, order no. 1636.

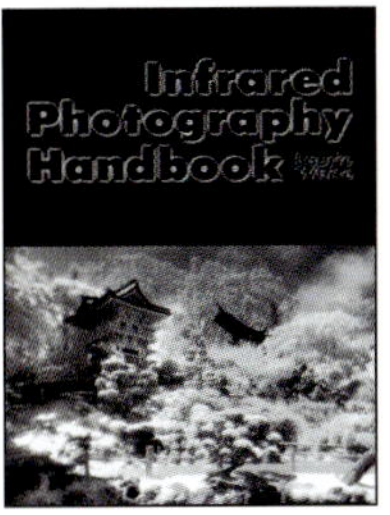

Infrared Photography Handbook

Laurie White

Covers black and white infrared photography: focus, lenses, film loading, film speed rating, batch testing, paper stocks, and filters. Black & white photos illustrate how IR film reacts. $29.95 list, 8½x11, 104p, 50 b&w photos, charts & diagrams, order no. 1419.

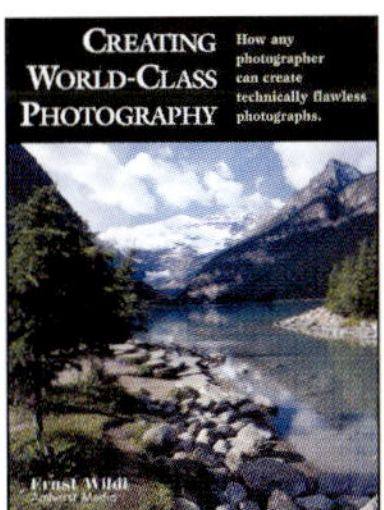

Creating World-Class Photography

Ernst Wildi

Learn how any photographer can create technically flawless photos. Features techniques for eliminating technical flaws in all types of photos—from portraits to landscapes. Includes the Zone System, digital imaging, and much more. $29.95 list, 8½x11, 128p, 120 color photos, index, order no. 1718.

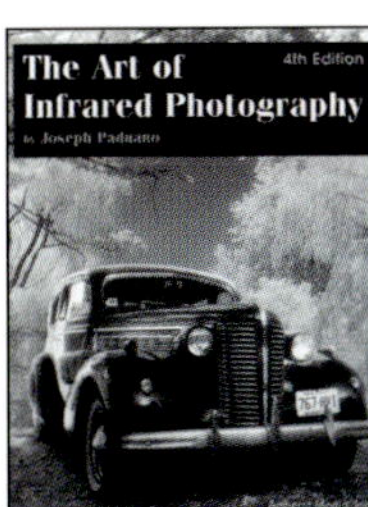

The Art of Infrared Photography, *4th Ed.*

Joe Paduano

A practical guide to infrared photography. Tells what to expect and how to control results. Includes: anticipating effects, color infrared, digital infrared, using filters, focusing, developing, printing, handcoloring, toning, and more! $29.95 list, 8½x11, 112p, 70 b&w photos, order no. 1052.

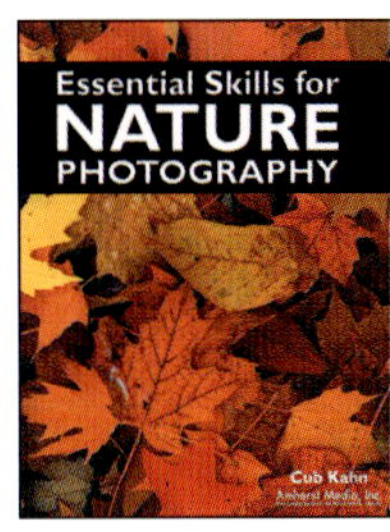

Essential Skills for Nature Photography

Cub Kahn

Learn the skills you need to capture landscapes, animals, flowers, and the entire natural world on film. Includes: selecting equipment, choosing locations, evaluating compositions, filters, and much more! $29.95 list, 8½x11, 128p, 60 b&w and color photos, order no. 1652.

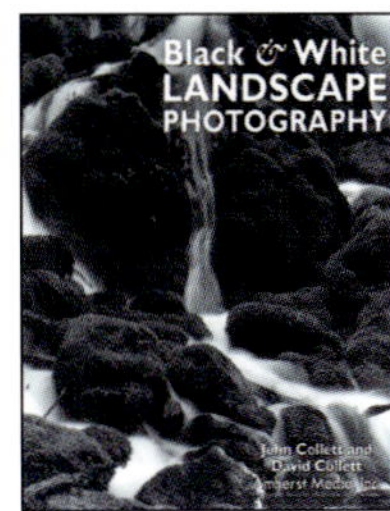

Black & White Landscape Photography

John Collett and David Collett

Master the art of black & white landscape photography. Includes: selecting equipment for landscape photography, shooting in the field, using the Zone System, and printing your images for professional results. $29.95 list, 8½x11, 128p, 80 b&w photos, order no. 1654.

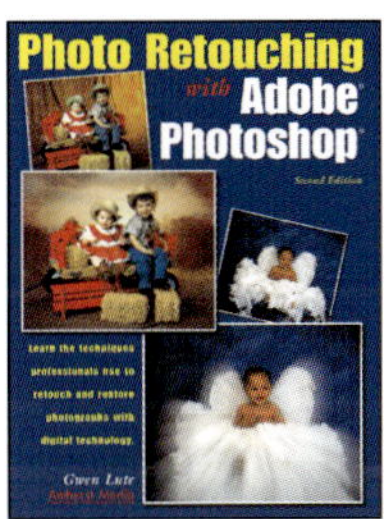

Photo Retouching with Adobe® Photoshop® *2nd Ed.*

Gwen Lute

Teaches every phase of the process, from scanning to final output. Learn to restore damaged photos, correct imperfections, create realistic composite images, and correct for dazzling color. $29.95 list, 8½x11, 120p, 100 color images, order no. 1660.

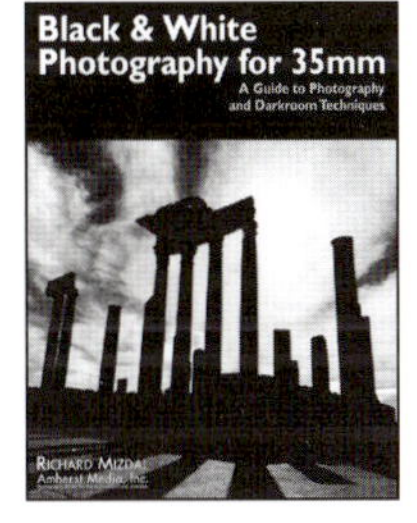

Black & White Photography for 35mm

Richard Mizdal

A guide to shooting and darkroom techniques! Perfect for beginning or intermediate photographers who want to improve their skills. Features helpful illustrations and exercises to make every concept clear and easy to follow. $29.95 list, 8½x11, 128p, 100 b&w photos, order no. 1670.

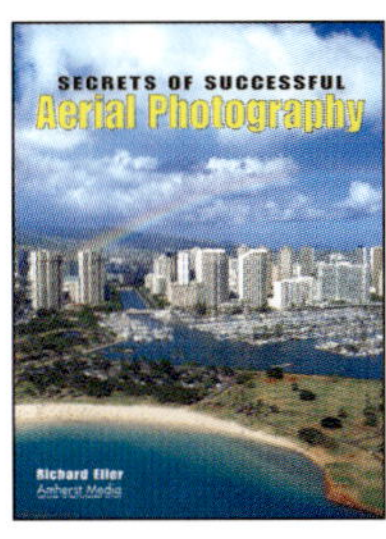

Secrets of Successful Aerial Photography

Richard Eller

Learn how to plan a shoot and take images from the air. Discover how to control camera movement, compensate for environmental conditions and compose outstanding aerial images. $29.95 list, 8½x11, 120p, 100 b&w and color photos, order no. 1679.

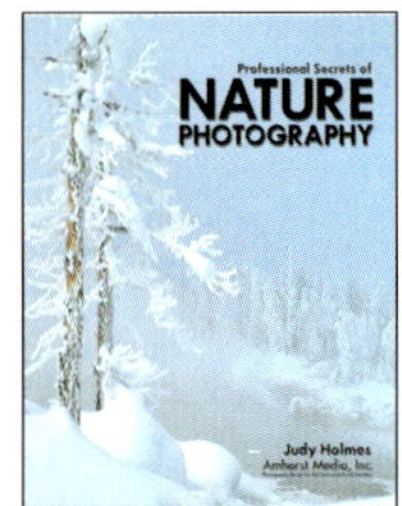

Professional Secrets of Nature Photography

Judy Holmes

Covers every aspect of making top-quality images, from selecting the right equipment, to choosing the best subjects, to shooting techniques for professional results every time. $29.95 list, 8½x11, 120p, 100 color photos, order no. 1682.

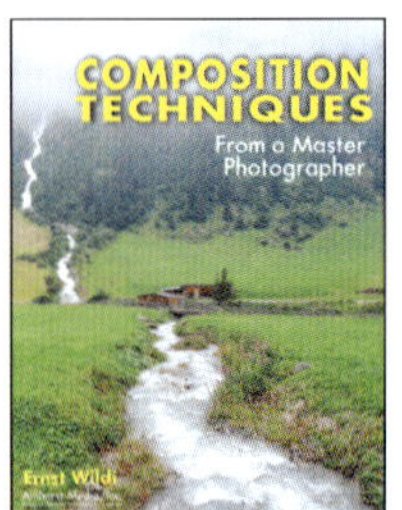

Composition Techniques from a Master Photographer

Ernst Wildi

Composition can make the difference between dull and dazzling. Master photographer Ernst Wildi teaches you his techniques for evaluating subjects and composing powerful images in this beautiful color book. $29.95 list, 8½x11, 128p, 100 color photos, order no. 1685.

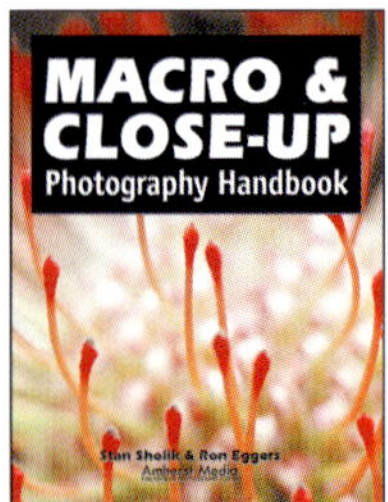

Macro & Close-up Photography Handbook

Stan Sholik and Ron Eggers

Learn to get close and capture breathtaking images of small subjects—flowers, stamps, jewelry, insects, etc. Designed with the 35mm shooter in mind, this is a comprehensive manual full of step-by-step techniques. $29.95 list, 8½x11, 120p, 80 b&w and color photos, order no. 1686.

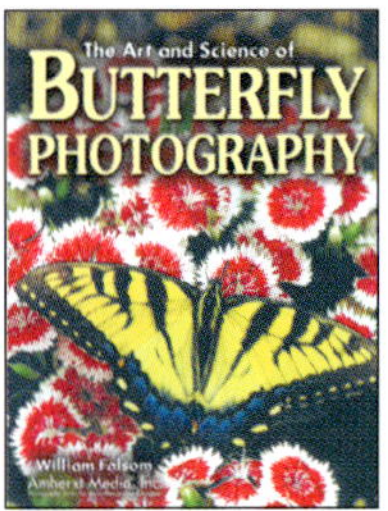

The Art and Science of Butterfly Photography

William Folsom

Learn butterfly behavior (feeding, mating, and migrational patterns), when to photograph, how to lure them, and techniques for capturing breathtaking images of these colorful creatures. $29.95 list, 8½x11, 120p, 100 b&w and color photos, order no. 1680.

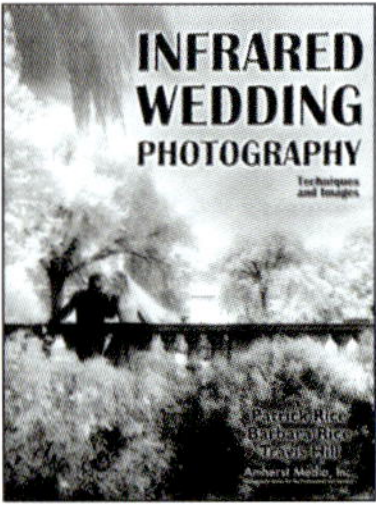

Infrared Wedding Photography

Patrick Rice, Barbara Rice and Travis HIll

Step-by-step techniques for adding the dreamy look of black & white infrared to your wedding portraiture. Capture the fantasy of the wedding with unique ethereal portraits your clients will love! $29.95 list, 8½x11, 128p, 60 b&w images, order no. 1681.

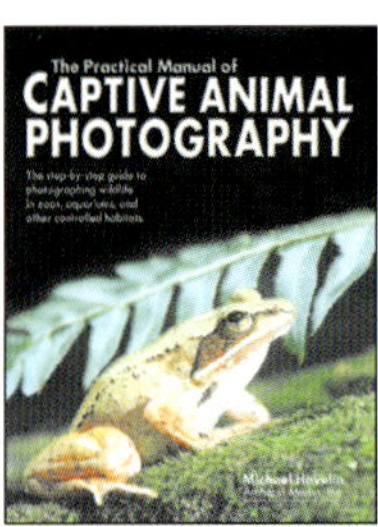

The Practical Manual of Captive Animal Photography

Michael Havelin

Learn the environmental advantages of photographing animals in captivity, and how to take natural-looking photos of subjects in zoos, preserves, aquariums, etc. $29.95 list, 8½x11, 120p, 100 b&w photos, order no. 1683.

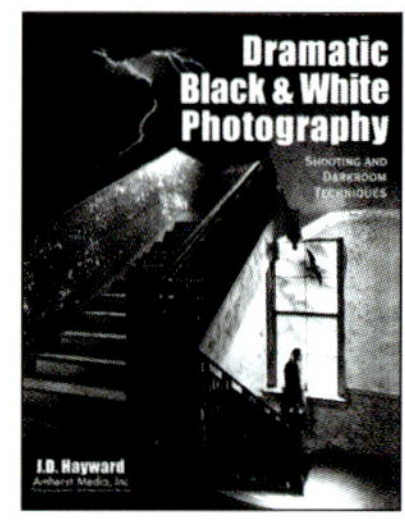

Dramatic Black & White Photography

SHOOTING AND DARKROOM TECHNIQUES

J. D. Hayward

Create dramatic images with these outstanding techniques for lighting and top-notch, creative darkroom work. This book takes black & white to the next level! $29.95 list, 8½x11, 128p, 80 duotone photos, order no. 1687.

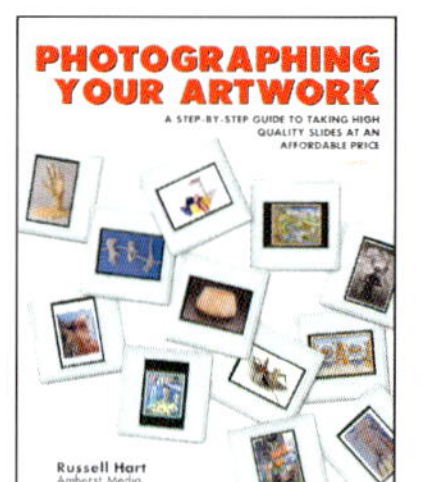

Photographing Your Artwork

Russell Hart

A step-by-step guide for taking high-quality slides of artwork for submission to galleries, magazines, grant committees, etc. Learn the best photographic techniques to make your artwork (be it 2-D or 3-D) look its very best! $29.95 list, 8½x11, 128p, 80 b&w photos, order no. 1688.

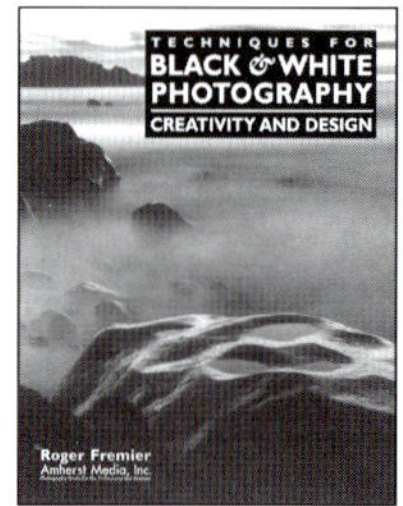

Techniques for Black & White Photography

CREATIVITY AND DESIGN

Roger Fremier

Harness your creativity and improve your photographic design with these techniques and exercises. A complete course for photographers who want to be more creative. $19.95 list, 8½x11, 112p, 50 b&w photos, order no. 1699.

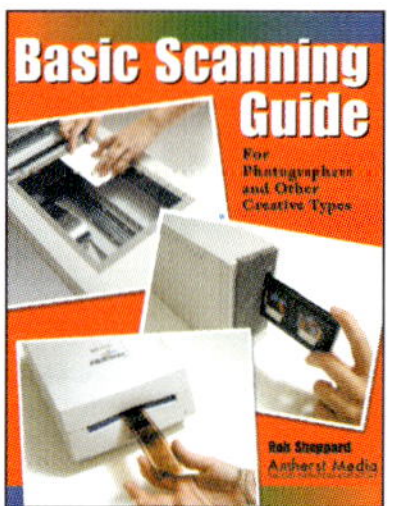

Basic Scanning Guide For Photographers and Other Creative Types

Rob Sheppard

An easy-to-read, hands-on workbook offering a practical knowledge of scanning. Includes selecting and setting up your scanner. $17.95 list, 8½x11, 96p, 80 b&w photos, order no. 1702.

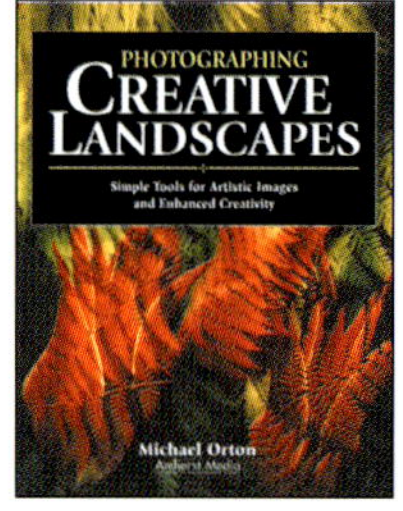

Photographing Creative Landscapes

Michael Orton

Boost your creativity and bring a new level of enthusiasm to your images of the landscape. This step-by-step guide is the key to escaping from your creative rut and beginning to create more expressive images. $29.95 list, 8½x11, 128p, 70 color photos, order no. 1714.

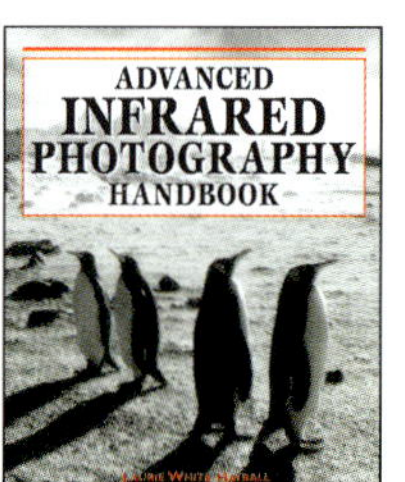

Advanced Infrared Photography Handbook

Laurie White Hayball

Building on the techniques covered in her *Infrared Photography Handbook*, Laurie White Hayball presents advanced techniques for harnessing the beauty of infrared light on film. $29.95 list, 8½x11, 128p, 100 b&w photos, order no. 1715.

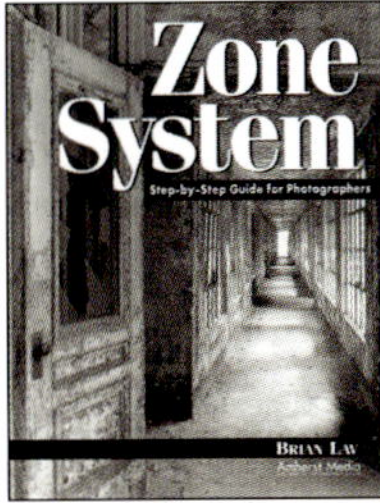

Zone System

Brian Lav

Learn to create perfectly exposed black & white negatives and top-quality prints. With this step-by-step guide, anyone can learn the Zone System and gain complete control of their black & white images! $29.95 list, 8½x11, 128p, 70 b&w photos, order no. 1720.

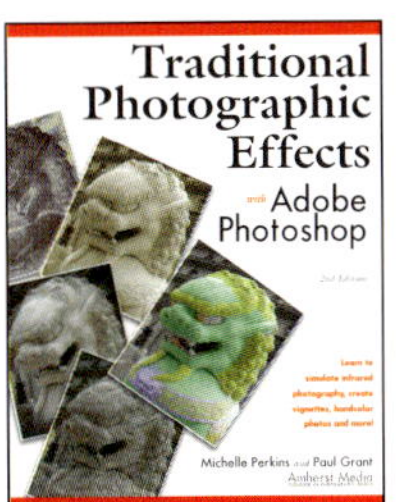

Traditional Photographic Effects with Adobe® Photoshop®, *2nd Ed.*

Michelle Perkins and Paul Grant

Use Photoshop to enhance your photos with handcoloring, vignettes, soft focus, and much more. Every technique contains step-by-step instructions for easy learning. $29.95 list, 8½x11, 128p, 150 color images, order no. 1721.

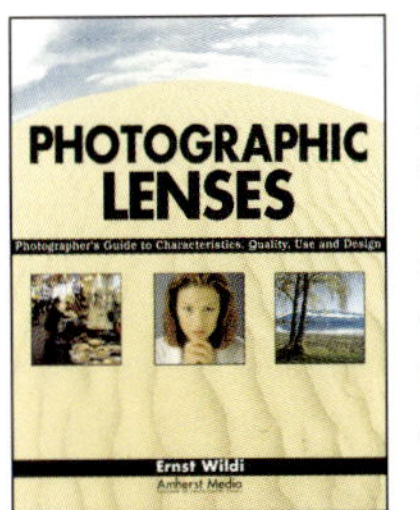

Photographic Lenses

PHOTOGRAPHER'S GUIDE TO CHARACTERISTICS, QUALITY, USE AND DESIGN

Ernst Wildi

Gain a complete understanding of the lenses through which all photographs are made—both on film and in digital photography. $29.95 list, 8½x11, 128p, 70 color photos, order no. 1723.

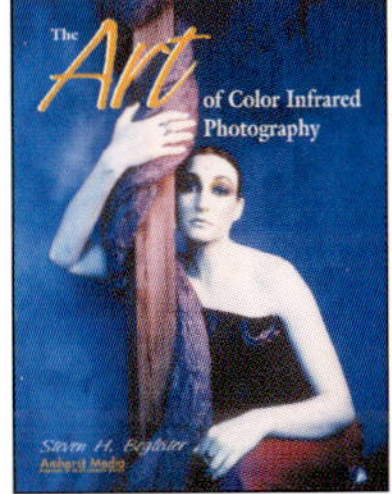

The Art of Color Infrared Photography

Steven H. Begleiter

Color infrared photography will open the doors to a new and exciting photographic world. This book shows readers how to previsualize the scene and get the results they want. $29.95 list, 8½x11, 128p, 80 color photos, order no. 1728.

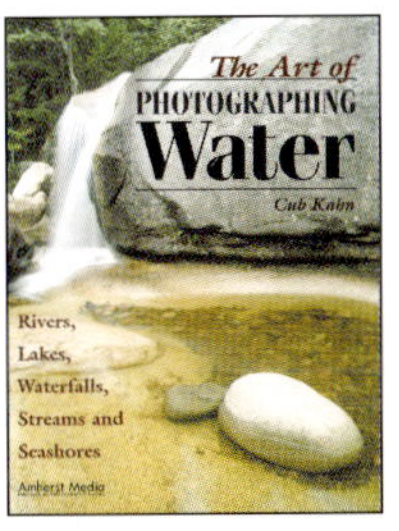

The Art of Photographing Water

Cub Kahn

Learn to capture the interplay of light and water with this beautiful, compelling, and comprehensive book. Packed with practical information you can use right away! $29.95 list, 8½x11, 128p, 70 color photos, order no. 1724.

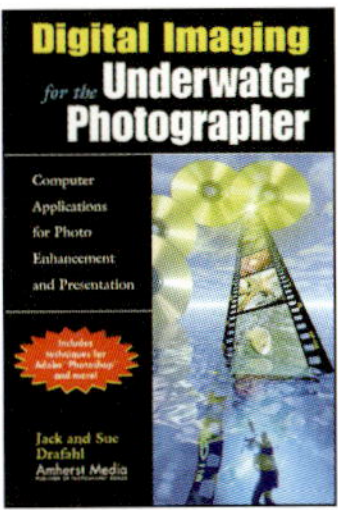

Digital Imaging for the Underwater Photographer

Jack and Sue Drafahl

This book will teach readers how to improve their underwater images with digital imaging techniques. This book covers all the bases—from color balancing your monitor, to scanning, to output and storage. $39.95 list, 6x9, 224p, 80 color photos, order no. 1727.

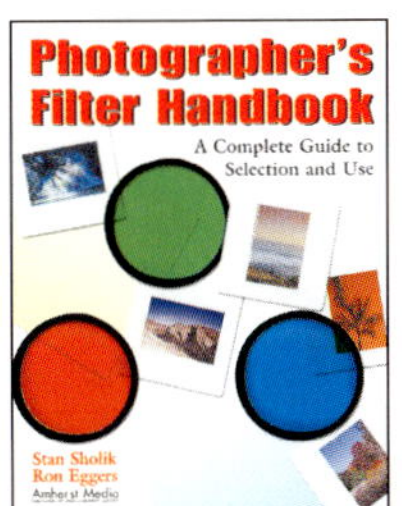

Photographer's Filter Handbook

Stan Sholik and Ron Eggers

Take control of your photography with the tips offered in this book! This comprehensive volume teaches readers how to color-balance images, correct contrast problems, create special effects, and more. $29.95 list, 8½x11, 128p, 100 color photos, order no. 1731.

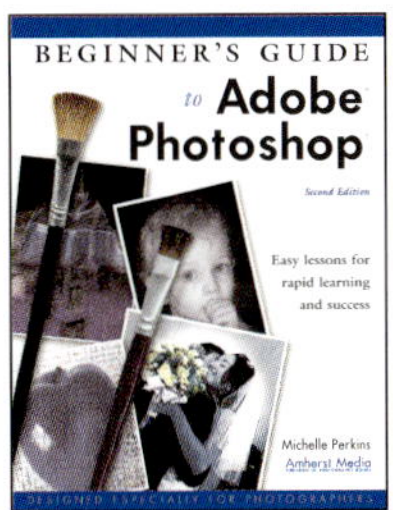

Beginner's Guide to Adobe® Photoshop®, *2nd Ed.*

Michelle Perkins

Learn to effectively make your images look their best, create original artwork, or add unique effects to any image. Topics are presented in short, easy-to-digest sections that will boost confidence and ensure outstanding images. $29.95 list, 8½x11, 128p, 300 color images, order no. 1732.

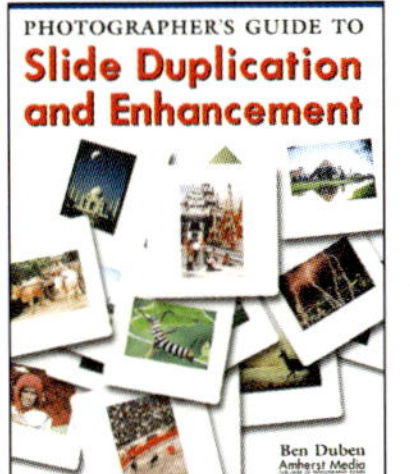

Photographer's Guide to Slide Duplication and Enhancement

Ben Duben

Whether you're looking to backup a slide or add impact to it, the advice offered in this book will make the process painless. $29.95 list, 8½x11, 112p, 130 color photos, order no. 1733.

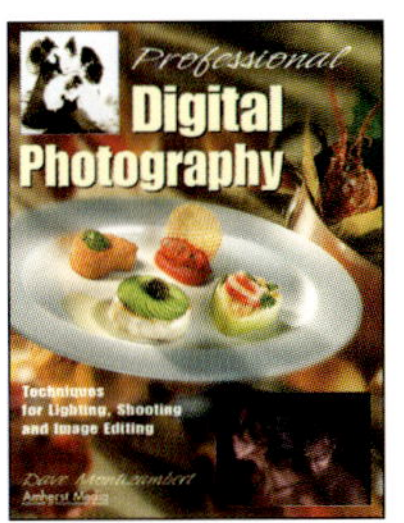

Professional Digital Photography

Dave Montizambert

From monitor calibration, to color balancing, to creating advanced artistic effects, this book provides those skilled in basic digital imaging with the techniques they need to take their photography to the next level. $29.95 list, 8½x11, 128p, 120 color photos, order no. 1739.

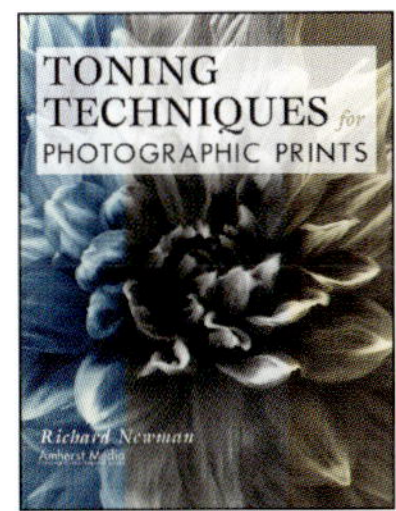

Toning Techniques for Photographic Prints

Richard Newman

Whether you want to age an image, provide a shock of color, or lend archival stability to your black & white prints, the step-by-step instructions in this book will help you realize your creative vision. $29.95 list, 8½x11, 128p, 150 color and b&w photos, order no. 1742.

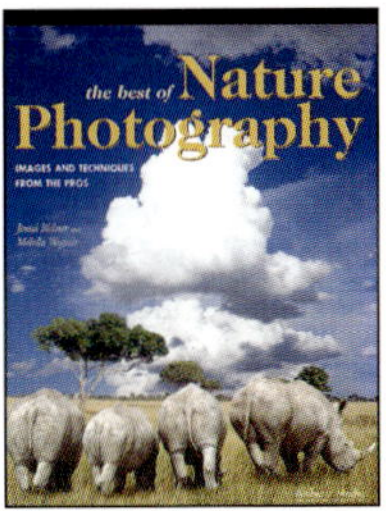

The Best of Nature Photography

Jenni Bidner and Meleda Wegner

Ever wondered how legendary nature photographers like Jim Zuckerman and John Sexton create their images? Follow in their footsteps as top photographers capture the beauty and drama of nature on film. $29.95 list, 8½x11, 128p, 150 color photos, order no. 1744.

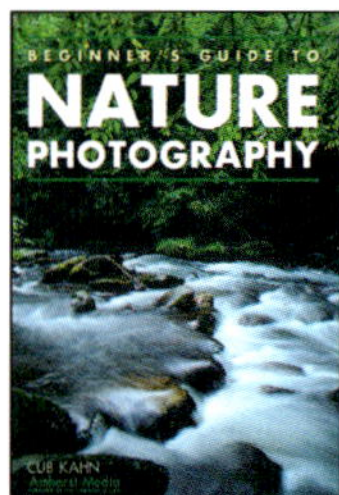

Beginner's Guide to Nature Photography

Cub Kahn

Whether you prefer a walk through a neighborhood park or a hike through the wilderness, the beauty of nature is ever present. Learn to create images that capture the scene as you remember it with the simple techniques found in this book. $14.95 list, 6x9, 96p, 70 color photos, order no. 1745.

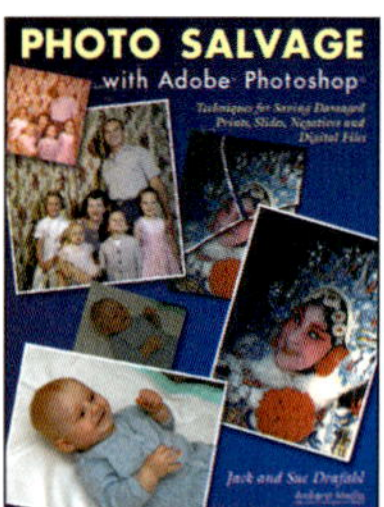

Photo Salvage with Adobe® Photoshop®

Jack and Sue Drafahl

This book teaches you to digitally restore faded images and poor exposures. Also covered are techniques for fixing color balance problems and processing errors, eliminating scratches, and much more. $29.95 list, 8½x11, 128p, 200 color photos, order no. 1751.

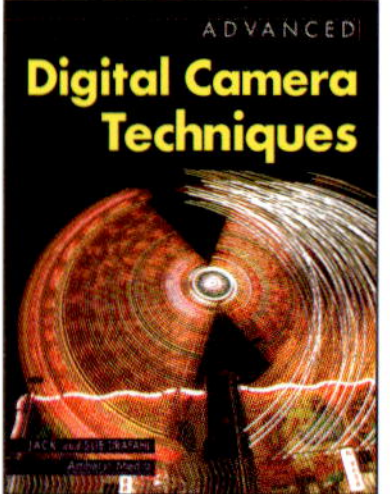

Advanced Digital Camera Techniques

Jack and Sue Drafahl

Maximize the quality and creativity of your digital-camera images with the techniques in this book. Packed with problem-solving tips and ideas for unique images. $29.95 list, 8½x11, 128p, 150 color photos, index, order no. 1758.

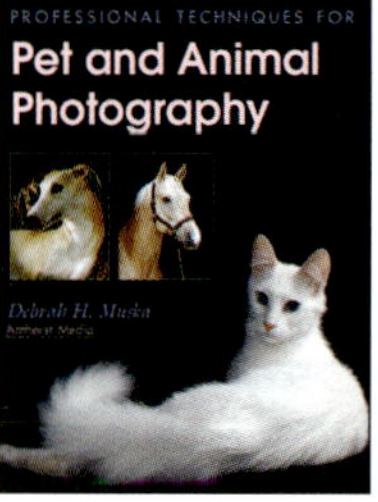

PROFESSIONAL TECHNIQUES FOR

Pet and Animal Photography

Debrah H. Muska

Adapt your portrait skills to meet the challenges of pet photography, creating images for both owners and breeders. $29.95 list, 8½x11, 128p, 110 color photos, index, order no. 1759.

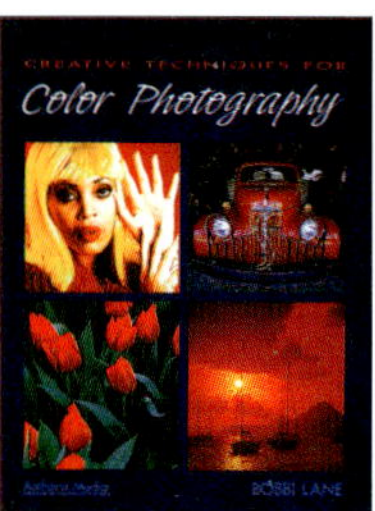

Creative Techniques for Color Photography

Bobbi Lane

Learn how to render color precisely, whether you are shooting digitally or on film. Also includes creative techniques for cross processing, color infrared, and more. $29.95 list, 8½x11, 128p, 250 color photos, index, order no. 1764.

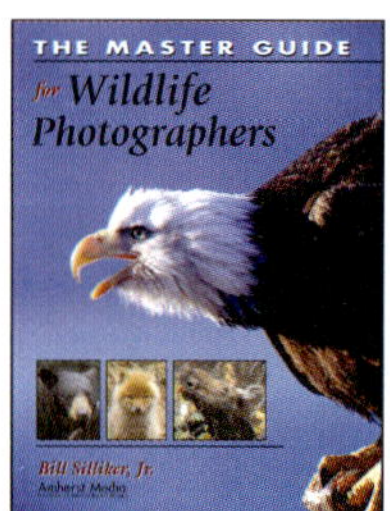

The Master Guide for Wildlife Photographers

Bill Silliker, Jr.

Discover how photographers can employ the techniques used by hunters to call, track, and approach animal subjects. Includes safety tips for wildlife photo shoots. $29.95 list, 8½x11, 128p, 100 color photos, index, order no. 1768.

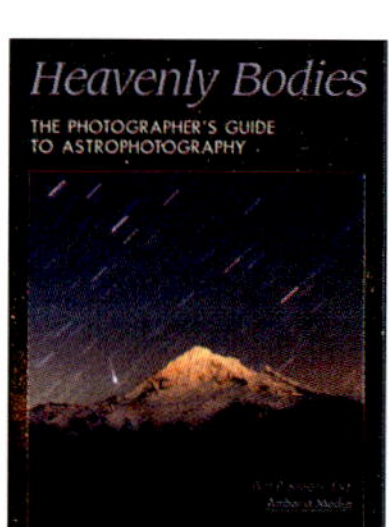

Heavenly Bodies

THE PHOTOGRAPHER'S GUIDE TO ASTROPHOTOGRAPHY

Bert P. Krages, Esq.

Learn to capture the beauty of the night sky with a 35mm camera. Tracking and telescope techniques are also covered. $29.95 list, 8½x11, 128p, 100 color photos, index, order no. 1769.

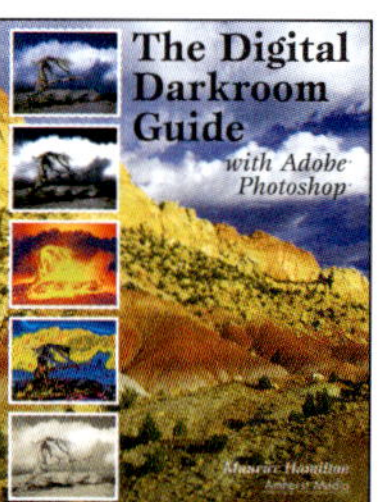

The Digital Darkroom Guide with Adobe® Photoshop®

Maurice Hamilton

Bring the skills and control of the photographic darkroom to your desktop with this complete manual. $29.95 list, 8½x11, 128p, 140 color images, index, order no. 1775.

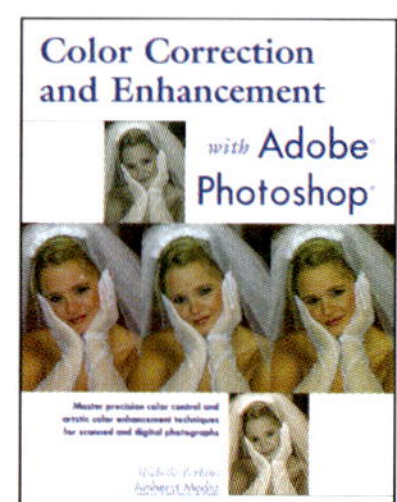

Color Correction and Enhancement with Adobe® Photoshop®

Michelle Perkins

Master precision color correction and artistic color enhancement techniques for scanned and digital photos. $29.95 list, 8½x11, 128p, 300 color images, index, order no. 1776.

MORE PHOTO BOOKS ARE AVAILABLE

Amherst Media®
PO BOX 586
BUFFALO, NY 14226 USA

INDIVIDUALS: If possible, purchase books from an Amherst Media retailer. Contact us for the dealer nearest you, or visit our web site and use our dealer locater. To order direct, visit our web site, or send a check/money order with a note listing the books you want and your shipping address. All major credit cards are also accepted. For domestic and international shipping rates, please visit our web site or contact us at the numbers listed below. New York state residents add 8% sales tax.

DEALERS, DISTRIBUTORS & COLLEGES: Write, call, or fax to place orders. For price information, contact Amherst Media or an Amherst Media sales representative. Net 30 days.

(800)622-3278 or (716)874-4450
FAX: (716)874-4508

All prices, publication dates, and specifications are subject to change without notice. Prices are in U.S. dollars. Payment in U.S. funds only.

WWW.AMHERSTMEDIA.COM
FOR A COMPLETE CATALOG OF BOOKS AND ADDITIONAL INFORMATION